Jean & Ken
    with much love from
  the editor
                July 2002

An American Journal, 1839–40

Outward-

Voyage Comm.ᵈ 13 Sep. 1839
Voyage Ended 12 Oct. 1839.

Homeward.

Voyage Comm.ᵈ 1 Oct 1840
Voyage Ended 17 Oct 1840.

Frontispiece of Rawlins' commonplace book drawn for his fiancée Mary Hunt.

An American Journal, 1839–40

Richard Champion Rawlins

Edited by John L. Tearle

Madison • Teaneck
Fairleigh Dickinson University Press
London: Associated University Press

Associated University Presses
440 Forsgate Drive
Cranbury, NJ 08512

Associated University Presses
16 Barter Street
London WC1A 2AH, England

Associated University Presses
P.O. Box 338, Port Credit
Mississauga, Ontario
Canada L5G 4L8

The paper used in this publication meets the requirements of the American National Standard for Permanence of Paper for Printed Library Materials Z39.48-1984.

Library of Congress Cataloging-in-Publication Data

Rawlins, Richard Champion, 1819–1898.
    An American journal, 1839–40 / Richard Champion Rawlins ; edited by John L. Tearle.
        p. cm.
    ISBN 0-8386-3929-1 (alk. paper)
    1. United States—Description and travel. 2. United States—Social life and customs—1783–1865. 3. Rawlins, Richard Champion, 1819–1898—Diaries. 4. Rawlins, Richard Champion, 1819–1898—Journeys—United States. 5. British—United States—Diaries. I. Tearle, John, 1917– II. Title.

E165 .R28 2002
973.5'7'092—dc21

2001040692

Contents

Preface   7
Introduction   9

 1. Outward Bound   19
 2. The New World   27
 3. New York to Lockport NY   43
 4. Lockport to Cincinnati   57
 5. Cincinnati   69
 6. New Year in Cincinnati   81
 7. Steamboat   90
 8. New Orleans   96
 9. To Washington   120
10. Back to Cincinnati   140
11. To Canada   152
12. Back to New York   163
13. Rhode Island, Massachussetts   170
14. The White Mountains   179
15. Homeward Bound   186

Postscript   196

Preface

"The most crowning event of the 1823–24 season," wrote George Odell in his *Annals of the New York Stage*, "was the first appearance in America of the famous William Augustus Conway . . . in the character of Hamlet." The American theater of the day welcomed leading English actors, who toured the country from Boston to Charleston and as far south as New Orleans, and when I was researching *Mrs. Piozzi's Tall Young Beau: William Augustus Conway* I was curious as to how they managed to get about in those early days.

A friend, Rowan Hope, provided the answer by showing me the diaries of her great-grandfather Richard Champion Rawlins, who traveled extensively, in the United States a few years later. The diaries are written in three duodecimo notebooks (6¾″ by 3¼″), each bound between boards and closed with a brass clasp, containing approximately 88 leaves separated by blotting paper, and they were written for the most part in a clear copperplate hand.

Apart from telling me all I wanted to know about travel, they introduced me to important people, institutions and events about which I knew little, and I am indebted to many agencies for their assistance in providing much valuable material. They are, in random order, the Historical Society of Pennsylvania, the Free Library of Philadelphia, the Cincinnati Historical Society, the Historic New Orleans Collection, the University of South Carolina, the Boston Public Library and the Harvard University Library.

I am further greatly indebted to Nigel Rees, deviser and presenter of the BBC's "Quote . . . Unquote" program (http://www.btwebworld.com/quote-unquote), who tracked down the origins of many of Rawlins' poetic quotations.

Introduction

I never imagined that Richard Rawlins' diaries would give me such a graphic, detailed account of the nature of long-distance travel in the New World, embellished by diversions into almost every aspect of life in the sixty-year-old United States. But by the time I had finished reading I wanted to know more about the diarist himself. He gave no indication of his age, but from his style and erudition he was evidently well educated. His interests were very wide: from history, politics and religion to architecture and engineering. He realized that his visit was likely to be a once-in-a-lifetime experience and he was determined to make the most of it, enthusiastically recording for his family everything he saw and heard.

Discussing the diary with the Rawlins family, I was astonished to learn that Richard was only 20 when he set off for America (though his twenty-first birthday was passed without mention). He had already acquired the diary habit when he wrote a record of a Scottish tour at the age of 15, and kept it up throughout his life. In 1884 he produced a leather-bound scrapbook and family record entitled "Recollections of Seventy Years" summarizing a full and varied life and telling the fascinating story which led up to his American adventure. A separate commonplace book, written for his fiancée Mary Hunt (MPH) during his travels, supplemented the three volumes of diaries, and all these lifetime records had been stored in a steel deedbox.

Rawlins' father Charles Edward was a typical nineteenth-century entrepreneur, who about 1815 became involved in the processing of smalt, a glassy blue material made by fusing cobalt ore with silica and potassium carbonate, which when ground to a powder was used in cotton-bleaching and paper-making. He married Jane Champion and had four children: Charles Edward, referred to in the *Journal* as Charles or CERJr., a daughter Juliet, and sons James and Richard Champion, who was born on 15 January 1819. He was brought up

9

with James, two years older, with whom he went to a progression of private schools. (There were no state schools in those days). They watched with great interest the tunneling under the Edge Hill during the construction of the Liverpool and Manchester Railway, and were given rides on the workmen's wagons. Three weeks before the historic opening event on 15 September 1830 the shareholders of the company were allocated seats for a rehearsal, and Rawlins preserved a ticket for Seat 46 on the "Arrow," one of the eight of Stephenson's trains which went in procession, led by him in the "Rocket."

When James left school at the age of 15, Richard pleaded to be allowed to leave too. He was apprenticed to one of the largest cotton brokers in Liverpool, and continued his education at the Mechanics Institute. He was already taking a keen interest in politics, and notable landmarks in his formative years were the passing of the Reform Act in 1832 and the abolition of slavery in the West Indies in 1834. He recalls the excitement of the debates and the divisions in Parliament, when he would join the crowds waiting for the arrival of the London mail coach with the latest news from Westminster. In 1838 the opening of the London-Liverpool railway speeded up communications on land, and Brunel's "Great Western," which Rawlins saw being built at Bristol, promised to do the same at sea.

He had been appointed cashier for his firm, handling large sums of money, and calculated that by the time he completed his apprenticeship £1m had passed through his hands. His indulgent parents allowed him to become engaged to Mary Hunt when he was only nineteen, and then, having served his time, he went into partnership with James, as Rawlins Brothers, cotton brokers.

Their maternal grandfather was Richard Champion, a Bristol merchant and ship-owner in partnership with his brother-in-law John Lloyd of Charleston, South Carolina, who looked after the American end of their transatlantic trade. He was related to Charles James Fox, the Whig member of Parliament, and was active in the Liberal cause himself. He was one of the signatories to the nomination of Edmund Burke for the constituency of the City and County of Bristol in the General Election of 1774 on a platform which challenged the policies of Lord North's government on the issues of the American colonies, slavery, and the British constitution.

He became Burke's constant adviser on matters relating to Bristol trade and commerce, but more significantly his long-standing association with South Carolina enabled him to act as a two-way conduit between the colonists and their supporters in England. Burke was in the vanguard of the movement opposing their taxation, and in a letter to Champion in July 1775 he acknowledged the contribution he had made to the cause by providing him with early intelligence [*The Correspondence of Edmund Burke* edited by Fitzwilliam and Bourke, 1844]. Champion's American correspondent was no less a personage than Liverpool born Robert Morris who was to finance the War and to sign the Declaration of Independence. Champion's letters, passing on British political intelligence, are probably to be found with Morris's papers in the Library of Congress.

Champion also made a name as the "Bristol potter" after he went into partnership with William Cookworthy of Plymouth, who had patented a method of making hard-paste porcelain from the white clay of Cornwall. Champion was so interested in the process that he invested £15,000 in 1770 to set up a factory in Bristol. In 1773 he bought the patent rights, which had only two years to run, and with Burke's help he petitioned Parliament for a 14-year extension. This succeeded in the House of Commons but was bitterly opposed by Josiah Wedgwood and other Staffordshire potters in the House of Lords, and was approved by Royal Assent in 1775 hedged around with restrictions.

In 1778 Champion presented George Washington and Benjamin Franklin with porcelain portrait plaques of themselves, thus combining in one gesture his support for the new republic with his promotion of the art and craft. The Washington plaque was seen in the possession of Mrs. B.W. Kennon, Martha Washington's granddaughter, by Charles Henry Hart, who recognized it immediately as the work of the Bristol factory, and he described it in *The Century* magazine in February 1892 as "a wonderful example of the application of hard porcelain to works of great delicacy and beauty. The entire design is in relief, the flowers being skilfully modeled with botanical accuracy. Above the medallion are the emblems of the revolted colonies, liberty cap and rattlesnake, crowned by a coronet with thirteen points for the thirteen original States, each capped by a star. Beneath the emblem is the shield of the Washington arms, and around it the flags of the Congress are festooned. When we remember that this was made by an Englishman in England in the heat of the war his daring and friendliness must elicit our admiration." Washington's letter of thanks has gone astray, but Hart wrote to Rawlins in November 1897 saying that he had discovered in the State Department Champion's letter to Washington presenting the plaque, together with the original draft of Washington's reply in his own hand. Unlike the Washington plaque, which is almost certainly unique, several copies of the less elaborate Franklin plaque where known to Hart, one of which was in the Edkin collection, later acquired by the British Museum and is on display in Gallery 47.

Porcelain portrait plaques of George Washington (left) and Benjamin Franklin.

To return to the point of Rawlins' journey to America: early in the War of Independence one of Champion's ships, en route from Charleston, had been captured by a privateer, but was recovered by an American man-of-war and handed over to Lloyd. The ship and cargo of cotton were sold, and the sum of £7300 placed to his credit, where it was held, rather than risking its repatriation to England during the war.

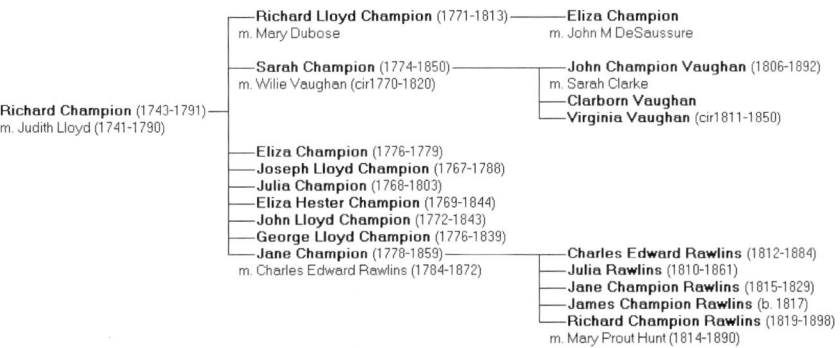

```
                                    ┌──Richard Lloyd Champion (1771-1813)────┬──Eliza Champion
                                    │  m. Mary Dubose                        │  m. John M DeSaussure
                                    │
                                    ├──Sarah Champion (1774-1850)────────────┬──John Champion Vaughan (1806-1892)
                                    │  m. Wilie Vaughan (cir1770-1820)        │  m. Sarah Clarke
Richard Champion (1743-1791)────────┤                                        ├──Clarborn Vaughan
m. Judith Lloyd (1741-1790)         │                                        └──Virginia Vaughan (cir1811-1850)
                                    │
                                    ├──Eliza Champion (1776-1779)
                                    ├──Joseph Lloyd Champion (1767-1788)
                                    ├──Julia Champion (1768-1803)
                                    ├──Eliza Hester Champion (1769-1844)
                                    ├──John Lloyd Champion (1772-1843)
                                    ├──George Lloyd Champion (1776-1839)
                                    └──Jane Champion (1778-1859)─────────────┬──Charles Edward Rawlins (1812-1884)
                                       m. Charles Edward Rawlins (1784-1872)  ├──Julia Rawlins (1810-1861)
                                                                              ├──Jane Champion Rawlins (1815-1829)
                                                                              ├──James Champion Rawlins (b. 1817)
                                                                              └──Richard Champion Rawlins (1819-1898)
                                                                                 m. Mary Prout Hunt (1814-1890)
```

Champion was obliged to discontinue his shipping business when trade with America was outlawed in 1775, and in 1782 he sold the porcelain factory. Then, on the recommendation of Edmund Burke, he was appointed deputy paymaster general to the forces jointly with Burke's own son, and was given an official residence in the Chelsea Hospital founded by Nell Gwynn. During the next two years he wrote two books, one entitled *Considerations of the present Situation of Great Britain and America,* and another on *Comparative Reflections on the past and present Political, Commercial, and Civil state of Great Britain; with some thoughts concerning Emigration.* By this time he had already emigrated, having sailed to America in October 1784 with his mother, wife and eight children whose ages ranged from six to thirteen. He settled in Camden, South Carolina, and acquired a cotton plantation at Rocky Branch, eight miles away.

With the approach of peace he had foreseen the need for the early appointment of a British Consul-General to the United States, and the coalition government under the Duke of Portland judged him to be eminently suitable for such a post. Unfortunately that administration was short-lived and the appointment did not materialize, but that did not affect his decision.

His support for the colonists had been a major factor, but the small fortune held by Lloyd on his behalf was another of the magnets that attracted him to South Carolina. Unfortunately Champion and his wife both died within eight years of emigrating, and when John Lloyd died in 1807, the balance to the credit of Champion's estate, with accrued interest, amounted to £11,400. He had died intestate, and his estate was to be shared equally between his five surviving children, the youngest of whom, Jane, had returned to England, where she married Charles Edward Rawlins in 1809. By the laws of the time married women could not hold property, which automatically belonged to the husband, and Rawlins naturally took an interest in his late father-in-law's estate. He pressed their claims with the executor, and when, by 1838, the case had been agreed in principle he sent his eldest son Charles Edward to finalize the settlement. The sum of $20,000 (£5,000 at the prevailing rate of exchange) was agreed as the Rawlins' share of the inheritance, payment to be made twelve months later; but when it became due the rate was so unfavorable that Rawlins senior decided to get the money out in kind, sending his youngest son, Richard, to America to buy cotton for shipment back to England. The family evidently had great faith in their twenty-year-old son, and with good reason.

Richard Rawlins briefed himself well before embarking on his journey. Charles had made many useful contacts during his visit, and armed Richard with introductions to people of importance, who in turn added to his list of the "great and the good." He also read the accounts of others who had toured the States, and one name that appears several times in the pages of the *Journal* is that of Harriet Martineau, a formidable figure who is still in vogue in scholarly circles, her most recent biography by Gillian Thomas having appeared in 1985 in Twayne's English Authors series, Northwestern University, Halifax, Nova Scotia. Her brother James was a celebrated theologian, moral philosopher, and a powerful preacher, who at this time was a Presbyterian minister in Liverpool and well known to Rawlins. Harriet (1802–1876) had just established herself against great odds as a writer on political economy and a leader of thought on a wide range of subjects when she made her tour of America from 1834 to 1836, mainly for relaxation, and with no intention of writing a book. For one thing she was well aware that the American public was tired of reading the patronizing criticisms by English travelers of their public and private lives, the most recent and provocative of which were Frances Trollope's *Domestic Manners of the Americans* (1832) and Captain Marryat's *A Diary of America,* published after his 1838 tour, both of which had aroused storms of protest. For another, Miss Martineau realized that her views on slavery were so well known that her very presence might be resented. She put it about that she had come to the States to learn and not to teach, and that her visit was not a "book-making expedition."

On her return, however, she was so besieged by publishers that she changed her mind: her *Society in America* appeared in 1837, and her

Retrospect of Western Travel the following year. *Retrospect* is a more-or-less chronological account of her travels, whilst *Society* deals at great length with the political, economic and social life of the people. These six volumes were required reading for Rawlins, who was to cover much of the same ground, meet many of the same people, visit the same places and institutions, and then to compare his impressions with hers. But the very spontaneity and youthful exuberance of his writing testify to the fact that he was his own man, with a keen eye and ear for detail.

For the benefit of the American reader I should explain that I have retained Rawlins' spellings, which differ in some respects from American usage as established by Noah Webster in *An American Dictionary of the English Language* (1828). These variations will be found in the *Journal* in examples such as "traveller," and words that came into English from the French: centre, sombre, spectre, theatre, etc. However, another class of words of French origin shared the same spelling on both sides of the Atlantic for many years. Rawlins had been brought up on "honor", not "honour".

An American Journal, 1839–40

Kosciuo Sep 13. 1839. 2. P.M.

Watched the last form
of y.e last friend until it
faded into the general hue
of all surrounding objects, and
then with a leaden spirit, descended to view my abode for
the next month —   'Tis a long
time to look forward to — but my
berth is roomy — which it would not
be in the Steamer — and I am well
satisfied. b.?.M Unicorn left us c 4 o'clock
Wrote home p Pilot — dined at six —
Everything rather confused at first —
Sundry children have been keeping
up a constant squall this afternoon
A good N.E. breeze is blowing. The Capt.
is a fine hearty looking man & appears
to be very attentive to the ladies.
How thankful I feel for my mothers
aunts' farewell letters — whose seals I
have did not break until now! They
are like another voice

First page of the diary (actual size).

1
Outward Bound

The diary begins on board the "Roscius," one of the 'Dramatic Line' of sailing ships established in 1835 by Edward Knight Collins to compete on the Liverpool/Atlantic trade, offering fast passages and luxurious accommodation. Others in the line were the "Garrick," the "Shakespeare," the "Sheridan" and the "Siddons."

Roscius Sep 13 1839 2 P.M. Watched the last form of yᵉ last friend until it faded into the general hue of all surrounding objects, and then with a leaden spirit descended to view my abode for the next month. 'Tis a long time to look forward to, but my berth is roomy, which it would not be in a steamer, and I am well satisfied.

6 P.M. Unicorn left us at 4 o'clock, wrote home per pilot—dined at 6—everything rather confused at first. Sundry children have been keeping up a constant squall this afternoon. A good NE breeze is blowing. The Captn. is a fine hearty looking man, and appears to be very attentive to the ladies. How thankful I feel for my mother's and Aunt's farewell letters, whose seals I did not break until now. They are like another voice from home!

7 P.M. A heavy drizzle of rain. The ship is so steady that she would not cause a ball to roll upon a table. None of the passengers look friendly. I shall endeavor to propitiate them with pears and their friendship buy with biscuits. Passed the Skerries about 7 P.M. and soon after turned in.

Sep 14 Passed Holyhead some time in the night and are now bowling down the Channel with a fine breeze from NE. Saw Tuskar Light at about 8 o'clock. Soon after overtook a barque that left the day before us. No bad sign for a beginning.

Sunday Sep 15 Wind freshened up a good deal, but still from the same quarter. Made Cape Clear before daylight this morning, so that we are now in the broad Atlantic. Went to bed early decidedly squeamish.

Monday Sep 16. Wind changed to N. last night & freshened up to a gale. Lay in my berth until 6 P.M. Crawled on deck & then back to bed.

Tuesday Sep 17. Gale still continues with little chance of abatement. Rose to dinner at 5 but soon went back again.

Wednesday Sep 18. No change in weather! Rose at 11 and kept the deck till dinner. Much better.

Thursday Sep 19. Wind same but more moderate. Breakfasted &c. &c. at table to my own surprise and the congratulations of several. No longer had to sing to self as the passengers went down at the ring of the bell "But me not destined such delights to share." With some surprise informed at dinner today that a man named Norris at Philadelphia made locomotives for England and has sent several over. The informant Dr. Wm. Gibson, a fellow passenger who says he crossed in the vessel that had them as freight. [*William Norris had acquired a reputation as a designer and builder with his locomotive, the "George Washington," in 1836, and the following year received an order for seventeen for the Birmingham and Gloucester Railway.*] So much have these squalls and this NW wind detained us that the Capt. says he could make Point Lynass in 48 Hours! I hear today that a ship evidently Liverpool bound passed us when we had made our utmost distance on Monday, and would doubtless report us. A small porpoise amused us for some time today, keeping up with the ship for two or three hours. The Mother Carey's chicks follow astern, but are too wise to entangle themselves in the strings some of the passengers have hung out. The wind has much moderated—we have frequent squalls requiring hasty shortening of sail.

Friday 20 Sep. 1839. A week at sea today and yet within 55 hours sail of Holyhead. Wind NW. Passengers all improve upon acquaintance. Some convn. with Dr. W. Gibson who has been on an extended tour through England, and intends to publish a book much of yᵉ same kind, I suspect, as Dr. Mullinger's "Curiosity of Medical Experience." He appears to have had some first rate literary and scientific introductions in Britain. The day is warmer than the last three have been, and some of the ladies have appeared on deck but only for a short time.

21 Sept. This has been a glorious day. Wind moderate and favorable. Last night I walked the deck by moonlight, which is now nearly full. The wind was fresher then and our good ship dashed most merrily through the waves. We have now been several days at sea without seeing a solitary vessel. We had some conversation this morning at nine o'clock about the "Liverpool," that being the time she was advertised to sail. [*The "Liverpool," one of the first steamships to be built for the Atlantic trade, was launched on 14 October 1837, in competition with the "Great Western" and the "British Queen".*] Professor Gibson showed us several autographs before dinner today. Many very valuable. Long. 19° 16′. Wind still rather unfavorable. Several porpoises have been playing about the ship, Mother Carey's chicks still follow our track. Long 19° 37′

Sunday 22 Sep. Rose early, a glorious day though very calm. Not a breath stirs our sails. We are "idle as a painted ship upon a painted ocean." At Breakfast thought of the service. 'Twas rallied by the passengers for dullness. They are mostly Americans and are going home, not leaving it, and that for the first time too! Thought again of the service at chapel time, and of Mrs. Hemans' last sonnet beginning "How many at this hour are bending" [*Liverpool-born Felicia Dorothea Hemans (1793–1835)*]. This afternoon the wind freshened and we have made a little way.

Monday 23 Sep. Wind adverse. Looked out long and oft for a ship. The Capt. says it is strange we have not seen one for such a time. The infant son of Mr. and Mrs. Lord has been taken alarmingly ill. Dr. Gibson has prescribed for it, but says there is little hope. It is a glorious night, the moon brilliant, sometimes forcing its light through the scudding clouds which cross it. Is it not Scott that says such a scene is the emblem of virtue, struggling with the cares and sorrows of life? Long. today 21° 23′.

Tuesday 24 Sep. Fresh breeze favorable. At 12 noon saw a most glorious rainbow far surpassing "all seen of old," by me at least, differing from the common, it appeared only just above the verge of the horizon. After dinner the breeze became a gale. Woke at 8 A.M. and went on deck. Ship flying, almost, through the water, with the close reefed topsail, foresail, mainsail and spanker. Sprays dashing over her bow. The scene was most exhilarating.

Wednesday 25 Sep. Slept until too late for bathing, which I commenced on Monday. This morning at ten when we were all reading under the bulwarks, a fresh breeze blowing from N., the Capt. sang out "Sail O!" "Instantly with a wild halloo/Each on his feet his body threw." We had seen no new object for several days, and the sight was very grateful. She proved to be a large brig and passed within 5 miles of us. We hoisted our signals, though she showed none in reply we hope she will report us. At 3 P.M. we discovered a large ship but she only came near enough for us to know her class. We have made but 50 miles since 3 o'clock yesterday. We are obliged to lie so close to the wind to keep our course & there is such a heavy head sea that much forward progress is not easy. Went on deck when dark and after making an allowance of one hour found that Dr. Nichol would be just lecturing. Looked long on the Great Bear (distinctly visible notwithstanding the brightness of the moon), and thought of that wonderful binary system therein contained whose period of revolution is 195,000 years! Oh! the nothingness of man and his works. Mighty and glorious some of them are.

Thursday 26 Sep. Squally—with a heavy head sea. The Capt says he never saw such a succession of gales and general bad weather. The poor infant was this morning released from its sufferings. At 3 P.M. the body was placed in its early coffin and we all attended to hear the last rites. The ship was hove to and the lower grating of the second deck was opened. The coffin placed on a long plank was then fastened to heavy weights, and Mr. Gordon, one of our passengers, read the service in a very impressive manner. The scene was very solemn— all the passengers—high and low—were present and seemed to sympathize with the parents. At the words "we therefore commit his body to the deep," the end of the plank was raised and with a heavy plunge the remains of the infant were for ever lost to sight, until the mandate shall be issued "Restore the Dead, thou sea"! The cold day and the incident of the afternoon damped the feelings of many. The sun not being visible, the Capt. could not take an observation. The evening was very cold with a gale of course from the SE, but the moon was unobscured. Night after night she becomes weaker and just a proportion of the light of eternal Ursa Major becomes more revealed, and consoled me for the diminished glory of the "Orb of Night."

Friday 27 Sep Our two days sailing have brought us on to 28° 22′ long. The intensely beautiful evenings have atoned for the cold foggy days of late, and tonight is no exception—though it has been very fine. Wind still adverse—the ship making a great deal of lee way.

Saturday 28 Sep A heavy gale of wind from the W, which commenced at 1 A.M. and gradually increased until 4 P.M. when the sea was at its greatest height. For more than two hours the ship was under less sail than she ever scudded under before. We did not dare to show more than close-reefed main, top sail and stay sail. We were tossed about after the fashion of a cork. We hardly expected to sit comfortably at table. Save and except a ludicrous incident or two, dinner ended well. I had two pairs of trousers on, and had the satisfaction of filling the pockets of both of them with some very good port that a lurch of the ship gave me the undivided benefit of. The weather continues too thick to take an observation.

Sunday 29 Sep. Dull day—horrid headache—stopped in my state room. Sat down to dinner to dispel ennui. Away on deck sung out "Steam boat in sight" [the "Liverpool"?] Every plate was deserted, and we all hurried away, some up one ladder, some up the other—some through the ladies' cabin and not a few through the pantry. We met on deck to laugh at each other's credulity—which the most rigid of the party could hardly help doing.

Monday 30 Sep The symptoms of an E. wind that showed themselves last night have not been realized. There is no change from yesterday. The sun broke through the fog at 12 o'clock, and the Capt. had time enough to take the Latitude which is 47° 50′. The Longitude we are still without and if the weather does not change we will still lack it. The oldest sea travellers on board do not recollect such a continuance of adverse winds. This is the 17th day out, and since we left the channel we have been running N. or S. or if not we have been beating to the W. close hauled. Nevertheless we managed to make some way and by Collins' calendar some 1000 miles or so from Liverpool.

Tuesday 1 Oct 1839 Dead calm—drizzling rain—the most "dull desolate and drooping." No observation of course.

Friday 4 Oct. Nothing to report since Tuesday. Alternate calms and squalls. Wind favorable for 4 hours, then chopped round to the old quarter of NW or SW. Today is very fine with a singular sky all round the horizon, which the dullest imagination could not fail to shape into land. Today's observations show us to be in long. 43° lat. 46° 42'. A day's running would bring us on to the banks, but it has fallen dead calm and there is no very definite prospect of a breeze. I have had much interesting conversation with a fellow passenger, my "form fellow" at dinner. He is lively and clever, his knowledge not derived from books—but society—of which he appears to have seen much in his travels, which have been to all parts. He criticizes the Americans with candor, thinks there are some noble minds amongst them but that the instances are rare even in comparison to the number of people. We had some skirmishing the other day, as to the proper situation of a man assuming the right of publicly criticizing a nation. Should he be one who has lived years amongst them and acquired an intimate knowledge of their manners, habits and customs, and the causes which have led to conventionalisms which at first startle, or should he note down at the first glance the opinion he then forms? I make this entry not for the purpose of answering my own question, but to refer to it at some future hour when that opinion will have become more mature by observation.

Sunday 6 Oct. Wind changes right about. A fine fresh breeze from NE sprang up this afternoon. Before 4 o'clock we had studding-sails set up [*narrow sails at the edges of the main sails*] and were progressing at a rate of 10 knots. Today's observation places us thus: Long. 47° 45' lat. 44° 49'.

Monday 7 Oct. We have been passing over the banks since 3 o'clock yesterday. In the middle watch one of those appearances which one regrets so much to have missed the sight of regaled the optics of one or two of the passengers. About 1 o'clock we passed a fleet of boats fishing for cod. The first one seen discharged a kind of rocket to warn the others of our approach. Each one exhibited a light and there were about 100 in number, and the Capt. describes the passage through their midst as strongly resembling the passage through a lighted street by night.

We were gratified on Saturday by the sight of two vessels—the smallest of which replied to our signals. We found her to be the "Factor," a schooner, trading from St. Johns to Liverpool. We had great hopes she would report us. Our yards are all square—our studding sails still set, and we are dashing through the waves at 10 knots at least. Long. 52° 41' lat. 43° 18'.

Tuesday 8 Oct. The glorious breeze still continues. The log run today gave 12½ knots equiv. to 15 miles per hour. The sea is most brilliantly phosphorescent tonight. Some of us amused ourselves this morning by assisting the Captain with taking the names ages and occupations of all our passengers. We have 57 in the steerage and 23 in the cabin. Our steerage passengers are most respectable looking people, almost without exception. They are chiefly Scotch—some few are however Irish and we had no small difficulty and amusement in obtaining the names of the latter correctly. Observation today: long. 58° 34' lat. 42° 56'.

Wednesday 9 Oct. Our good NE wind has freshened into a gale, but as it is behind us we can snap our fingers at it. At 2 P.M. we passed two ships—one supposed to be the "Cambridge" which sailed 6 days before us. The ship is rolling more than she has yet done. Hardly a single "spill case" occurred at dinner however—so the laughers were disappointed. Independently however of laughing at each other's miseries, we always manage to keep up some joke or other between the three who reign paramount at our side. Prof. Gibson, Mr. Lewis and myself. As we are now within 500 miles of N.Y. an observation would be acceptable, but the day has been very foggy. The log was run two or three times at 12½ knots.

Thursday 10 Oct. A change has come over the spirit of the scene. Today is almost calm. What wind there is, is from W. and in despair of reaching New York by tomorrow evening, as some of us expected. However we have done too well already to grumble. Long 68° 24' Lat 40°.

Friday 11 Oct. The glorious breeze has returned—a fine N.E. and we are going 10 knots through it. Everyone is preparing for shore. The gentlemen are in their berths—the Dr. firing off his new gun— the Captain in a good humor as well he may be after such a splendid passage. The cow has commenced lowing—the pony neighing. Land birds flit about the vessel. All tells of our approach to our wished-for port. The wind lulled at 3 P.M. but soon after again sprang up, reviving our hopes of tomorrow's landing.

Sat 12 Oct. Greeted with the exclamations of surprise at my laziness by some passengers at my state room door at 7 this morning. Oh joyful news! The pilot boat was standing down for us. I was soon on deck—gazing at the highland of Neversink, "so long sung in song and told in story." At nine o'clock we were off Sandy Hook. It poured with rain, but who would care for rain—entering the port of N.Y. The view was unfortunately obscured in many places, however. And now every face seemed glad, smiles and dimples quite the rage. Had to wait half an hour for the lazy doctor to come on board and punch the sailors in the ribs to see if they were well. And now the hateful Customs House officers came on board. Stopped the package of presents. Passed an English brigantine with a slaver she had captured lying close beside her, the "Hercules" steamer towing us. Saw for the first time a first-class ship of war in complete rig. Every object now excited my utmost attention and kept it at the stretch until we anchored in the East River opposite Brooklyn.

Luggage and passengers were then transferred to the "Hercules" and we said our mutual adieus to each other on the passage to the shore. On the way (as Miss Martineau experienced) Mr. Clifton, a last passenger, asked me my opinion of New York. [*It was an old joke that was to persist as long as ocean travel itself.*] I was sorry to part with some of the passengers. Who can be so placed with regard to 20 others without feeling some regret at leaving them (save a misanthrope). Dr. Gibson asked me for my company. I was too glad to have to say nay. So amidst pouring rain we had our luggage stowed upon a cart, ourselves in a carriage, and drove to the American Hotel, next to Astor House. The doctor knew the owner would accommodate him, whoever else he excluded—he, (Mr. Cozzens), being under early obligation to the former. Every inn and place almost is full. Some of the passengers were coursing up and down the street for more than an hour.

2

The New World

Cozzens' Hotel is second only to the Astor House (which is right opposite) in size and importance. All my previous ideas of the massive pile of buildings so called were insignificant compared to the reality. It is said they can accommodate 400 persons at once. Our cicerone waiter first led us to one landing of our hotel, and then to the next and next and next, on which our room was, "a chair-lumber'd closet just 12 feet by nine" [*Goldsmith,* The Haunch of Venison] in which there were two beds.

Oh! the delights of a good wash, where you can use your arms and not have to bend your body double as on board ship. I indulged in as good a splashing as ever nurse gave child on a Saturday even. Down with the window and looked out—opposite is the Astor House— rivaling our own in height, and far surpassing it in size. Looked upon the walking pygmies below.

Halfway down hangs one that "gathers samphire" [*Shakespeare,* King Lear], I was going to say, but by the aid of a powerful telescope I find he is only cleaning a window! Every moment I hear the bang of the Park gates. Opposite, over the park, is one of the theatres. [*The Park Theatre, naturally.*] Hurried away to Mr. Persse's for my letters— find some missing somewhere. The hotels all have hairdressers' shops communicating with them. Went to ours and came back some pounds lighter. The gong gave its portentous sound at half past three, but we prefer dining at the second table (of both ladies and gentlemen). At five we accordingly entered the dining hall. We had almost the only two vacant seats left—so quick had everyone taken them up. We were distant three from the head of the table, where General McComb (commander in chief of the U.S. army) presided. Opposite to us sat Colonel Worth—engaged in several of the late battles [*RCR adds a footnote: "also in Mexico 1848"*]. Dr. Gibson knows them both intimately. After the ladies left, Mr. Cozzens, who presided at the other table, joined us and an hour passed pleasantly. Opposite to me at dinner sat the most faultless beauty I ever saw, and there were quite enough pretty women generally in the room to give me a favorable first impression of American beauty. Although there were at least 170 people in the room, the dinner was very well managed. Ice is in great abundance—a very big jug, on the butter, and under every chair, in a cooler. In an American hotel there appear to be only two retirements—that of Mr. Jinks within yourself, and that of your own bedroom. Chose the latter, and read, and re-read dear [*sister*] Julia's letter. Found Mr. Prince in the same hotel with myself. He has a book for me in his trunk, which he will get at soon. The letters, by some mistake, he put into the bag—where they are I know not. At nine another gong reached through the halls, landings, and passages for a kind of continuous tea and supper mixed, which remains on the table until 11 or 12. We slept three in our room, though it had but two beds, Number Three being the Dr.'s little King Charles spaniel Rose which he bought in London.

Sunday 13 Oct. Mr. Persse was to call for me this morning. but I missed him somewhere—to go Mr. Dewey's. I thought I never should have arrived at it. It is in Broadway which must be five miles without a turn. Arrived in the middle (or later) of the sermon; very tired (in consequence of walking on land). No one offered a seat! After standing quarter of an hour I spied a bench and crossed the end of the Church to it. Very handsome interior—every window stained glass. Back of yᵉ pulpit painted to imitate Gothic cloisters—savours of scene painting in theatres. Walked back and met Mure, with whom I walked until dinner time, when he was engaged. [*William Mure was a young Scotsman, now a New Orleans merchant and commodity broker, whom RCR had known in Liverpool. He was later to assist him in his assignment, and had evidently traveled to New York especially to meet him.*]

After dinner went to the Tabernacle—an immense Presbyterian Church said to hold 5000 people. Heard a fair sermon. Hymns not exactly chanted, nor yet sung, by a large no. of singers—very few of the people joining. The same thing at Mr. D's this morning. Many persons smoke to the church door, throwing their cigars away as they ascend the steps thereof.

Monday 14 Oct. Mure called after breakfast, and took me to Napan St.—Saw Mr. Campbell and presented my letter. Walked to Wall St. and found great numbers of people talking together—on the present crisis evidently. Nothing is talked about today but the Bank suspensions. There was a great run upon the banks here on Saturday. From one, kegs of bullion were taken one day last week! Called on Mr. Persse who had the box of presents. Apprised and paid the duty. Met Mure at the reading room—introduced me to Mr. Frith, a gentleman from Sheffield England who promised me a ticket to the room. Walked down with M. past the scene of the fire—all new stores now. Passed the store of Lewis Tappan, a great Abolitionist, for whose head $20,000 was advertised by the planters—who being afraid the Southerners would fire his premises, built them of granite to the top—all the others have only granite basements.

Dined with Mure at his boarding house—very comfortable, but there is not room for another—I am pining away in this vast house with no-one to speak to—tasted American oysters, which are finer, fatter and larger than English. Mure introduced me to Mr. Hicks, N.Y. agent for H. Mure & Co., and Mr. Dixon, New Orleans agent for J. Holford & Co. He also pointed out Vincent Nolte whose speculation of 34,000 bales cotton astonished the New Orleans people so much <u>before</u> they knew him, and some of them far more <u>since</u>.

<u>Tuesday 15 Oct.</u> To the "Roscius." Fish'd my box out of the hold and sent it to the Public Store. Called on Fryatt and Campbell—had a long confab. on the banks, cotton &c. I am told that if the usual fall business was doing in this city, the stores would be open till 3 in the morning and the pavements all block'd up completely. Nothing like it now. Fever physical in the South—fever monetary here. How will it end?

To Mr. Persses to tea. Mrs. P. pretty—very young—pleasant. Mrs. Lyne—lively—Mr. L. ditto. All nice people—very handsome house [*on the blotting paper interleaf RCR wrote "$11,500 Mr. P.'s house"*].

Went to American Institute Fair at Niblo's Gardens—one of the most extraordinary exhibitions that ever was conceived—in a large garden is erected an immense number of continuous wooden galleries and booths—in which will be found specimens of almost every man's wares in New York. Here is silk from its first formation to the high state of beautiful manufacture to which the Americans have brought it. Here are all sorts of new inventions—ingenious folding bedsteads, shutting up into sideboards (£7) Kitchen ranges, printing presses in operation—specimens of sign painting—portrait painting—marble painting—tailors' work—shoemakers' work – hatters' work—silver coffee and tea urns—wigs—books gorgeously bound and emblazoned—brushes of all kinds—railway propelled by

electromagnetism—handsome race gigs—sleighs and fire engines—
the specimens of the latter cost $1500 and decorated and seem fitter
for a drawing room than a fire. The object of the American Institute
is to encourage native talent by giving prizes to the most beautiful
work in each department of trade—but I understand that foreigners
settled here have generally carried them off.

Wednesday 16 Oct. Down to Wall St. Presented E. Davies' introduction to Jasper Grosvenor—pleasant man—thinks the N.Y. banks will
stand—but the parties wishing a suspension are very strong. Went to
Custom House—miserably slow dogs. One of the clerks, while numbers were waiting for him, turned round and occupied some time in
sharpening an old knife! Mr. Persse tells me the C. H. officers are
always the most active politicians, as the rule has become to turn out
those who are opposed to the "powers that be"—down to the very
lowest—(in the city it is carried down to the scavengers). Of course in
this way many a man must either sacrifice his conscience or his situation. The English law is better than this—no C.H. officer being allowed a vote at all. The ballot of course here protects a man's actual
vote [*RCR adds a later note in pencil "NO!"*] but then he is obliged to
exert himself for the party that is most likely to win.

Walked with Mr. Persse up Broadway—beauty (and wealth apparently) in abundance. Not much outward sign of a suspension. American ladies dress generally better than ours in the street. The more
handsome the kerchief the more it is displayed. Mr. P. introduced me
to Mr. Corring to whose boarding house I go this evening. Took a last
look out of my room window at the Astor House &c. I can command a
view almost into the dining saloon—when the waiters and eaters too
are very busy. The Astor House gong sounds almost as loud as ours
and I have been deceived several times by it. In the street beneath, in
the basement of the Astor House is a barber's shop with a very pretty
sign, merely bearing "wigs, inimitable wigs"!

Went with Mure to Peale's museum containing specimens of min-
eralogy, geology and natural history—a variety of curiosities—
cosmoramas, and portraits of almost every distinguished American.
Here too is a little dwarf 40 inches high only, very gentlemanly in his
dress. We first advanced to a kind of theatre, where a man extempo-
rized Blitz, Sutton (and every other black art man) showed us tricks.
Then a Dr. Valentine gave us specimens of American people from
different parts, changing his dress in a most magical manner—by
merely popping his head under the table. I weighed myself here and

found myself 7 pounds lighter than when I left England—Oh! what a falling off was there!

Thursday 17 Oct. 1839. Firmly fixed in my new boarding house—very glad to be rid of the noise and bustle of the American Hotel, not to mention the having to mount to the 5th or 6th storey. There were about 50 people to breakfast. Gen. Hamilton of S.C. (afterwards Gov. of Texas) is staying here. I do not know any of the people yet. To the Exchange in Wall St. at change hour, 1 o'clock. A low damp vaulted hall is used temporarily as a meeting place. Change is over at 2 o'clock and instead of closing the door, they sound a gong at that hour, which effectively prevents any more conversation at any lower breath than shouting.

Strolled up Broadway with Mure—into the Astor House. Here they wash by steam with a vengeance—a shirt to be given out to be washed at 11 o'clock may be on your back at ¼ past 12! All cooking is done by steam ranges. After dinner, visited the Battery with Mure. Went to call on Miss Throckmorton—Miss T. not at home—saw her sister very like her. Turned into a book auction and bought a few books—not so cheap however as I expected. We pass'd two soldiers (officers Mure called them) drunk—reeling along the Battery Walk. [*Here ten lines are heavily scored out.*]

Procrastination is indeed the thief of time. I have put off writing my private letters until this evening. It is now pouring—but prospect for the "Liverpool" tomorrow at 2.

Saturday 19 Oct. Took a Drydock stage with Mure to see the "Liverpool" away. Left her after waiting half an hour after her proper departure, leaving my own and Mr. Persse's parcels with Mr. J. Pegg. Mure dined with me and we went to the National [*Theatre*] in Niblo's Gardens in the evening—"La Somnambula"—Miss Sherrif as Amina.

Sunday 20 Oct. Went with "mon ami" to Mr. Dewey's [*Rev. O. Dewey*]. More civility in showing us into seats. Heard a sermon from Ecclesiastes—"Behold I have seen all things under the sun and all is vanity" or words to that effect. Brought forward some ideas and sentiments both new and strange. Amongst them was the choice of the world as it is in preference to its being perfectly innocent—because it has been the glorious scene not only of the sufferings of martyrs but those of Jesus Christ. His opinions appear to belong to the class of moralists called optimists. He quoted two or three times from

Shakespeare—once largely from Hamlet's soliloquy "To be or not to be."

After dinner we found it too late for Dr. Hawks, and walked round by some parts of the west end. We passed the houses of several millionaires, amongst them the handsome mansions of Mr. Coster and Mr. John Jacob Astor—the builder of the house bearing his name. It is said that the latter is a most profoundly miserable man—subject to both nightmare and somnambulism. Who would be wealthy at such a cost? Mure told me an anecdote of him. One day a clergyman called on him for a subscription for some charitable purpose. Astor knew his errand but affected not, and commenced with: "Oh sir, I am so sick." "Indeed sir, where do you feel pain?" "Oh no pain bodily, but I am sick to death of beggars dunning me for subscriptions. What can I do for you, sir?" The clergyman saw there was no use, and took the hint and his departure.

We visited Lafayette Place—a row of houses built of white marble entirely—which costs, laid down here $8 a ton. These houses are built with beautiful Corinthian pillars of great height. The rent is said to be from $2000 to $3000 per ann.

This evening we went to the Tabernacle, and heard a good sermon on the life and character of St. Paul, and some very beautiful singing. Today has been very cold—quite as much so as a December day in England. This afternoon we met a singular funeral in Broadway: Hackney coach hearse, about 80 men (2 & 2), 35 hackney coaches— an Irish funeral evidently. We could not learn whose funeral it was— but the driver who closed the procession said it was that of "an ould country man." Many of these coaches had no person in them, and the majority had not more than three—generally women—laughing and making merry.

Monday 21 Oct 1839 Cold thermometer ranging somewhere about 35°. Clear blue sky. Letters from [*many names scored out*] Aunt V. and John S. [*John de Saussure, grandson-in-law of Richard Champion, and one of the surviving beneficiaries of his estate*] very kind from both. Called on Miss Throckmorton, one of my fellow passengers on Roscius. Sister married to Mr. Van Hook, all boarding at Mr. Plinta's, Whitehall St.

Tuesday 22 Oct. Some interesting conversation at breakfast this morning with Mr. Kelly for whom I had a letter from Mrs. Ames. He boards in the same home with me. Whilst we were yet arguing, Mr. Corring, keeper of our boarding house, joined us, and when Mr.

Kelly left he amused me much by saying "Mr. Rawlins, don't listen to him, listen to me, and then you will get at the truth!" Mr. Kelly tells me he has certain fixed sentences which he regularly brings out if the subject matter in hand be law, love or larceny, politics, phrenology or physics.

At one o'clock Mure and I took tickets for a journey to Harlem— the extreme point of Manhattan Island. The railway goes along the centre of the street from the City Hall to the outer boundary of the city. To this point it is drawn by horses. The locomotive was then attached and we were whizzed along at the rate of some 12 or 14 miles per hour. Harlem is a pretty country place. We strolled over the bridge into Westchester County. Men and boys were hauling up bass fish (with rod and line) very quick. Ordered dinner and amused ourselves with rambling about until it was ready. A most gentlemanly-looking host and a genteel looking girl (that we scarcely liked to mention the word money to) waited upon us. Bass fish and a fowl that we heard crowing as we entered the hotel an hour before, served us for our meal.

The day was gloriously fine, and as we took our seats in the stage coach to return, we saw that the night would be equally so. The moon was completely at its full, the sun set, for there is very little twilight here. After leaving Harlem we ascended a gentle acclivity and soon gained a view of the East River with the moonlight sleeping on its placid surface. It was long, very long since I had such a view before, and by tacit agreement we enjoyed it in silence. The weeping willows line this avenue almost from Harlem to New York—and with the white wooden houses give a picturesque scenery to the road. This constant habit of painting everything white (steamboats, palisades, churches, houses) must be very trying to the eyes on a day in July.

To the opera of Gustavus the Third [*of Sweden*], beautiful singing. Aurora Borealis was visible about 11 o'clock.

Wed 23 Oct. Crossed over to Brooklyn and had a fine view of New York therefrom. The sky blue and clear, this bay is certainly a magnificent one. Just below me was a 74-gun ship with boats crowded around her and at least a thousand blue and red shirts drying amongst her rigging. Returned by the Whitehall ferry having first crossed by the Fulton.

Thursday 24 Oct. Looked as usual at evening bulletin board for the "Orpheus," in vain. Oh! what blessings letters from home are.

Strolled to the Battery with Mure through Broadway. Mr. Grosvenor called in his carriage to go to his house to tea. Very pleasant man— the interior of his residence handsomer than the exterior. Mrs. G. vivacious, pleasant—pretty. Miss G. possessing the second quality at least. Mrs. C. G. very handsome and tolerably well informed so far as an hour or two could show. Spent from 6 to 10 in pleasant confab. Invited by Mrs. G. to return, and by Mr. G. still more pressingly.

An hour's amusing argument between Mr. Kelly, Mr. Corring and myself. We made C. contradict himself over and over again, and underwent almost pain to avoid laughing. Poor Mr. C.—he thinks the United States are going to rack and ruin!

Friday 25 Oct. "Orpheus" 34 days out today, and still no sign of her. Crossed to Brooklyn again—a glorious day. The weather indeed is far superior to any I saw in England. Such an intense blue sky we rarely have. Watched the "Garrick" towed out from the heights above Brooklyn and could not avoid a passing wish that I was in her. Met Mure at 5 and we spent the evening together. At coffee we had the celebrated buckwheat cakes so much lauded by Americans. They somewhat resemble our pancakes, but have no eggs in them. They are baked on a kind of griddle over a quick fire. They are more than passable, they are very good.

Saturday 26 Oct. Glad to leave Gorrings, where the waiters are scanty in number and wanting in sense. You might almost starve in the midst of plenty, if you did not keep up a constant call until you secured a waiter.

Embarked at 9 in the Jersey steamboat—booking previously for a trip to Philadelphia. By a good arrangement wagons are placed in the packet to receive the baggage, and upon landing are wheeled straight away on to a lorry attached to the train. Extraordinary carriages, built very long, all one apartment with seats transverse and holding between 50 and 60 persons each. There are 8 wheels to each carriage—4 at each end, above which is a swivel to allow the wheels free play at the curves, which are very great. We first passed Newark— where I looked in vain for "Yarrow's birchen bower," [*Wordsworth?*] though to atone for the want thereof hundreds of the gently weeping willows relieved the intense whiteness of the houses.

We stopped for a few moments at N. Brunswick, when some of the passengers actually moistened their whistles, though it was but half past 10. Princeton (celebrated for its battle) and Trenton, were then passed, and a very small place called Rahway, where however I saw an immense sign with BANK displayed on a dilapidated looking brick house. After leaving Newark I found there was only one line of railway and surmised that it would be very awkward if we met a train. About two miles beyond Princeton this happened and we were obliged to turn back to that place before we could find a road to receive our train and allow the other to pass. Rather annoying to the impatient. [*RCR was intrigued by the differences between American and English railways. The London to Liverpool line was double-tracked.*]

Some 7 or 8 miles from Philadelphia most beautiful views of the Delaware broke through the trees, with here and there a bright white sail stealing along. The day inexpressibly lovely. No cloud has changed the sky's deep azure of the last six days, while a gentle breeze has during that time been sufficient to prevent too much heat. Views of the Delaware delighted me until we arrived in Philadelphia which was at 3 P.M.

This was an exceedingly pleasant trip—sometimes for two or three miles dashing along the side of a canal—astonishing the slow-going barge—at other times careering over a river in a wooden bridge rumbling and shaking as if it would let us in. Now driving our way apparently through a dense wood with lofty boughs arching far above us, and the leaves varied with every hue, almost, which the painter's art could fancy. Bright red (the maple), brown green (willow) and yellow relieved one another as you looked along the thicket and amply atoned for the want of hill and dale in many places along the road.

The locomotive left us outside the town, and horses drew our train through the centre of the street—a circumstance which I have before mentioned as appearing in N.Y., and which we should deem so strange. The streets are, however, very wide. Sometimes the railway turns a right angle, and it gives one the idea of firing a gun round a corner. This could not be done if the axles of the wheels were fixed to the body of the carriage, which I have before stated they are not. When the train stopped I picked up my valise and posted away for Chestnut St. On the way on the corner of the street I saw a very amusing sign over a tea dealer's shop door and under which was written "Boston Tea Party 1773." Above was a representation of the Bostonians throwing the tea into the sea—for the importation of which England wished to tax her American colonies, and from which primary act "the great revolution" may fairly be dated.

Took up my quarters at the U.S. Hotel immediately opposite the U.S. Bank from which has emanated transactions so important to the commercial world. The bank has a noble front of 8 columns of the purist white marble—fluted Doric order—resting on a basement reached by 12 steps. [*The meticulous RCR had left a space here and later inserted the figures in pencil.*] The marble is of course unpolished. The street is a great thoroughfare and I surmise is the Broadway of Philadelphia. Strolled down it as far as the Delaware and crossed to Camden (New Jersey) by one of the numerous ferry boats which go every five minutes.

The machinery, like that of most of the river steamers in N.Y., is above deck and the vessels are about as long as they are broad. They are admirably adapted for carrying horses and carriages over. The carriage is driven on to the deck of the steamer, and just drives off again on the other side. In the middle of the river we passed a lovely island covered with willows and other trees. All round the wharves or landing places at the different ferries these beautiful trees grow in rich profusion and add a charm to the view.

As I returned, the last rays of the sun were just departing from the golden horizon and lighting the Delaware with their blessed beams.

At 8 o'clock called upon Dr. Gibson and accompanied him to Prof. Hare's where the conversazione was to be held. The Dr. soon introduced me to Mr. Vaughan (the "Man of Roses of Philadelphia"). He immediately recollected Charles—we conversed together for some time. Prof. Dunglisson (a native of England) joined us and Mr. V. introduced me to him. He too remembered Chas. well. Presently our group recd. the addition of Dr. Poulterson, President of the Mint— to whom I was also presented, as well as to many others [. . . .]

At about 10 o'clock the folding doors of the dining room were thrown open, where a splendid supper was laid out "with all the delicacies of the season"—as the newspapers have it. There were about 60 persons present. At 11 they had thinned to about 20 or 30— when Dr. Gibson and I took our departure—the latter very much pleased with this specimen of a Philadelphia conversazione. These meetings, which are held every Saturday evening at some member's house, are called Wistar Parties in honor of the late Prof. Wistar, who first commenced them. [. . .] No native or citizen of Philadelphia is admitted unless he is a member of the Philosophic Society, but a member may introduce as many strangers as he chooses. When members of Congress are passing through Philadelphia on their way to sessions, these parties are very crowded.

Punctual to the moment this morning <u>Sunday 27 Oct</u> at 10 o'clock Mr. Vaughan's old servant came to conduct me to his house. He welcomed me kindly and pointing to Charles' name in a book asked me if I knew that name? I then entered mine in the same way. "There is no fire here, you perceive" said he. "My servant asked me if I should light one, and I told him to look at the thermometer. He found that it was 70°, so you see he has judged wisely." Round his room were the portraits of the wise and good. The "Pater Patriae" over the chimney piece (as in many places I have been in). He showed me the portrait of his father and of the Rev. John Yates, father of his namesake R. Vaughan Yates [. . .] Mr. Vaughan then told me some particulars about his early life. He left school at Warrington [*Lancashire*] in 1776. Went to the West Indies and returned in 1779. To France and Spain the year following. In 1783 he was captured crossing the Atlantic and taken to New York, where he remained on his parole until the peace. As I afterwards learned he is a relation of Petty Vaughan, an English counsellor.

[*A fuller account of John Vaughan's life appears in* The Pennsylvania Magazine of History and Biography, *which indicates that he was one of the most distinguished men Rawlins was to meet. His father Samuel had been a member of Benjamin Franklin's London Coffee House Club—the "honest Whigs," and frequently entertained Franklin at his London and country homes. Samuel and the rest of the family followed John out to America in 1783 and soon established themselves among the elite of Philadelphia. Both were elected members of the American Philosophical Society, and John became its secretary, a position he held for fifty years. Records show that "every traveling foreigner of distinction and every American of note was entertained at his Sunday breakfasts." It is not clear how Rawlins and his brother before him qualified for such attention, but it is likely that their grandfather Richard Champion had been most welcome there.*]

<u>Monday 28 Oct</u>. This morning I went straight away after journalizing to the Chinese Museum. With this collection of Chinese "everythings" I was much pleased. I spent more than three hours here and then came away without seeing all. At 2 o'clock I called upon Mr. Smith at the Philadelphia Library and presented my letter from CERJr. He first showed me through the Library founded in 1731 by Benjamin Franklin and now containing upwards of 50000 vols. Behind in a separate room is a library of 8 to 10,000 vols. presented by Mr. Logan, Mr. Smith's great grandfather, with an endowment for its increase—a farm worth $500 per ann. and which will before long be

worth 10 times as much. Of this Mr. Smith is the hereditary librarian. He then showed me the library of books embracing the original editions of Cowper, Goldsmith &c presented to the Philadelphia library by Dr. Preston, an English rector. [. . .]

After leaving the Library Mr. Smith took me to the Athenaeum where Mr. Vaughan had entered my name. [. . .] From this place we crossed into the State House and in a few minutes I found myself in the room where the Declaration of Independence was proposed, debated upon and signed. Fancy was busy as I pictured each noble spirit rising in his majesty and approaching the memorable document. I felt overawed by the recollection of the intellectual glory and moral courage for which those great men have been, and shall be, as long as time shall last, distinguished. I longed to be alone to give open vent to my feelings. Alas! thought I, is there among the Americans themselves the deep reverence I feel so deeply now? I have not seen enough of them to answer Yes. From what I have seen I should give a reluctant negative to the enquiry. They lose, in the spirit of party, the welfare of their country. They forget all that is due to the imperishable glory of Washington, and would seek to build upon a pedestal of the purest marble,—white, chaste unsullied—an image of gold, an idol of metal for which the virgin innocence of the former is neglected; and to which they sacrifice alike their reason and their judgement. But is it not ever thus with that withering demoralizing principle, "party spirit," well said to be "the [illeg.] of many for the gain of a few." There is a very fair statue of Washington at the end of the room cut in wood by Mr. Rush a native artist. [. . .] In this room too is a portrait of Wm. Penn, a fine full-length painting and another of the noble, disinterested La Fayette for whose services the Americans were so grateful; and never was gratitude so amply due as to him, who in the hour of the greatest danger confronted it for the cause of honor and virtue.

[*Marie Joseph La Fayette (1757–1834) was a nineteen-year-old captain in the French army when the American Colonies declared their independence. He was so taken with their cause that he volunteered to fight on their side, and on 31 July 1777 Congress passed a resolution "that his services be accepted, and that in consideration of his zeal, illustrious family and connections, he have the rank and commission of major-general of the United States." He served with distinction until after the Battle of Yorktown when he returned to France to become a prime mover of revolution in his own country.*]

From the Hall of Independence as the celebrated room is called (and which by the way is sacrileged by the elections being held therein) we crossed the passage to the steps fronting Independence Square, which rang to the shouts of a free people, when they were called to hear the Declaration read for the first time. Mr. Smith then took me upstairs to the summit of the steeple—taking me into the Circuit Court on the way up, and pointing out to me Judge Hopkinson, author of the national melody "Hail Columbia"! From the exalted position above, the city appeared of great extent. Mr. Smith pointed out to me its rapid growth by showing me what was once his father's country house, the ground of which is now occupied by the Chestnut Theatre, and beyond which Philadelphia now extends more than a mile.

After dinner I walked up to Mr. Furness's [*a Unitarian minister*] in Pine St and had an hour's pleasant conversation with him. [. . .] Spent the remaining hours at the Athenaeum to which Mr. Vaughan had given me the privilege of entrée. It is a double room, the one containing newspapers only, the other reviews, books maps, charts &c.

Tuesday 29 Oct Met Mr. Smith at 9, by appointment, at the Museum round which he took me hurriedly, as I could come at my leisure and inspect it. We then entered his carriage—a light one-horsed vehicle—and he drove me to the water works—passing on the way the Laurie Charity School for the Blind, of which last Mr. Vaughan is Treasurer—as he is indeed of several charities. The Schuylkill Water Works afford another instance of a simple contrivance being neglected for years—buried so to speak, in its own simplicity. The water was originally forced up to the immense reservoirs above the Schuylkill by forcing pumps worked by steam. This was found inefficient and expensive, but no way was suggested until the present simple but effectual contrivance was proposed by Joseph D. Lewis, a connection of Mr. Smith's, who with a few other gentlemen built him a monument of his great work. The forcing pumps are worked by six immense water-wheels, which cause a continuous roar, and the water is projected into the first of six large reservoirs on the summit of Fair Mont above. From the first pond, it passes into the second and so to the last. The level of this hill is higher than the highest roof in Philadelphia. Water is consequently most abundant in all parts of the city.

From the water works we went to the Girard College, passing the gloomy baronial prison on the way, called the Eastern Penitentiary. . . .

[*RCR goes into a long description of the half-built college and its purpose—
the education and residence of orphans, but he thought much dispute would
arise as to whether an orphan was a child deprived of one or both parents.*]

We soon arrived at Laurel Hill cemetery, the most beautiful spot,
perhaps in the neighborhood of Philadelphia. [. . .] On returning to
the city I spent an hour in the Philadelphia Museum, of which Mr.
Smith is the curator. The most interesting objects to me were the
skeleton of mammoth, (found by Peale the originator of this museum, in 1806 in Pennsylvania), and a collection of Indian dresses,
ornaments, implements of warfare, brought together by Capt. Lewis,
one of the celebrated Lewis and Clarke explorers.

After dinner I sauntered up Chestnut St. [. . .] and arrived at Mr.
Furness at half past 6. Mrs. F. welcomed me kindly—I have to thank
Charles for all this open sesame. After tea, however, I did not see Mrs.
F. as we adjourned to the study. [. . .] I have seldom passed so pleasant a conversational evening. Upon remarking the Boston Tea Party,
Mr. F. told me that Mrs. F.'s grandfather was one of the parties
concerned—at least it was at his warehouse the disguises were assumed and doffed. His wife made a vow that she would drink no
more tea until the duty was removed. This she faithfully kept—
though exceedingly fond of the beverage—until 4 July 1776. This
family, closely pressed by a party of British, were compelled to take to
an open boat in which they made their escape down the coast. When
the conversation turned on oratory and eloquence we mutually condemned Brougham's fulsome flattery of the Duke of Wellington.
From this I mentioned the comparison between the former &
Webster—Mr. F. thinks highly of Webster and mentioned a circumstance of his power of language, characteristic of the man.

When Jackson sometime since wanted money to carry on the Indian war—without much notice he pushed into the Senate at 10
minutes to 12 a bill authorizing the expenditure of $1,000,000. Now
the Senate, which at 12 would close for the session, were evidently in
favor of passing this bill, when Mr. Webster rose, and for 8 minutes
spoke with a force and energy that electrified the house. The consequence was the bill was ejected.

Mr. Furness told me some further particulars about the venerable
Mr. V. He was the friend, the intimate friend, of Jefferson, and accompanied Franklin on his visit to Europe. No-one knows what are
his politics. The only time he was ever known to betray himself, if it
might be so termed, was when riding out with Jefferson once—when,
having a new horse it stumbled and nearly fell. "Ah!" said Mr. V. "this

fellow's a Democrat." "No," said Jefferson in reply, "or he would have thrown his rider before this." Mr. Vaughan made no rejoinder at all confirmatory of his first exclamation. Mr. V. is vice consulate of the Brazils, and Spain and Portugal, treasurer of the Chamber of Commerce, and of the Athenaeum, president of the Blind Asylum and vice president and freeman of half a dozen other societies and charities. [. . .] So well is he generally known that a letter posted at Quebec and directed "John Vaughan, United States" was not long in finding him. [. . .]

Wednesday 30 Oct. Joined Mr. Smith this morning at the museum and walked with him to the Eastern Penitentiary. [. . .] From the prison we went to Asylum for the Blind. The Principal was very obliging and showed us everything that was worth seeing in it. [. . .]

At 7 this morning Thursday 31 Oct. I embarked on the steamer for Borden Town [*near Trenton, N.J.*] at which place we arrived at 9. The sail up the Delaware was pretty—and the water was without a solitary ripple, the reality and shadow deceiving the eye and baffling its attempt to identify each separately. At Borden Town we entered the railway car, precisely similar to those on the other railway—and rode away to Amboy, passing some rather dense woods, tinged as they all are with every varied hue. At Amboy, which is at the mouth of the Raritan, we had a most delightful sail through the winding straits which separate Staten Island from the main. At New Brighton on Staten Island there are some very handsome erections, wooden, of course, but in better taste than most of the villas are built.

At 2 o'clock I arrived in New York after spending four days in the regularly built, hospitable, intellectual city of Philadelphia, which numbers within its walls more interesting institutions, and handsomer public buildings than it ever was my lot to see before. Had a most stringing disappointment on finding no letter per "John Reynolds" and only one per "Independence" and not a single newspaper by either. Spent the evening in Mure's room—after calling on Miss Squire—a pleasantish sort of body, who with her nieces asked me to tea tomorrow.

[*RCR spent the next few days with Mure and other New York acquaintances, before embarking on a long journey. The "Great Western" brought a letter from Charles, and one from his aunt ("with a P.S. from my mother").*]

Wednesday 6 Nov. Made an expedition with Mure to visit the "Patrick Henry"—the splendid new Liverpool packet. I think she has a more convenient cabin than the "Roscius." From the "Patrick Henry" I went up to the "Gt. Western." She does not look to my eye any larger than the "Liverpool" and, I think, inferior to the latter in appearance outwardly. Her cabins are much more elegant—each panel beautifully painted with some pleasing device. I went below and inspected her engines—the largest I have seen save those of the "British Queen." I had not a fair inspection of the "Gt. Western" as she has but just come in, and everything was in the confusion generally attendant on a recent arrival.

After dinner I went into the Battery and saw the sun set with a brighter glory than the last night at sea—and that is saying what I never expected to be able to say with truth. And now to pack up for a farewell from New York tomorrow morning.

What shall I say of this heart of the United States, from which all its commercial veins and arteries seem to be nourished? New York is not what would be called a handsome city. There are very few fine buildings—and those which are so are more elegant than imposing, being petite, at least compared to some of the noble Philadelphia erections. The chief of these are in Wall St.—banks and insurance offices. When the Merchants Exchange is finished it will doubtless be a very handsome building. The same may be said of the new Custom House, which is also in the course of erection. The principal street in New York is of course Broadway. This is about 100 feet wide, and some 3½ miles long. [*This would reach only as far as 42nd St.*] The upper part contains a great many of the best houses in the city—though these are by no means in Broadway only—being distributed about the upper part in squares and handsome streets.

The lovely trees, chiefly weeping willows, which line so many of the streets in New York and Brooklyn give these cities a foreign air to an Englishman. Residents in the city must know the value of them on a hot day. Broadway is most crowded about 2 o'clock when I think all the ladies in the city must be abroad. This city can boast of very many pretty faces, but I have not seen a single fair figure. [. . .] The boarding house I am just about to leave is the most comfortable I have ever been in. Tea in the evening is handed round just as it is at parties in Liverpool—the first time I have seen it in this city. And now, packing being completed—bills paid—and farewells said to my only friend in the city let me turn and anticipate the Hudson tomorrow by dreaming of it tonight.

3

New York to Lockport NY

New York to West Point by steamboat

Thursday 7 Nov. Called at 6 this morning, dressed myself by lamp-light, and hastened down to the Albany steamer—the "Champlain"—a very fine looking boat with double engines, over deck of course, fitted with expansion valves. These engines are, I believe, not connected. I cannot see how they can cause them to work uniformly separate, however. The cabin of this steamer runs her whole length from stem to stern, and here, round a suffocating stove sat groups of passengers, and here too they remained whilst we were passing the most splendid scenery of the river. Some two or three miles from our starting point we had to take up passengers and I could not but admire the speed and dexterity with which the boat, which hung by blocks over the side, was lowered and hauled up after doing its office.

The noble views in this noble river soon commenced—and for several miles rocky precipitous banks lined the west side of the river, with here and there an apparently inaccessible cottage at their base. These heights are called I believe "the Palisades." I was very much gratified shortly after this by a beautiful instance of refraction which kept the point opposite N.Y. suspended in the air, long after it had really disappeared. We soon after passed Sing Sing. The State prison is visible from the boat. It is said to have 800 cells for solitary confinement. There is a large quarry inside the quadrangle of the prison in which the convicts work.

Past Haverstraw Bay, the river becomes very narrow, and not the closest investigation of the approaching highlands could enable me to determine between which of them the Hudson took its course. At length it appeared—totally opposite to the slight speculation I had formed—and now a sudden turn of an acute angle brought West Point into view. West Point—the beautiful par excellence. I was soon landed and my baggage tossed over the side, and away went the steamer. I had my trunk &c. deposited in the packet house—a small shed—and a soldier presented a slate requiring my name. As I thought he might present something else if I did not, I gave it to him, and taking my valise in my hand wormed my way up the steep bank to the hotel accompanied by a U.S. officer who had been my fellow passenger and who kindly offered to be my cicerone. The hotel looked more like a private house, no name appearing on its side or door, and had I been alone I should have hesitated not a little in making my entrée. It was now only 11 o'clock. We had run the entire distance, 52 miles, in less than 4 hours from N.Y.

After ascertaining dinner to be at the early hour of one, I walked out—the day not so fine as the clear sunrise promised. I was first attracted by the tomb erected in honor of Kósciuszko—a chaste white marble erection—a base supporting a Doric column, bearing simply the patriot's name. [*Tadeusz Kosciuszko (1746–1817) was a Polish soldier who had fought for the colonists in the American Revolution.*] From thence I went down to the secluded spot known by the name of "Kosciuszko's Garden." The autumn leaves almost hid his name, which is carved upon the marble basin of a little fountain. I mourned to see the benches cut and marked with the names of fools who had not enough to think of and view from this gentle spot, but were compelled to fill up their time with this odious practice.

Passing through the opening between the military college and chapel and the barracks of the cadets, I sought the road to Fort Putnam, and in ¼ of an hour found myself upon its ruined heights. Surely there cannot be another spot on earth as West Point viewed from the Fort. Up and down the river, which is covered with little craft with bright white sails, shown whiter by the afternoon sun, the eye can range—resting for relief on the rocky headlands and slopes covered with evergreen trees.

If the ingenuity of man were taxed to alter this place to make it more beautiful, it could not make change in a solitary shrub—so lovely it is already. I was sorry to descend, but I could not but be conscious that the wind was bitterly cold—so I turned my back upon it after seeing—or fancying I saw—the cell in which the unfortunate Major André was confined. It is doubtful, it appears, whether he ever was here at all. The place where he was discovered and seized is some miles further down the river on the same side as Fort Putnam.

[*In 1780 the American general Benedict Arnold approached the British offering to disclose the dispositions of the fortress at West Point, and Major*

John André (1751–1780) was appointed to negotiate with him. The handover went wrong, André was arrested in civilian clothes with the plans in his boots. He was tried and condemned to death. General Washington refused his appeal for execution by firing squad, and he was hanged. Arnold escaped and was commissioned as a British officer. Miss Martineau, when in Boston, met a Mr. Sparks "who brought with him the pass given by Arnold to André, and the papers found in André's boots. He possesses also the reports of the West Point fortifications in Arnold's undisguised handwriting. The effect is singular, of going from André's monument in Westminster Abbey, to the shores of the Hudson where the treachery was transacted, and to Mr. Sparks' study where the evidence lies clear and complete." Jared Sparks' Life and Treason of Benedict Arnold *was published the following year.*]

The hotel is kept as a boarding house for the officers who are teachers at the academy, but it is open to as many more as it will accommodate. At mess (to speak <u>militarily</u>) I found that I was the only diner out of uniform. A gentleman, the engineer who landed with me, and whom, I soon found out, had been educated here, and myself were the only strangers present. They all seemed very gentlemanly men. After dinner they all left for the college—departing to their separate duties, and I was left alone with the young engineer. He told a few things about the academy. The cadets live very plainly— roast beef three times in the week and boiled the other three days— Sunday some other dish with a greater variety of vegetables. He said he never had his health so well as at West Point . . .

At 4 o'clock I went to the exercising ground to see what is called dress parade—i.e. a mustering of all cadets in full uniform to go through their evolutions and practice with muskets. There are about 250 now at the College. They were arranged in two lines of 125 each and looked extremely well. After going through their exercises, during which a band played a number of airs, the officer drilling them read over the list of those who had offended in any way against the rules of the establishment, which are very strict. The principle on which the cadets are taught musket exercise is good—viz., that before a man is an officer he should learn to be perfect as a soldier.

At tea I found the same parties assembled as at dinner—but as my fellow passenger of the morning left West Point after tea, and the officers dispersed—where I don't know—I had a brilliant lamp—a comfortable room—and a glowing fire all to myself, whilst the autumn wind whistling through the piazza and blinds outside made me value the blessings inside the more. I spent the evening in reading, writing and thinking of home and friends.

Friday 8 Nov. I threw open my blinds at 6 this morning and scarcely repressed the shout of delighted surprise with which I had astonished the servant who showed me into my room yesterday. We breakfasted at 7—we, that is the officers and myself only—the night boats whose lights I saw as I lay in bed last night had brought no visitors to West Point.

After breakfast I paid another visit to Kosciuszko's tomb and garden and then set out for the cemetery. Returning, I struck my path through the woods by way of changing my ascent to Fort Putnam. Here I was rather entangled and after a while sat down to rest. Just below are the barracks of a regiment quartered here and occupying about 50 pretty white cottages, almost the whole extent of the village of Camp Town. Behind me, feeding amongst the grass and brushwood were a number of cows each having around its neck a bell to speak of its whereabouts. These bells, some far and near came tinkling through the wood and added to the charm of the spot. Renewing my walk I came upon a little lonely charcoal burner. The cattle hung with bells, and the charcoal burner, called me back to many an early fairy tale of the Hartz Mountains.

In a few minutes I was again on the heights of Fort Putnam. The morning was more lovely than the night had promised, and I wanted but a companion to enjoy the glorious beauty of this perfect panorama. I was more sorry than before to descend, but I had to see to the cares of life—to have my baggage ready for the steamer, which will not stop for more than ½ a minute for anyone. This duty done I went down to Kósciuszko's Garden from whence I could see the Hudson for three or four miles, and enjoyed this lovely retirement until I saw the blue smoke of the 'Leviathan' curling above the gaudy foliage of the distant headland. The strict military surveillance obliged me to give my name again on leaving West Point—which done I leapt in the packet and soon left the village, academy and the hotel far behind.

West Point to Albany (by steamboat) 50 miles

I went down to the moving hotel beneath to deposit my cloak. Here resigned to a Knight of Suds was a gentleman whose beard he thought it would be better to leave on board than carry ashore. Round the stoves were groups of Americans, some reading the newspapers, and others arguing, and not a few gazing on the heated stove with "lack lustre eye." Behind the vessel was the ladies' cabin with careful injunctions to gentlemen who did not accompany ladies not to enter its precincts. These places were of course always forbidden to me.

If I do not get to Cincinnati soon I certainly shall become a Visigoth and shall retire to Rome. That is to say Rome N.Y., shut out the world and go wild. I booked myself for Catskill and was not sorry to see, as I thought, the Mountain House stage waiting on the wharf. I jumped on shore with my travelling case, my large trunk and little trunk came slowing trotting after. By way of caution I asked the driver of the stage if that was for Pine Orchard. "No stages at this season, sir, but we might manage perhaps to get you up there in a wagon." I looked to the plank. It was not removed. I ran back into the vessel and was horrified to see my trunk being left behind. "Stop!" I shouted. Fortunately I was heard and in two seconds, sadly disappointed, was once more on my way up the Hudson. Not only the Captain but the landlord at West Point had assured me that there were stages still running, so I felt the disappointment more from having my hopes fed by them. I could not help thinking, however, as I looked on the snowy range of mountains, upon one of which Pine Orchard hotel stands, that my night's rest in Albany would be warmer than if I slept on that eagle perch—or perhaps in the farmer's wagon on the way up.

In the boat I met with an English rector, Mr. de la Hooke, whom I found had a living in Bedfordshire, journeying to Toronto for the winter with his son, wife and daughter—the latter a merry-looking black-eyed girl. I saw that they were English people before I fell into conversation with the father. I was sure the young man's complexion was too rubicund to belong to American soil. The color in my face has also betrayed me several times since I entered the States. I found both father and son pleasant, and when we landed we went to the same hotel, Congress Hall. I also met with a young student of Schenectady College, who was on his way to spend his vacation in Buffalo. He had a happy, laughing manner with him and I could not help being pleased with his good-humored remarks about his College—and the City of Schenectady.

Albany to Utica (by railway) 93 miles

Saturday 9 Nov. Breakfasted at ½ p 7 and at 8 entered the car at the depot in State Street, from which, two and two, they were drawn by horses up the hill about 2½ miles out of the town [*where, presumably the locomotive was attached. This was the beginning of the Hudson and Mohawk Railroad, which had been open since 1831]*.

The State Hall and Academy are prominent and handsome buildings and not surpassed by any buildings in New York. When I had started about ten minutes, I found I had left my cloak at the hotel. I fortunately had kept my case in my hand and had plenty of room in my car. I quickly indited a letter to the landlord and gave one of the drivers a doucement and strict injunctions for a speedy delivery. I hope it may meet me at Utica. While giving the man directions, another gentleman with another letter came up with precisely the same purport as my own! We mutually laughed at each other's minor misery. We reached Schenectady in an hour and then changed cars. My new fellow passengers were two debating politicians, who argued for 30 or 40 miles—a stout farmer, nation and politics doubtful— and "John Browdie and his wife" (either them or their ghosts!) [*Dickens*, Nicholas Nickelby]. John Browdie's wife took my seat which I had chosen next the door to see the country. John sat opposite and as 'Tilly' had taken my seat I asked him for his. He gave me an indignant "no" and said that "the lady" had as much right to my seat as I had myself. There was no refuting so obvious a truism, but at length Mrs. Browdie was taken ill, and John was obliged to take a seat next to her, so I soon acquired an outside place.

We passed through the lovely valley of the Mohawk—on the other side of which is the Erie Canal with its comparatively slow-moving barges—indeed I may say superlatively slow. At length we came to the village of Little Falls, as romantically situated as one could desire. High banks lined the river on each side, with the grey mountain limestone peering through at intervals, and varying the perhaps otherwise monotonous green of the firs and cedars. On the opposite bank, supported in arches, an aqueduct leads the canal over the very bed of the river which foams and dashes below, whilst we were carried over a similar work on the railway track. Little Falls can boast of two or three woollen factories and some flour mills. What are called falls in this place are nothing more than rapids.

All through the valley of the Mohawk—on the steep bank over the canal are built hundreds of temporary little houses—rough, unpainted miserable-looking erections—hastily and temporarily knocked up for the Irish laborers who are employed in widening the Erie canal, and will be in deepening it, when all the water is out, which will be done shortly. [*The Erie Canal connecting Lake Erie at Buffalo with Albany on the Hudson river, opened in 1825, was the main artery connecting the northern Atlantic ports with the States of Ohio, Indiana, Illinois and Michigan. Freight could be carried between Albany and Buffalo in six days, compared with 15 days by horse and wagon. Passenger boats, drawn by relays of horses could cover the distance in 3½ days. The work of enlarging the canal, which RCR noted, had begun in 1835.]*

The snow lay upon all the mountains bounding our prospect—and a kind of biting sleet, or showers of little icicles made us glad to find ourselves in Utica a few minutes before 4 o'clock.

Here I was doomed to another disappointment. No coaches within 2 miles of Trenton Falls. I looked to the sky—it was black and lowering—to the mountains—they were white with frozen snow, and I was somewhat reconciled. Nevertheless, here I must stay for my cloak. I said farewell to the rector and his family—whom I have some chance of meeting at Auburn, if my cloak comes on, which I hope it will. The train leaves at 4 in the morning so I must take sleep by the forelock and away to roost.

Utica to Syracuse (by railway) 60 miles

Sunday 10 Nov. The faithful porter roused me at ½ past 3. "Has my cloak come?" was my first question. "Not seen it" was the reply. However, in hopes of finding it at the station, I jumped out of bed, and on looking out of the window, discovered (alas) a white world. The morning was biting cold. At the railway I found my cloak and I never gave a porter 25 cents with so much pleasure as when I once more clutched my warm companion. Our course lay for miles through woods and cedar swamps—the fallen trees thickly covered with frozen snow presenting a most dreary aspect. We reached Syracuse about 9 o'clock with nothing hardly of interest so far—save the dashing before daylight of sparks past the carriage windows—a sight that served to amuse me until darkness disappeared. Notwithstanding my moccasins, I was very cold when we arrived at Syracuse and was not sorry to see "Warm breakfasts upstairs" painted outside the hotel. This little inn has evidently only just been knocked up—yet it was very well furnished, and I do not recollect having seen anywhere a larger or indeed as handsome a couch as the one in the breakfast apartment of this little place.

<u>Syracuse to Auburn by railway 22 miles</u>

After remaining here for ½ an hour I entered the Auburn coach, built on the plan of the Philadelphia Railway carriages which I have elsewhere described—but larger and more handsome than those. A stove placed in the middle of the car made it so comfortably warm that most of the passengers doffed their hats and overcoats. A few miles from Syracuse we passed the Onondaga Lake with its <u>town</u> of Liverpool (I beg its pardon, <u>city</u> I mean) plainly visible on the other side. This is I believe a great place for salt.

At 11 o'clock we arrived at Auburn. We should have been there much earlier but the carriages remain sometimes as much as 10 mins. at a resting-place to allow the passengers to enter the "hotel," as many of these little dram shops are called—and go through the leg-stretching process as originally performed between York and London by that amiable pedagogue Mr. Wackford Squeers. [Nicholas Nickelby *had been published that year.*] My heart sank within me when we landed at the station, the sky black and threatening. The snow deep on the ground. The village of Auburn ½ a mile off, and no stage or wagon to the Auburn House, where I had agreed to meet the English family I had met at Albany.

I picked up my small valise and travelling case, and enquired the way. There was the prison, its black stone walls contrasting with the white snow, and making by association the scene more dreary still. I never recollect having such a walk as I had through the melting snow and soft wet clay as I had from the railway to the inn. Until fairly in the village there was nothing in the shape of pavement or even stepping stones. Long before I arrived at the Auburn House, my arms ached with my burden, for the valise had books in it and was very heavy. Here I found no name like the rector's. These people had been so kind that I was determined to see if they were at the American House, though it was still some distance. I was the more willing to do this, as the Auburn Ho. looked anything but tempting. It was not 12, yet several men were smoking and drinking brandy toddy in the bar, or office as it is called—so I again grasped my baggage. What became of the English people I do not know, but I did not find them at the American.

After dinner sallied forth for the Episcopal Church. Never since the day I left home had I felt so dreary as I did then. A cold wintry sky—snow everywhere—except right in the path where the constant passing had melted it over the soft clay—not an individual to speak to—yet I should not say so, for a gentleman seeing that I was trying the gate of the locked Episcopal Church kindly invited me to walk to his church and he would give me a seat. On the way he explained to me the reason of its being locked—the minister, a talented popular preacher had died the week before and there was no one to officiate.

In the evening I brought out all my letters and passed some time in reading them over again. Unless I have some more soon I shall certainly have acquired these by heart.

<u>Monday 11 Nov.</u> My heart bounded this morning as I saw once more the clear blue sky—the bright sunshine gleaming upon and melting the snow. We breakfasted at ½ past 7 and I then went over to view the prison. Never have I seen in any place such bolts and bars and locks as appeared on every door at this place. Entering the office I obtained an order for admission, paying 2 shill. therefor, and thro' a door locked by a key <u>one foot long</u> was led into an interior passage. Surely there must be more appearance than increase of strength in these massive locks. I was first shown the cells—small confined little holes which however are only occupied during the night, as all the prisoners work together during the day.

The cells are warmed by steam pipes passing outside—effectively preventing any conversation by night. The young man who showed me round was as stupid a person I ever met with in a public institution. He either would not or could not tell me anything I wished to know respecting the conduct of the prisoners &c &c—so that I came away after all without knowing anything but what my eyes told me. The first place this bright cicerone took me was the cooperage. Here I suppose about 50 convicts were at work. I took care to look at them when they would not see me—but those I glanced at by stealth confirmed generally Miss Martineau's account of their paleness.

A superintendent was seated at a high desk which overlooked the whole apartment. This I found to be the case in all the workshops. In addition to this, a passage runs behind the whole range with holes cut in the sides. From behind these the over-lookers can detect even a movement of the lips which is carefully noted down, and some punishment—additional labor, perhaps, inflicted on the prisoner. From the cooperage we passed to the plane-making room, thence to the shoemakers' and tailors' rooms. Crossing a court I entered the workshops of the carpet-makers, comb-makers, blacksmiths, tin-smiths and machine makers. I made two small purchases and then discovered that the profit did not go to the prisoners, but to the

State. The machinery necessary to the extensive operations which are carried on here, is propelled by water power. The Owasco Creek, which flows into the lake of the same name 2 miles below Auburn, runs past the prison walls.

I left the prison with feelings of deep regret and pity for the poor men who are there confined. There they work open to the stare of every stranger who has not delicacy enough to avoid encountering their eyes—dressed all alike—as if to hold up to public view which are the convicts. Surely all this must tend to harden them to every sense of kind feeling toward their fellow man. And then too, the pain that must be endured in restraining themselves from the verbal intercourse they have from birth upwards been so accustomed to delight in. Oh! who could visit this place with anything but the deepest pity for the poor men who are confined to so hard a bondage.

[*Rawlins had evidently studied Harriet Martineau's chapter on prisons in* Retrospect, *in which she wrote:* "I have shown in my account of Society in America *that after visiting several prisons in the United States I was convinced that the system of solitary confinement pursued in Philadelphia is the best that has yet been adopted. So much has been heard in England of the Auburn prison, its details look so good and satisfactory on paper, and it is so much a better system than the English have been accustomed to see followed at home that it has a higher reputation amongst us, but I think a careful survey of the institutions on the spot must lessen the admiration entertained for this mode of punishment. The convicts are almost without exception pale and haggard . . . . " Miss Martineau continued with an account of the regime at Auburn.*]

As I walked back from the prison the village appeared more respectable than when I viewed it yesterday in its snowy garb. I ran up to the Cupola (my general custom) and soon found that Auburn was an extensive place. Opposite the hotel is the Court House—its dome sheeted with tin—shining brightly in the morning sun.

Auburn to Canandaigua (by stage) 39 miles

At 12 the stage drove off, with myself and three others. One I soon found from his twang was a "Paisley body." Conversation turned between us on English politics, and he told me that he and his brother were compelled to fly to the Highlands in 1820, for their attachment to, and open advocacy of, universal suffrage—and other ultra opinions of which Government was at that period so jealous.

Nothing of interest occurred until we came to Cayuga, a little hamlet bordering a lake of the same name—over which is a wooden bridge one mile and some yards in length! The passage across in the stage affords some pleasing views. Passing the pretty village called Seneca Falls we halted at Waterloo and dined. It was about ½ p 3 and the sun's glory was beginning to fade when we came in sight of the lake of Geneva. I do not think that Lake Leman itself could have afforded me more pleasure than this delightful little spot. The stage drove round the head of it, which afforded increased opportunities for viewing its beauty. The afternoon, indeed the whole day, has been without a solitary cloud—so different from the austere mood of yesterday. At the lovely little village of Geneva we received an addition to our load, making up the full number of nine.

The night was so fine, the new moon having risen, that I resolved to go on to Rochester and take the chance of sleep on the road, but not having given my name, the stage drove off while we were at supper and left me behind—so I was obliged to call for the book, and book myself for the night. I wrote my name in a pet—quick and scrawly—and I was amused by finding that curiosity was busy when I returned to the bar, endeavoring to decipher the hieroglyphics. "Liverpool, England," however, and "Niagara" were plain enough. "Gentleman's a stranger" said landlord to porter and so I was marshaled into a room which I found after examination of the book had had the honor of harboring no less a personage than [*President*] Van Buren himself not many weeks before. I went to sleep pondering the greatness of the little man who had caused perhaps the same mattress to bend. How lowered is its dignity tonight! "Sic transit, &c."

I wandered down to the lake side along which the new moon was casting its long line of silver light. I have been every bright evening on the lookout for the meteoric appearances observed in so many Novembers, but my watchfulness has not been repaid. I saw the new moon sink behind the hill, and then walked to my hotel.

Canandaigua to Rochester, by stage, 27 miles

Tuesday 12 Nov. A stroll down again to the lake to see the sun rise in the morning repaid me for encountering the keen frosty air. At the lake I went on to one of the horse ferry packets—boats propelled by paddles, which are caused to revolve by the weight of horses continually tramping over an endless chain platform. I cannot see why they should be so cruel as Miss Martineau describes them. [*She had called it "a device so cruel as well as clumsy, that the sooner it is superseded the better. I was told that the strongest horses, however kept by corn, rarely survive a year of this work." Rawlins was yet to see a horse ferry in operation.*]

My fellow passengers in the stage that morning were a New York pedlar and another Scotchman. The latter, I soon found out, was superintendent of mills in Rochester. and he kindly offered to take me through them when I arrived there. We passed several villages, of which one called Victor was the prettiest. The pride of these villages is to build their houses of cobbles—round stones such as we use for paving our streets.

When we arrived in Rochester, which is a very respectable-looking place, I went down to the Genesee falls from which Sam Patch made his last fatal leap. They cannot be called very pretty. The rocks are not rugged enough to cause admiration, divested of trees—and the mills of all kinds which crowd around have rather an anti-romantic effect! I crossed from rock to rock, and gained the point of rock from which Patch created the platform—soon to prove his death scene. This rock completely overhangs the gulf below and I could not look over without a shudder.

I then went into the mills and my obliging fellow passenger was my cicerone through them. They are the largest mills in this part of the country and are propelled by two immense water wheels—60 ft each in circumference and 20 ft wide. Step by step I was taken through the process and taught the difference between fine and superfine—and bolting and grinding.

I then went to the splendid new granite aqueduct over 180 ft long constructing for the Erie Canal. It is a work of great beauty. The arches are flat and solid looking. The principal bridge is covered by houses on one side (wooden of course) which were built to allay the jealousy existing on both sides of the river for its half on the other side of the Genesee.

Rochester to Lockport, by canal, 64 miles

Removed my goods and chattels to the packet boat at 7 and wrote a general letter home (No. 2) per "Great Western" to sail 16th inst. At 9 o'clock we hauled out of basin the boat pretty well filled with passengers, so much so that I gave up the idea of occupying one of the confined shelves in the side of the vessel, technically called berths by the captain, and determined to walk the deck and watch for the meteors. I saw but two—I found I could not walk the deck, the bridges were so numerous, and so low, and the night was intensely cold. At length, very reluctantly, I was obliged to be put on the shelf, an operation performed by the steward with considerable applause. I lay in a kind of doze all night, sleep I could not, the place was so confined. At length, about 6 A.M. a voice cried "Sleep no more!" We were hurried on deck to wash in canal water, the shelves were taken down and breakfast succeeded—save me from a canal boat.

The only pretty place we passed was Medina where there is a fall of about 50 ft high, descending into a prettily-wooded ravine better worth seeing than that of the Genesee. I found an agreeable fellow passenger in a young man who had traded a good deal with the Indians, some time as the agent of the North American Fur Co. He interested me much in the hair-breadth escapes he had occasionally had; and from him I heard the original story of "Sir William's dreaming land" [*source unknown*]. He strongly advised me to visit the Wisconsin territory and see the Indians in their native condition. A horse, he stated, could be purchased from them for $10, and a comfortable Spanish saddle for 2. The roads would be good, he assured me, and the territory was not the least unsafe.

The cabin has presented a singular scene all morning. Four have been playing whist, since ½ past 11, and as I am now sitting by the bar, I can tell how many come up there and partake of the fire water which the steward keeps in a place which will scarcely allow of his turning round, so narrow is it.

We have some ladies on board, and $40,000 in specie [*coin*] going to the Toronto bank, with P. W. & K.'s seal upon the casks, which it is easy to interpret into Price Ward and King. The passengers say there is constantly specie going both up and down the canal, but seldom so large a quantity as at present. We arrived at Lockport at 2, ½ an hour too late to take the train to Niagara. A gentleman, his wife and daughter landed with me, and upon our mutual explanation, that we were bound to the Falls, he proposed I should join his party. After surveying the locks we went to the hotel and he introduced me into his private parlor, and to his wife and daughter. We had a good deal of conversation, during which I discovered that he was a geologist and that he had well instructed his daughter in that science, as well as botany. His name was singular, Coffin, and I think he is professor of geology in the college at Jacksonville, Illinois.

When we were hot in an argument, the door of the parlor opened and two ladies entered, and in a moment I heard my name from one of them, in too clear and melodious a tone to leave any doubt of the word. In another moment I had joyfully recognized Mrs. de la Hooke and her family—and they appeared equally glad to see me.

They have had a sad time of it since I parted with them. They took the canal at Syracuse for Oswego and after arriving there after a long and fatiguing passage, found there was no steamer for Toronto, without taking the one going the whole circuit of the lake first. They then hired a stage to take them to Rochester. Nearly the whole of the distance the horses had to be walked, and they were all compelled to alight and make the best of their way on foot at the worst parts of the road. They arrived at Rochester at one P.M. and immediately set out for Lockport where they did not find themselves till 6 o'clock. We passed the remainder of this pleasant evening in narrating what we had seen since the Saturday evening we parted at Utica.

4

Lockport to Cincinnati

Lockport to Niagara Falls, by railway, 22 miles

Thursday 14 Nov. After an abundant breakfast we entered an omnibus with our luggage and were carried to the railway. Here we had to wade down a steep muddy bank, an operation which completely soaked the ladies' feet. There is a great variety on this road. Forest scenery is the most abundant. We passed the Indian village on the way—with its neat little church. Here and there a squaw was visible standing in her parti-colored dress at the door of her distant log house. At Lewiston Junction I once more said goodbye to my kind friends from England and our cars were whirled off from one another—separating parties whom circumstances had made almost intimate, but who in all probability will never meet again.

In 20 min. I caught the first glimpses of Niagara. I suppressed a rising exclamation—they were too common to those around me in the carriage, and at length we alighted at the Cataract House. My first look at the falls was taken hurriedly with Mr. Coffin and his family—who had to proceed by the Buffalo train at 3 o'clock. When I parted from these pleasant people I went down again—the only visitor, solitary and alone. There is no one else in this vast hotel—and the ample halls and passages re-echo to no stranger's step but mine. I felt the intensity of loneliness most deeply when I went as far as I dare venture under the sheet towards the Cave of the Wind. Oh! Never since childhood's earliest hours have I felt so awestruck as at that moment. My limbs trembled violently—my heart beat so perceptibly as to be painful—and with feelings of fear which I could neither suppress, nor conceal from myself, I hastened from the deafening thunder of this awesome chasm.

I wandered from view to view until it was dark, and then sought my lonely dwelling to write my first thoughts and impressions. But where is the language which will illustrate my thoughts at this moment?

Oh! for an angel's pen to write the glories of the Deity so magnifi-
cently revealed in this eternal flood of waters. From age to age—
onward and onward—its ceaseless roar as changeless, it has sped—
and ages more will tell the same unvarying tale. Generations will pass
away—the millions who tread this globe in life and vigor now, will be
laid in their last long home—but still and ever that mighty torrent
will roll—the lasting emblem of the Almighty's power. Yet there
are some who can visit this spot unmoved. Their ears are deaf to
the thunders which have awakened within me so much awe—their
minds are not elevated, though the finger of God himself is raised
before them.

I wandered away to the great cataract and ascended the tower, built
over the brink. The bridge was carried away last winter by the ice—
but two beams of timber still rest firmly on the edge. I scrambled out
upon them and gazed into the deep abyss below—a mighty caldron
ever sending forth clouds of light spray and veiling the final fall of the
roaring waters. The noise which this cataract produces is not so loud
perhaps as the American Falls. This may be owing greatly to the
reverberation caused under the latter by the Cave of the Winds.
When I first saw the fearful rapids the sky was densely shrouded
with heavy black clouds. Against these the white foaming crests of
the angry waters appeared to be tossed with wild and convulsive
motion—reminding me very much of a storm at sea—and seeming
as if each particle of water were conscious of its destiny, and was
endeavoring to avoid it by struggling with the rocks below.

I was again on the Terrapin Bridge at 9 o'clock, Friday 15 Nov. How
different the day and the scene. The sun was still too cloudy to cause
a rainbow, but the clouds were light and promising. Before 12 every
vestige of a cloud was gone, and then the rainbow became gloriously
visible, spanning the whole cataract. I spent the afternoon chiefly on
the Table Rock, whence the view is almost too much to bear. Landing
on the American side I strolled down the river's bank throughout the
dense wood, and then up again to the Terrapin Bridge. From this
spot I watched one more of those glorious sunsets which western
climes only can show. Oh! it is a spot from which it is meet to watch
"the day depart to God." I sought once more my lonely inn. There are
none to echo my feelings. I am glad it is so, as I cannot hold communion with those whose thoughts would resemble my own.

At 7 o'clock I was again crossing the bridge over the rapids, which
the peaceful moon lit with her radiance. I think their snowy whiteness looked even more fearful than yesterday. At last I reached the
Terrapin bridge and keeping my eye with cautious care on no object

but the frail planks beneath my foot, gained the base of the tower, and in another moment was in its lonely summit. Oh! Heaven, what saw I then! There was the mighty cataract white in the moon beam, and spanning its whole extent from Table Rock to Iris Island the lunar arc lay stretched. Oh! peaceful vision, amidst the eternal roar of the waves! The wild wonder—the soul-stirring admiration—the "awe-stricken praise" of yesterday were all surpassed. I lost consciousness to all surrounding associations—I saw but the halo before me. For many minutes I felt as one in a trance, spell-bound by a power over which no influence of mine could prevail.

It was long, however, very long, before the fascination was over. Oh! if there be a man, who denies the existence of a Creator, let him stand alone where I did, above the abyss of that vast cataract, when the subdued light above shall form an arc of glory—adding beauty and sublimity (for once made twin sisters) to the scene, and his pale philosophy will fly in a moment. Whatever his first impulse, his last will be to worship and adore!

There are a hundred views of Niagara each different from another, that an attentive observer will rejoice at. These are too varied and minute to be described—but if there is one more beautiful than another—it is that obtained in crossing the river at early morn. You then see the edge of the American fall—one line of gushing, silvery light. I watched it long in crossing the river the following morn and I was amply repaid. The finest panoramic view is I think from the Clifton House. You can from thence without any great effort, take in the falls on both sides—with the green wooded Luna and Iris Islands in the centre. [. . .] I walked slowly up to Table Rock, slowly because I had determined to go behind the fall, and was protracting the adventure as long as possible.

Arrived at the guide's house—he appeared himself and offered me his own companionship, or that of the colored man who had conducted Miss Martineau. I chose the former, and then spent 15 minutes in putting on a dress—which would have proved a disguise for me even within the Terrace gates. The "overall" was a huge oilskin coat which Mr. Starkey overlapped and then tied close to my body with stout ropes. An old straw hat, also fastened with rope completed this strange costume. Before leaving the house I told him I should like to write my name upon a card against Termination Rock. He laughed at what he said was the novelty of the proposal, but promised to aid me. A card and pencil were produced and he carried them under an inverted can to keep them as dry as possible.

All being ready, we were soon at the bottom of the winding stair and on our way to the fall. The wind was not exactly the right way for the experiment, but the sun was—the whole of its light falling upon the water. I held up my head until the driving mist compelled me to droop it and trust to my guide—upon whose heels I kept my eye fixed. In another minute I felt my breath suddenly checked and a shower came over me with a force which compelled me to cling to the rock. I lost sight of Mr. Starkey and I think I must have remained there three or four minutes. Presently he returned, and giving me his hand led me on some distance. He then told me to look up as this was the clearest place we would have. With one hand forcibly impressed upon my hat I did so, and saw distinctly the commencement of the falling sheet. Presently we resumed our walk over the slippery rocks—over which a continuous stream of water was coursing. The hurricane seemed to increase every moment we advanced and I was almost beginning to repent the adventure, when Mr. Starkey turned round—took my hand put it on Termination Rock. Short as my breath was, I got up a small huzza—which however my own ears could not catch. "Look up!" said the guide. I essayed but found it impossible. "Now," thought I, "if I could manage to write here, it would be something new." I shouted at the very top of my voice "The card, the card!" The moment it was taken out it was soaked. I put it up against the rock down which the water was pouring two three inches deep, and trusting more to feeling than sight.

I was glad to turn my back on this fearful spot and hasten once more to the regions above. Surely this place may be called the "Cave of Horrors." The hurricane of wind and water—the deafening roar of the boiling caldron beneath (each pulse sounding like another thunderclap)—the difficulty in breathing, the absence of anything to support or steady the progress onward—all conspired to make that name the most appropriate that can be given to it.

Long before we were clear of the fall I was drenched to the skin and my fingers stiff and numbed with the cold. And there I found time to acknowledge to myself that I had not been very prudent in going in at all. The force of the hurricane under the fall may be imagined when I found that both the flannel shirts were soaked, and that too underneath an oilskin coat. The certificate of my exploit was duly made, and I registered my name and hung up my card next to that of my worthy brother Charles—as one of those who had visited Termination Rock. It is not a little amusing to read the register at Table Rock—I could not see either CERJr.'s [*he was to find it on a later visit*] or Miss M's names. [. . .]

NIAGARA FALLS, U. C.

THIS IS TO CERTIFY THAT

Richard Champion Rawlins

HAS PASSED BEHIND THE GREAT FALLING

SHEET OF WATER,

TO TERMINATION ROCK,

Being 230 *feet behind the Great Horse-Shoe Fall.*

Given under my hand, at the office of the General Register of the names of visiters at the Table Rock.

This *16* day of *Nov.* 183 *9*

Isaiah Starkey

[*Miss Martineau had written about Niagara in very similar terms, but unlike Rawlins, who thought the falls would go on for ever, she thought that it was only a matter of time before the erosion of the rock would continue all the way to Lake Erie. He had evidently taken note of Miss Martineau's misfortune in losing her hat, and held tightly to his. She wrote her name in the register, and received a certificate confirming her exploit.*]

To Lewiston and back, on horseback, 14 miles

At one o'clock on as lovely a day as ever I saw I was on my way to Lewiston. I allowed my nag to take his own pace, partly because it was so pleasant, but chiefly because there was no prevailing on him to hasten one jot. Just before the road descends upon Lewiston a most beautiful view is visible, which includes both the American and Canadian shores of Lake Ontario. I crossed to Lewiston in a horse ferry boat, and now having seen the plan in operation I can add my testimony to Miss Martineau's of its clumsiness and cruelty. The view from Brock's Monument above Queenston is very fine, as might be expected from its great height—being nearly 400 feet above the level of Lake Ontario. [*Sir Isaac Brock (1760–1812) commanded Upper Canada against the invasion by the United States in the war of 1812 and was killed at the battle of Queenston Heights.*]

The low grounds bordering this lake on both shores are covered with dense black forest extending on the Canada shore for I should think, 40 or 50 miles. The lake lay completely over the northern part of the horizon, but I could not obtain the slightest glimpse of Lake Erie, which is, I believe, sometimes seen from this point. The setting sun warned me not to stay any longer on the Monument, as the strict surveillance of our Government will allow no crossing after sundown. I had, however, to walk some little time, during which I entered into some conversation with the solitary sentinel who was pacing before the ferry house. He told me the strict watch at all the ferries was to prevent desertion from the British Army. More than 1500, he said, had deserted from our troops since the Canadian Disturbances [*of 1837: see Chapter 12.*]

The ferry house on the American side I found to be kept by an Englishman from Gloucestershire. I was sorry to hear him say he wished himself back again. His parents had written to him, but he did not like to go without his younger brother (like Joseph and his brethren of old) and his brother would not leave the situation he held. The sun set whilst I was talking to him, but after ascending the heights above Queenston, I also saw the glorious orb sink below the horizon, without one solitary cloud surrounding "his death bed," imparting a tint to the whole west that an Italian sky would, I think, fail to equal. I had a fine distant view of the Falls by the clear, cold moonlight on my return home from Lewiston.

Sunday 17 Nov. I visited the little Presbyterian church. The minister made no allusion to the Falls, though we distinctly heard the distant roar whenever the portals were opened by late-comers—of whom there were not a few. [. . .]

Monday 18 Nov. This was to be the last day at the Falls and I rose early. I do not know a finer time to see the aweful rapids than when they are lit by the first rays of the rising sun. I saw them so this morning. Directly after 9, I set out through the woods down to the west bank of the Niagara to see the whirlpool. There is not so much of this to look at, but the rapids well repaid me for the trouble in reaching the bed of the river. The morning was very lovely and I had a most delightful walk. I made one more visit to the Table Rock, from which one of the many rainbows was visible, and then spent the last hour on Iris Island. I visited each spot which for the last three days had been my favorite haunt, and sadly spent this farewell hour.

Independently of the Falls, the rapids and the unrivalled scenery of this beautiful river are well worthy of all the praise lavished upon them, and the profusion of fir and cedar trees make the view as acceptable as it would be in May.

Niagara to Buffalo, by railway, 22 miles

The sun was setting over the wide expanse of the fresh water sea, Lake Erie, as we entered Buffalo. The drive to our hotel rather surprised me in the character and appearance of the houses, which are really very superior to anything I have seen out of New York. At 8 o'clock we had a tremendous storm of hail, accompanied by thunder and lightning, in the midst of which the cry of "Fire, fire" was raised throughout the hotel. I hurried my articles together, drew on my boots, donned my coat and cap, and was soon out in the hall. Quick as I had been, I found many out before me with their valuables and small trunks in their hands. Very luckily it was but a small affair, and soon subdued, and each crept back to laugh at the haste he had come out with. The cry sounded certainly very alarming, and those who saw this hotel in flames last winter would dread a second such exhibition this year.

Well, my situation is singular. Here I am by a fine fire, "taking mine ease in mine inn," [*Shakespeare,* 1 Henry IV] very comfortable for the time, but then I have to wait here until this gale abates, which may not be for days. Eheu! Eheu!

I strolled through the principal street this morning (Tuesday 19 Nov.) to enquire about the stages from Cleveland, and was offered a seat in an extra going to Westfield, which would place me 60 miles on my way down the lake. I cogitated for a while, and then determined to take my seat in it, as the gale still continued, and the steamers would not dare to face it.

Buffalo to Westfield, by stage, 60 miles

I had the stage all to myself for some time—the only advantage was that there were none to hear the piteous groans every rut brought from me. I really expected my skin would be black and blue before night. The road from Auburn to Rochester, of which I had complained so much, was like a railway compared with this. About 4 o'clock we passed the ten-mile-square settlement of the Seneca Indians. I was then sitting with my back to the horses when the vehicle went into a deep hole. My poor fellow passenger was sent head foremost against the back of the stage behind me like the head of a battering ram, and the driver was whirled from his seat. Fortunately neither was hurt, and five minutes repaired all damages.

Thirty miles only have been attained today, and we have stopped at a place called Catterangus—about ½ a mile from the shores of the Lake. I cannot but congratulate myself I am not upon it—as I am writing by a blazing log fire, and the wind is howling outside most mournfully—leaving little chance for a steamer sailing from Buffalo tomorrow morning as advertised.

Wed 20 Nov. Set off with an improved road this morning—at least as compared to that through the Seneca forest—passing through the villages of Silver Creek, Fredonia and Coldwater to Westfield, where the stage left me to make up for the day's abstinence, with the best fare I have had since I left England. The landlord's daughter, a pretty Hebe, waited upon me and told me she was very fond of reading. At this little inn I found the Rev. Mr. Barnard's Exposure of Freemasonry, a book which also contained a full account of the abduction of the celebrated Wm. Morgan and the trials which followed.

At 9 o'clock the coach arrived, with but one place vacant, which I was too glad to occupy to complain of the tight packing which the extreme smallness of the vehicle occasioned. At the village of North East, the boundary line of Pennsylvania, we left three behind us. At 5 P.M. we arrived at Erie after a bitterly cold night's travelling during which we had frequently to alight and walk. The hills were so steep, and rendered so slippery with the frozen snow that the horses literally slid down the whole distance—their muscles rigid, and feet turned out to suit the motion! Over a blazing fire at Erie I enjoyed a nap of two hours and was then roused to a breakfast of musty tea, bad bread, sour milk, sandy sugar and intensely salt butter. I was very hungry but not enough to swallow much of this execrable fare—more particularly as there was not even the glimpse of a fire in the room. Of all the places, avoid Eagle Hotel at Erie.

This town is "considerable." There is a hotel building, two-thirds the size of the Astor House, and after its model, and the port which I walked down to see is commodious, and well protected by a natural breakwater of some extent. I found one of my fellow passengers in the stage was a gentleman who had landed from the "Columbus," one of the Buffalo steamers, which had put into Erie the previous night. This steamer and two others left Buffalo on Monday morning and had only made 20 miles at dusk. The captain, afraid to take a chance of reaching Erie, turned tail, and, the storm still continuing, lay for 30 hours under the lee of the land opposite Buffalo. Early on Wednesday morning he was again on his way and succeeded in making Erie at 7 the same evening. During all this time the passengers were suffering much from the cold—particularly those in the steerage where there were at least 150—many of them Germans and Swiss. This gentleman, who afterwards gave me his card (Mr. Boggart of Boston), and several others, left the steamer at Erie and filled the vacant places of those who had left us at that town.

Erie to Cleveland, 104 miles

We dined at a place called Girard [*still following the lake shore*] and after another night's cold travel, entered Ohio, and having supped at place called Ashtabula, and passed a number of pretty-looking farm houses, white in the moonlight, we breakfasted at Willoughby—a pretty village, where there is an extensive medical school. This breakfast certainly atoned for the miserable one of yesterday and cast promising shadows before of good Ohio fare. We had not only hotcakes, bread, toast, biscuits and cakes in variety, but apple and mince tarts, pumpkin pies, preserves, cheese, potatoes, pickles, beefsteak, roasted fowl, tea and coffee. Who could not make a breakfast here?

Notwithstanding this conveyance carries the mail, we stopped at several places without actual necessity, and when in motion, from the time of leaving Westfield, did not attain a greater average speed than 4⅛ miles per hour. What should we think of such mail conveying in England?

The approach to Cleveland is very pretty, and the Lake was then "peaceful at rest" at last, giving it an additional charm. We passed several country houses, some few in very good taste, the majority in the very worst.

Cleveland to Columbus, 139 miles.

Saturday 23 Nov After a slight survey of the town and lake from the cupola of the American, an excellent hotel, I entered the stage for Columbus at eight o'clock. My fellow passengers were a gentleman and his lady—three young men and a man of color from Mississippi—a very shrewd and tolerably well-informed individual. At the first inn we came to, however, I found that a separate table was laid for him, at which he ate apart from the other passengers. At Wooster where we changed coaches at 5 P.M. I noticed some very excellent substantial-looking buildings. Here we found that it had commenced raining, freezing as it rained—and heard at the same time that there were some very steep hills on the road.

This information on a cloudy night with a coach crowded with heavy luggage and passengers was anything but pleasant. I suppose it was about 11 o'clock, just as I was settling down to a very comfortable sleep, that the first notification from the driver was heard, very civilly requesting us to dismount from our warm pinnacles and walk up the hill. This was no easy task, for the road was one mass of ice, and the rain was still descending in sufficient quantity to damp our coats, and make them very uncomfortable when we again entered the stage. I have frequently wondered since how we ever attained the summits of these minor mountains—and far more, how the horses got the great lumbering vehicle up. However it was so, and the same operation had to be repeated more than once—with this difference, that it became so common that the originally civil request of the driver by degrees became less and less so, until it at last subsided into the short dry expressive phrase "Now tumble out!"

Sunday 24 November We were glad enough when morning came, for it at least gave us more light to guide our steps over the slippery path, and I had already kissed Mother Earth more than once. It was almost as bad rattling down the hill on the other side—although we had the advantage of descending the southern aspects, on which the ice was neither so thick or so slippery as the northern—and the coachman possessed the means of locking the two hind wheels at pleasure.

The day presented a series of the same kind of scenes—but not so numerous as those of the previous night. We endured another change of coaches at Mount Vernon, and having supped at Liberty, entered the stage with the comfortable information that in the road through the woods there were holes so deep that the coach might be upset. Fortunately no such accident occurred—though I and others were roused at midnight to jump out and prize the vehicle out of one of these holes.

Monday 25 November At our next change of horses, we found the door of the hostelry on the latch, and on entering piled up the slumbering log fire until we had achieved an invigorating blaze. It was ½ past 4 when we landed at Columbus, 139 miles, a journey, which, inclusive of stoppages occupied 43½ hours, showing a bare average of 4¾ miles per hour the whole distance—and this with the mail. We did not meet with the slightest accident, and the ladies seemed to have sustained comparatively little fatigue. Jubilate!

Rest and food did their office at a tolerably good hotel. After breakfast I was introduced to Mr. [*name omitted*], the architect of the new State House, which is about to be erected here. He took me to the foundations and showed me the plans. We then went to the old State House and had a good view of the city from its summit. At some distance west, the penitentiary shows its extensive front, and large buildings have been appropriated for the blind, deaf dumb and lunatic &c—all of which, seen amongst the woods bordering the city have an imposing appearance.

Columbus to Cincinnati, 106 miles

At 11 our stage came up, three hours later than promised. It was of the largest kind, holding 12 inside. Our way was along the National road, a Macadamized causeway, whose level is generally preserved, constructed by Government of the very best materials. This road caused the coach to run much easier than the Buffalo and Niagara railway. The day, though still intensely cold, was cloudless, and we had a very pleasant journey to Springfield where we dined at dusk. A change of coaches, and one of the greatest troubles to a traveller occurred here—for next to the danger of losing one's baggage comes the having it placed in danger of being lost. I was always very watchful, and though I often lost a warm, or the opportunity of refreshment, I was compensated by the perfect confidence that my trunks were safe in the boot.

At 2 in the morning we picked up a lady and her two children, who could not ride in a coach without the window was open! Oh! fancy this going through the air at 9 miles per hour, with the thermometer somewhere about zero. [. . .] I found myself gradually relaxing into stone, in which rigid state I remained until morning light appeared and we stopped for breakfast. I braved the cold for the last six miles outside, to obtain a view of the country, which is exceedingly beautiful before you enter Cincinnati—and I was well repaid. The road is continually winding and is surrounded on all sides by high banks and mounds covered with wood. I gave a cry of pleasure when I had the first glance of the city—looking indeed very like a queen, with the green hills of Kentucky bounding the prospect, and the Ohio winding through a valley possessed of a city whose situation can scarcely be equalled. A few minutes served to deposit myself and my luggage at my cousin's door—right glad to pause in my wanderings.

Here let me rest.

5

Cincinnati

Except for his contacts with bankers and cotton brokers in New York, Rawlins had not so far applied himself to the main objective of his visit to America. That, apparently, could wait until he had paid an extended visit to his cousin John Champion Vaughan and family, who were not, it seems, related to the John Vaughan of Philadelphia who had been so attentive to Rawlins.

In the introduction I mentioned that after the deaths of Richard and Judith Champion their daughter Jane had returned to England where she married Charles Edward Rawlins. The Champions' eldest daughter Sarah remained in Camden, S.C., and married a Virginian, William Vaughan. They had four children, including John Champion, born in 1806, and Virginia born 1811. John's mother (referred to as "Aunt Vaughan") and sister ("cousin Virginia") had apparently traveled to Cincinnati to see Richard.

From the very first entries in the diary after Rawlins had settled down, it is evident that John Champion Vaughan was a substantial member of the Cincinnati community, but the diary shed no light on his history and background. Nor strangely, in view of Vaughan's later achievements, did he get a mention in *Recollections*.

An unpublished address delivered by a Samuel Bernstein at Vaughan's funeral in 1892 disclosed a great deal about his remarkable life. He had been to school in England, and studied law under Judge Pettigrew at the College of Charleston. When he graduated in about 1827 the whole class was addressed by Governor Hammond and Vice President Calhoun, both of whom were unshakable believers in slavery, and determined to defend it against all comers. They regarded the new graduates as their front-line troops in the battle of minds, and the Governor had already prepared their commissions to join his staff. Vaughan pointedly declined. His family background and education had led him to detest slavery, and he had no intention of strengthening the forces of oppression.

He had grown up at a time when the Union was facing up to new, internal, problems. Having seen off the British in the Revolutionary War, and again in the "unnecessary" War of 1812, people began to feel the call of the West. New territories opened up and sought admission to the Union, and there was much debate as to whether slavery should be allowed to spread too. The northern states objected to its extension, whilst the southern states saw slavery as the natural and only system for the maintenance of white supremacy. There was already rough parity between slave and free states: in 1818 there were ten slave and eleven free states, and when, the following year the territories of Alabama and Missouri both sought recognition as slave states, the North accepted the entry of Alabama as a slave state, but objected to Missouri, which would tilt the balance the other way. The dispute was finally resolved in the Missouri Compromise of 1820, whereby Maine was admitted as a new free state carved out of the Commonwealth of Massachusetts.

Even without the benefit of hindsight the compromise could be seen as no more than a temporary solution, and the forces on both sides of the debate pursued their cause with every weapon open to them. It was in this atmosphere, on fiercely defended slave soil, that Vaughan rejected the offer of state employment. Within five years he had sold up the estate he had inherited, freed its 21 slaves, and moved north to set up practice in Cincinnati where the freedom movement was strong.

It was not long before his skills and dedication to this cause were tested. Governor Vance, without proper warrant, had approved the deportation to Kentucky of a man alleged to have enticed slaves across the Ohio to freedom. Young Vaughan, heedless of warnings that he might be lynched himself, followed the sheriff's posse to Mayville and secured the acquittal of the accused.

Thus by the time RCR arrived in Cincinnati his cousin was one of its foremost citizens, a highly respected member of the community, and of the First Congregational church. As well as being a trustee, tutor and examiner of the Common Schools, he was a keen supporter of the Mechanics' Institute, and a leader in the anti-slavery movement.

There was a wide spectrum of opinion even amongst the anti-slavers, from the outright abolitionists at one end, to those who aimed simply for containment, amongst whom there were many who merely wanted to keep the North white: from those who saw themselves as moral crusaders, to those who thought political action was the only way forward. John Vaughan was in that camp.

* * * * * * * *

[*Rawlins took a three-week break from his diary before resuming:*] Thursday 5 Dec. Today we had an afternoon drive up a hill about 3 miles from the city from which the view, if not equal to the Hudson from West Point, partakes of many beauties. Far to the west, where the afternoon sun lit up the placid waters with its declining glory, the Ohio appeared meandering through its fertile valley, causing an impress upon the mind of that loveliness of nature, whose gentle influence is never lost—and to which in after years it will turn with the same fondness that gladdened it at the first glance. The eastern prospect also commands the river, appearing in shadow from the opposite hill of Kentucky.

Our return home was through a pretty village called Mount Auburn, where many of the Cincinnati people congregate in the summer. Dined with Mr. Walker, the gentleman alluded to in Miss Martineau's book as "the accomplished lawyer." No ladies were present except Mr. W.'s sister. In almost all points dinner was conducted as with us. Through some mistake (for the people at table were mostly intellectual) the conversation fell upon wine, and remained at that the greatest part of the dinner-time. It was rather wearisome to sit for so long and hear canvassed the comparative merits of grape juice—a subject which I neither understand nor care to take part in.

[Friday] 6 Dec. Walked down to the river and through the business part of the city. At 2 dined with Mr. Stetson [*President of the Ohio Life Insurance and Trust Company*]. There were about 12 to dinner—but no ladies save Mrs. Stetson. Indeed it was not the custom to invite ladies at all. What tendency this custom has it is easy to see. The last fifty years in England might read the gentlemen of Cincinnati a lesson on this subject, that would teach them the value of a restraint—at once gentle and effective.

Our host and hostess on this occasion were most delightful people and certainly entertained their guests most sumptuously. After dinner coffee was handed round in the drawing room, as with us. The same routine and customs took place at a dinner party at Mr. Lawler's, another friend of my cousin.

[Saturday] 7 Dec. The drawing room at the house of Judge Miller, we found on entering on the evening of this day, to be chiefly occupied by the choir of one of the churches, which meets regularly in this sociable manner to practise music. This occupied an hour and was succeeded by ballad, music and dancing—all very pleasant. [. . .]

<u>Tuesday 10 Dec.</u> I was present today at the semi-annual examination of the Common Schools of Cincinnati. These are noble institutions. Here is a city with but 48,000 inhabitants yet it has eleven of these public schools, supported by a general tax of ½ per cent on all property in the city, in which children are educated without any

Grade I.

The *Alphabet*, thoroughly—spelling easy words of *one*, *two*, *three* and *four* letters, progressively—spelling easy words of *two* syllables—spelling and reading easy sentences—spelling and reading more difficult lessons.—The teacher giving the necessary *oral* instruction, and teaching the pupils to use their eyes as well as their ears.

Grade II.

Spelling, correct pronunciation, reading accurately, modulation of the voice, accent, emphasis, stops and marks in reading, spelling sentences, simple tables in arithmetic, learning to count, &c., writing after copies on slates and blackboards.—The teacher giving the necessary *oral* instruction, and guarding against error.

Grade III.

Spelling—higher reading—analysis of words and learning their meaning—analysis of sentences—spelling sentences—writing after copies on slates, black-boards and books—copying words and sentences from books and manuscript—*oral, mental,* and *written* arithmetic—tables in arithmetic.—The teacher giving the necessary *oral* instruction and insisting upon correctness.

Grade IV.

Spelling—reading with definitions—stops and marks—analysis of words and sentences, the nature and power of letters, modification and influence of words upon one another—writing after copies on slates, black-boards and books—copying from books or manuscripts—higher arithmetic— geography and history of the United States with maps—the definition of grammatical terms—simple parsing—classification of words, and their constructive influence on one another—modern geography and history, with maps and globes—chronology.—The teacher giving the necessary oral instruction.

Grade V.

Analysis and definition of words more extended—rhetorical reading—penmanship as applied to forms of business, such as copying from books or manuscripts—letter writing, bills, notes, receipts, &c.—higher arithmetic with all its kindred branches, as applied to business—English grammar, parsing, correction of false syntax, writing with grammatical accuracy—rhetoric and composition—modern and ancient geography, and history with maps and globes—algebra, geometry, trigonomtry, mensuration, surveying, chymistry, botany, natural history, geology, natural philosophy, and rural economy—to these may be added, as circumstances may suggest, the study

Course of instruction pursued in Common Schools.

charge to their parents. This may be objected to on the ground of its causing the parent to undervalue the blessings of education—but it is surely far better to incur the risk of such a feeling, than by placing a charge, however moderate, possibly preventing some children from partaking of it at all.

The department that most interested me was that embracing the youngest classes. They were taught by two young ladies, who kept up a gentle yet strict discipline over their youthful scholars. They more particularly directed attention in their pupils' reading, to emphasis and intonation, so lamentable a want in everyday education generally. The total number of children instructed in these schools is about 4000, but the teachers do not exceed 40 or 50. These are said to be quite adequate to the duty. [*The Common Schools of Cincinnati were then only three years old, the culmination of years of effort by a number of like-minded individuals from the professions and other institutions who formed an unofficial "educational directorate." In parallel with members of the legislature who saw the need for public funding, they promoted the cause of free education for all.*]

Sat 14 Dec. This was the day appointed by the Governor of the State for a General Thanksgiving, and many of the churches were consequently open for Divine Service. In New England, where the Pilgrims originated this annual practice to avoid keeping Christmas, of which, on account of its Romish origin they had so much horror, it is the custom to assemble friends and relations together and spend the evening in social festivity. We spent this particular evening at Mr. Walker's, whose handsome suite of rooms was thrown open for dancing and musical entertainment. The old Virginia reel, known with us as the Haymakers, is a popular dance, and went far to enliven a very pleasant evening. I was introduced to a Miss Rives, said the be the city belle. I did not think her beautiful. I have seen more than one more worthy of the title, certainly. One good point in the Cincinnati dances is that they break up at, or soon after, eleven o'clock. [. . .]

Cincinnati to Columbus, by canal and stage, 116 miles

Sunday 15 Dec. Before four o'clock we were in the canal boat on our way to Dayton, admiring one more of those glorious sunsets which no pen can describe. Every variety of land is seen from this canal—and the passage affords an insight into the fertility of this noble State. There were but few passengers—and the cabin was spacious—so our trip was very pleasant as far as Dayton—a manufacturing town of considerable extent, which numbers amongst many other works a cotton mill of considerable size.

At Dayton we hired a light carriage to take us to Springfield, 25 miles. It was fortunate it was light, as we travelled upon a road not yet open to the public, and had to lift the said carriage over immense logs placed across the road to prevent traffic. This road, which may be said to be quite an experiment in this State, is constructed of nothing but gravel. If it should answer, it will be of special advantage to all that part of the country, as the gravel abounds in every direction. [. . .]

We arrived at Springfield at 7 and enjoyed a good sleep till two, when the same immense coach which had conveyed me down before (having 12 inside) was once more on its way, with us, to Columbus, where we arrived (45 m.) at 8 o'clock.

At 10 o'clock I went to the House of Representatives, and spent some time watching the course of business there. There were no speeches this morning of any length. At the adjournment of the House I went up to the Senate where the subject of debate was a petition from certain individuals who had purchased land from the State to postpone the payment from 1 Jan 1840 (the day the contract becomes due), to some future period, the parties paying interest at the rate of 6 percent on the purchase money. [. . .]

The Senate adjourned at ½ p. 12 to 3 o'clock. At dinner we sat opposite, and were introduced to, Mr. Buchanan, the Speaker of the House. [. . .] When I entered the Senate in the afternoon I heard a fine sensible old man addressing the chair upon the same subject that occupied the morning. This was Mr. Vance, who has been Governor of the State. His full deep tones were followed by the sharp squeak of a Yankee lawyer, who spoke on the opposite side. His voice was "between that of a guinea pig and a bassoon," partaking of the qualities of both.

In the course of the day both House and Senate went into Committee and passed several Bills—three of which were for divorce—one to permit a man to change his name, and several to incorporate Turnpike Road Trusts. [. . .]

Wed 18 Dec. Divided the morning between the Senate and the State Library. [. . .]

Thursday 19 Dec. Various Bills came before the Senate this morning, and the subject of discussion yesterday was referred to the Committee on Finance, which honorable Senators generally believed was equivalent, as one of them said, "to slaughtering it outright."

In the afternoon we accepted an invitation to visit the Penitentiary, and proceeded there, accompanied by Mr. Faran, Senator for the Cincinnati District, and our friend Mr. Greene of that place. The Governor informed us that the best time to see the discipline of the prison was at four o'clock. [. . .]

I spent the evening at a political meeting. Both Whigs and Democrats held meetings, the former to signify their approval of the nomination of Gen. Harrison for the Presidency, and the latter partly to counteract the effects of that meeting, and partly to receive the Democratic Vice-President of the U.S.—Col. Johnson, who was passing through Columbus en route to Washington.

There were several good speeches at the Whig meeting, among which was one from Mr. Greene of Cincinnati. [*The Hon. William Greene (1797–1883) was the son of a US Senator, grandson of a colonial Governor, and great-grandson of the Governor of Rhode Island.*] The speakers generally abused the opposite party most unmercifully—one or two calling them by the epithet of banditti!

Friday 20 Dec. Divided the morning between the rich shelves of the State Library and the Senate. [. . .] Dined at the house of Mr. Kelly—a spacious stone mansion about ½ mile out of the city. Our party consisted of Mr. Vinten, an ex-member of Congress, where he served 14 years, Mr. Greene of Cincinnati, J. V., myself, and four others. Our host, himself an ex-member of Congress, and his wife and daughter made up our party at table, which went off pleasantly, as all other dinner parties do—for who is ever dissatisfied with turkey, venison and champagne?

At four o'clock we again visited the Penitentiary, and witnessed the melancholy form of locking up the prisoners. When a bell rang, they all left work and hurried across the yard to the Rendezvous, where they were classed according to height, and arranged themselves in single file close to each other, in number about 40. As they crossed the yard to the dining room they appeared to be joined to each other by an external band, so regular was movement in walking. As they passed through the room each picked up from the table as much Indian bread as he chose, and then they wound around the staircase leading to their cells, and as each one came to his own he disappeared and pulled the iron door behind him. The feeling can hardly be described, as the jar of each door strikes upon the ear. At this early hour of the day, when in a few minutes will obscure every object from their eyes, even the narrow walls of their dungeons—they are confined, and twelve long hours, the greater part perhaps happily consumed in sleep, will elapse before they again behold the light of heaven, and then but for a moment. After their hasty meal they are hurried across the yard to their respective workshops, again to repeat the tasks of yesterday, and again to perform the same degrading ceremony in the evening.

Saturday 21 Dec. I spent this morning in the Houses of Legislature, and after dinner, which is here at the good old hour of one o'clock, accompanied Mr. Greene on a visit to the Lunatic Asylum, chiefly interesting from its being an institution erected and supported by the State. From this abode of misery we went to the Asylum for the deaf and dumb. We found that there was no school, but on looking about us discovered one of the pupils and one of the teachers in the garden. I found it difficult at first to revive my manual alphabet—but the necessity therefor was obviated by their taking us into a room furnished with a large slate and chalk.

Mr. Greene conversed with the pupil and I with the teacher. His first question was "Where are you from?" The next was "Is Victoria going to be married?" It is strange that there should be so much interest expressed in this country, about the person of our little Queen—yet it is so, amongst all classes. A variety of questions followed—I asked if the pupils generally were contented and happy. He said "Yes, but there were some that would rather be at home."

We attended a preliminary meeting of the Historic Society of Ohio—a society formed for the purpose of collecting from all parts of the State statistical information of its early settlement—in fact, of all matters relating to the advance of civilization and the progress of improvement. J. V. introduced me to Judge Lane and Judge Wood, both of the Supreme Court. The Society adjourned its meeting—through some mistake there was no one ready with an address.

Sunday 22 Dec. I accompanied to the Episcopal Church this morning an elderly gentleman, Col. Johnson, who settled in Ohio among the very first. He was formerly Government agent, in trading and negotiating with the Indians. He told me he could recollect the country before a white man was settled in it—and when a person was never safe without keeping a strict watch at night, and being constantly armed by day. How different has this State become in less than 50 years—wealth, and population too, still increasing. The last census shows 900,000 inhabitants. [. . .]

Monday 23 Dec. Mr. Shannon, the Governor's brother, and a member of the Senate, who for some reasons known only to himself, took an uncommon fancy to me, introduced me this morning to the Governor. I found him a very pleasant and exceedingly gentlemanly looking man. We conversed for some time on sundry matters connected with England. He enquired particularly concerning the Penny Postage Bill [*Rowland Hill's Bill was enacted in 1840*], and seemed much interested in its success—but assured me that the experiment would not be attempted in this country for many, many years, as the Post Office is at present no source of profit—and all extra revenue that might possibly arise must be devoted to the object of increasing the number and speed of the mails. [. . .]

After taking leave of the Governor I went into the House of Representatives. [. . .]

On the evening of this day I accompanied a very pleasant girl, Miss Buckingham, and her sister Mrs. Converse to the Historic Society. [. . .] The preliminary business being arranged, John Vaughan delivered an interesting speech. He opened with sundry remarks on history which he showed to be based on a wrong foundation. Of what interest or importance is it to us, said he, how many hours such and such a battle consumed in the bloody work of destruction, compared with the account which the true historian might furnish us with, were he to dilate upon those characters who have wrought the moral revolution, whose effects are around us? While Hume consumes 6 pages in describing the Battle of Blenheim, he dismisses John Locke with a brief notice of 3 lines! Do we know anything of the Roman people—the people themselves—by reading the pages of Gibbon? Do we know aught of their passions—their joys, their hopes, their social communion? That man is the true historian who will give such a picture of the people as will give a deep interest to a future generation—in their character and habits—and enable it to draw the line of comparison between their own manners and customs, and the manners and customs of their fore-fathers.

Mr. Greene followed Mr. Vaughan and gave us an interesting account of the Common Schools of Cincinnati.

Columbus to Cincinnati, by stage, 106 miles

Tuesday 24 Dec. Booked a place for Cincinnati this morning. My companions on the coach were a merry black-eyed damsel and her aunt, and an English Tory of the Sam: Easton stamp. The worst part of the road, some sample of which I had on my way down before, we had to walk. [. . .] Sleeping on such a road was of course impossible, so I spent the night in the hopeless task of endeavoring to reclaim my countryman from the errors of Toryism. It was like sawing marble with a penknife.

Christmas Day The first Christmas day I have not dined at home, and if I was always true to the season, the first that I have not ate more or less of that compound of all that is rich and indigestible, yclept [*Old English: "called"*] a Plum Pudding. But brother Jonathon, alas, has no taste for such delicacies, and if he had I suspect he would not make one of the real English stamp.

There is every sign of a holiday in town. Many shops are closed, all, very likely, except those of New Englanders who dread the idea of showing respect or what might be construed into respect for a day, the appointment of which emanated from the Church of Rome. Guns are firing in all directions and boys in the streets in defiance of City regulations—which by the way are not much enforced here— are discharging pistols. [. . .]

Thursday 26 Dec Every day adds to the tribute I can pay to the society of this city. I have endeavored to find, but have not yet discovered, any of that illiberality that Miss Martineau seems to fear as the greatest evil with which Cincinnati has to contend.

[*Miss Martineau had observed, after three days in the city, that although the residents share that concern for the poor and afflicted that was typical of Americans, "the most threatening evil to Cincinnati is from that faithlessness which manifests itself in illiberality." There was sectional prejudice between the two leading classes of inhabitants, violently-held positions for and against abolition, and a bigoted opposition by Protestants to the growth of Catholicism.*]

I can only say that as far as John Vaughan's friends go there is not a shadow of such a feeling. I have several times seen people of very opposite opinions in religion on the most intimate terms, and each seeming as much pleased with the other as if their sentiments were the same. The enquiry naturally arises, why should it be otherwise? But to one so long accustomed in a different constitution of society, it appears with double force, and gives a double satisfaction.

There is a division of classes here, not as with us by the herding together of sects, but a division well explained by the old adage "Birds of a feather flock together." There is an intellectual class— chiefly of members of the legal profession, but amongst whom you will find merchants and men in general business. This class I have had the best opportunity of observing, and so far as my little experience of men and society generally, and as far as my abstract idea of what such society should be will guide me, I should say that this description of society in Cincinnati would stand as high as any our own country can afford.

Another class consists of merchants, and others whose tastes disincline them to enter into what I should call the highest class. They have their dinner parties, card parties, hunting clubs, and no doubt have a great deal of pleasure in their own way. The Germans in this city must make a class of their own—as they form more than ⅕ of the population.

Everyone knows that Cincinnati is celebrated for its pork—in quality and quantity. I this morning paid a visit to a countryman of my own who has a most extensive establishment for carrying on an exterminating war with the Swinish Community. However the 'H.T.' (hard times) seal was upon his concerns—the mallet and knife slumbered upon the block, and the porkers still grunted in quiet satisfaction. All joking apart, this is a sad time for everyone. This Englishman, with an essentially English name, Smith, (not John Smith—his parents escaped that temptation) but Henry Smith, has one of the most extensive establishments here. Last year he was killing and packing [*blank*] hogs per day, all the week through. This season he has only certain days for that operation, and then only operates on very few in comparison.

On taking my leave he very politely invited me to witness the various operations, killing, cutting, and packing up &c. I accepted the invitation for all but the first department. [. . .]

Friday 27 Dec. Walking up Main Street this morning I perceived my cousin engaged in a conversation with an individual who was "whittling" with considerable energy. As it was the first time I had seen that Yankeeism I looked at the Whittler. If it had not been for his hat, which was a white one, without hair upon it, you would have called him "shabby genteel." He wore an old cloak that no-one would give a dollar for, a dirty shirt, and shoes down at heel. I was introduced to him and found that he was the city "Croesus," Nicholas

Longworth. His extensive vineyards are some two or three miles from the city. [*Nicholas Longworth had arrived in Cincinnati in 1803 as a budding lawyer, who by accepting gifts of apparently worthless land in lieu of fees made a fortune by their appreciation, leaving $10 million when he died in 1863.*]

On a previous occasion I had become acquainted with his son— the very antipodes of Mr. Longworth—pleasant, gentlemanly, and withal well informed, particularly in natural history. My cousin Virginia and I went with him through his father's extensive range of green and hot houses where we saw some of the most beautiful plants and flowers I ever beheld. He also showed us his sister's extensive and interesting collection of shells and minerals.

I saw West's picture from Hamlet—but as there was no light, hardly, upon it, and what there was, not of the right kind, I could form no judgment thereof. It is of immense size, and occupies almost the whole of end of an immense ballroom. [*Benjamin West (1738– 1820), born in Springfield, Pennsylvania, settled on London in 1763, became history painter to George III, and president of the Royal Academy (1792– 1820). He studied in England with Peale.*]

Returning from Mr. Longworth's we passed Mrs. Trollope's Folly— the bazaar which she built and never paid for. It is one of the most singular buildings I ever saw, and is of every variety of architecture— from a Musselman's mosque to Gothic gloominess. It is now used partly for a Mechanics' Institute and partly for a boarding house. Mrs. Trollope has, I think, on the whole, excited more amusement than censure from the American people. It is universally allowed that she has done some little good here. If a man displays his feet when he should not, in a theatre or other place, I am told the cry of "a Trollope, a Trollope" is raised until the nuisance is abated. If you mention Mrs. Trollope's name in any way to an American, the chances are 10 to 1 he will smile before he replies to your remark. [*Frances Milton Trollope (1774–1835), mother of Anthony (1815–1882), opened a fancy-goods shop in Cincinnati, and later achieved notoriety with her* Domestic Manners of the Americans *(1832).*]

Tuesday 31 Dec terminates the year and the first part of this Journal.

6
New Year in Cincinnati

<u>Wednesday 1 Jan. 1840</u> There is a custom observed here on this day, which if not perverted as it sometimes is, adds one other delightful trait to the habits and customs of society in Cincinnati. The young men (and old men too, by the way) call on all their acquaintances and give them their good wishes. The women of every household are expected to remain at home. The perversion of this exceedingly pleasant practice consists in making it a day for feasting—and as everyone, or almost everyone spreads a table—with wine—there is great fear that in some cases, perhaps quite unintentionally, excess is the consequence. Amongst those whom I know here there was only one lady who had the courage to set her face against the practice of offering wine and other refreshment—for which there is no real call—as in almost all cases the business, or rather pleasure, is over before dinner time.

Augustus Clarke and myself accompanied one another to the houses of those I knew, amounting to about a dozen. The extent, variety and expense of the entertainment varied with the household. In some places simply wine and cake, in others the addition of those delicacies which seem especially relished here—chicken salad and oysters. The latter article cannot be procured here without great expense—particularly just now when the river is closed and the only conveyance is by stage. In the afternoon I spent two hours at a meeting of the Friends of Gen. Harrison. The impression seems to be very general that at the next Presidential election there will be a change of Government.

<u>Thursday 2 Jan</u> We this evening attended a lecture on Credit delivered by Judge Walker. Nothing more than a history of the introduction of credit into the commercial world, and a few comparisons between the United States and other countries, was attempted by the lecturer. He strongly advocated perfect indulgence in usury—the

81

laws of Ohio against which, he thought should be repealed. He spoke for some time on the advantages which would accrue to a law permitting limited partnerships—as in New York. He explained the nature of the Stay Law as it prevailed in Kentucky by which no creditor could sell, although he might sieze, the land of a debtor, for three years, on the principle that at the time land was so deteriorated in value in consequence of the scarcity of money that if sold at once it would be sacrificed. This law is supposed to have destroyed the credit of Kentucky for [*blank*] years, and that State can hardly be said to stand as high as others at the present time from this cause.

Mr. Walker then explained the Appairment Law as it exists in Ohio. By this law no land can be sold by a creditor for less than two thirds of what it had been valued at by Commissioners appointed by Court. The principle of this law is of course the same as that of the Stay Law of Kentucky—to prevent a sacrifice of the property. The lecturer then advocated a Bankrupt law, which he showed would place credit on a much higher basis than that on which it rests at present.

Today I was introduced to the father of the Common Schools system of Ohio—Mr. [*Nathan*] Guilford. He is tall, venerable, and intellectual looking. [*He introduced the Bill to the Ohio State Senate in 1825 which established the public school system. As a publisher he became a major supplier of standard texts to the schools, and in 1832 was accused of abusing his position as a member of the Schools Board. The charges were repudiated, however, and he continued to play an active role, becoming the first superintendent of the schools in 1850.*]

Saturday 4 Jan Rode out into the country to visit a farmer, residing about 5 miles from town—by name Clopper. The day was intensely cold, and notwithstanding I had two coats and a large heavy buffalo [*a bison hide rug*] for protection from it—it penetrated through all. I found the said Mr. Clopper to be a very intelligent man, and his daughters decidedly above their sphere of life in manners and appearance.

Thursday 9 Jan At one o'clock, with just enough frost to make the ground pleasant for walking, I set out for Belle Air Farm near Cheviot—distant five miles, the residence of Mr. Briant, an Englishman with whom I had dined at a house in the city the day before, and who then invited me to take the same meal with him today. I had an exceedingly pleasant walk out. Much as I thought of the beauty of Cincinnati and its neighborhood before, I found it raised much higher on this day. The road winds through the valley of the Ohio with hills on either side—not running continuously the whole distance, but made up, so to speak, of a series of small hills, each possessed of its own little valley—presenting its vista to the eye, terminating only by exhibiting another series of these minor hills which give to the view a never-ending variety and charm. I saw this scenery when the snow lay deep under the trees, yet admired it greatly. Its beauty in summer must be overpowering.

The party at dinner were all English, and it was pleasant enough. After dinner Mr. Briant took us to see his horses, his cows, his pigs, his poultry, his dogs, and his children, with all that sort of feeling which an English country gentleman with us would manifest. Mr Briant's father is still living, and he has a country place in Yorkshire.

I remained here until the following morning and then left my kind host and hostess. This lady has the misfortune, real or supposed, (which of the two, it would seem, is of little consequence) to be tinged with Negro blood. This is enough to bar the doors of the people of Cincinnati against her—in which city, as I understand Mr. Briant, they only visit with one family, that of the gentlemen at whose house I met them at dinner. Now I can understand perfectly, nay I can almost, if not entirely, sympathize with the common dislike, manifested by Americans, for what is called amalgamation—yet here is a case in which such feeling in my mind cannot be brought to bear.

I had a fair opportunity of observing Mrs. Briant. She is very pleasant, often intelligent in conversation—she plays and sings very prettily (according to my comprehension) and is as ladylike in manner as nine tenths of the women I have ever seen. Yet because her appearance, though but skin deep, is darker than the fellow beings of her own sex by whom she is surrounded—they wave the sceptre of exclusion round their dwellings—and help to stimulate that power of public opinion which bars for the time as effectively as "the flaming sword which turned every way"—the free passage of that fellow being to the society which her education should be a passport.

I recollect very well how often I recurred to the conduct of the only man in Cincinnati with whom this lady and her husband visit, and how highly I thought of the coinage he displayed—yet reckoned I without my host. I called upon him one morning. In the course of conversation we were led to speak of the Briants, and he told me that there was a prejudice against the family from many persons supposing that Mrs. B. was slightly tinged with African descent—but that it was quite a mistake. And then he went on to offer some proofs (which

I do not recollect), that it was not so! Fortunately they are some way out of the town, and appear very happy amongst themselves—with their extensive farm which Mr. B., I think, cultivates more for amusement than profit.

Saturday 11 Jan At an evening party a short time since I met and was introduced to General [*William Henry*] Harrison, the anti-Van Buren candidate for the Presidency. The gentleman is not very venerable or dignified in his appearance, but his face accorded his mind to his character. It bespoke sterling honesty of heart, and if ever that quality was wanted in any country at any time, the United States is that country, and that time the present.

The people seem to be sickening of an administration whose acknowledged motto is the "the spoils belong to the victors," i.e., who ever will play the partisan to the greatest extent and with the most effect shall be rewarded with place and power, no matter how unfit for the office to which he is named. Deep is their consideration of one side of the matter, "that the office shall do for the man," forgetting the other necessary and co-relative position, "that the man shall do for the office"!! Now all governments might be accused of this by their opposers, but instances in this case are tolerably apparent. I recollect observing in a newspaper soon after my arrival that a receiver of public money in Missouri had embezzled upwards of $40,000. I appealed to a staunch Democrat for the truth thereof. The reply was that it was perfectly true, but they found him too useful a man to take any notice of his defalcation!

We this evening attended a lecture delivered by John Vaughan at the Mechanics' Institute. His subject was "The Influence of the Subject on Society, and the Action of Society on the Individual." He showed that wealth, from the power which it possesses, may procure what commands some respect, yet by far the greatest part of the respect shown to it does nothing worthy to rest upon, and while we deplore the ascendancy which wealth sometimes possesses over intelligence, we should recollect that we ourselves are the cause of it. The lecture was throughout interesting. As an illustration of what may be done by the force of moral suasion he instanced the formation of the Athenaeum, and its affect upon the Slave Trade, for which Liverpool was then so famous, or rather infamous! At the request of some of the Mechanics J. V. continues the subject on Saturday following.

The Institution seems to be in a flourishing condition. They have [*recently*] purchased Mrs. Trollope's bazaar which cost $6000, a part of which however only has been paid up. From the report which was read it would appear that there is at least one, R. V. Yates, amongst the donors to its funds and apparatus.

Friday 17 Jan. The birthday of Benjamin Franklin, commemorated in this city by a lecture on his life and character by Mr. Perkins. Mr. P.'s sketch was interesting and as comprehensive as the time would allow. In analyzing those parts of Franklin's character, which appear to have exercised an influence over him, hardly compatible with other and nobler qualities, the lecturer was of the opinion that the ruling principle of Franklin's life was not the high one of right and wrong, but of expediency. In fact the germ of the Utilitarianism of another and later period. [*James Handasyd Perkins (1810–49) was minister-at-large of the Congregational Church and was to become the first president of the Cincinnati Historical Society, and vice-president of the Ohio Historical and Philosophical Society.*]

Saturday 18 Jan On last Monday evening I was taken to what was called a soirée at the house of a lady in the fashionable part of the city. Here I met with what are called the fashionable of Cincinnati. The rooms were crowded, and moreover small. There was dancing all evening. I tried it once, but as the only exertion was turning round in your place, the crowd being so great, I gave it up in despair. This was called, I was told, a social, neighborly party, but several of the young dames appeared in full dress, white satin shoes &c. The manners of some of these young people, who doubtless consider themselves very fashionable, reminded me very strongly of what one would see at a second-rate ball in England—certainly anything but gentlemanly or ladylike.

On this evening John Vaughan continued his lecture of last Saturday evening. His remarks were on the relative social condition of employer and employee. He enlarged upon the duties of confidence and kindliness. This whole lecture breathed the true spirit of brotherly love. As an instance of what may be done by kindness he quoted the example of CERJr. and his workmen. [*Charles had joined his father in the smalt business.*] His lecture was well-attended by the Mechanics and other members.

Monday 20 Jan John Vaughan introduced me this morning to the Hon. Judge Hall, author of "Letters from the West" &c, with whom I had a few minutes' conversation. Speaking of the security of property in Cincinnati the judge told me that he was one of an exploring party in Illinois in 1819—when through the whole State there were but 50,000 inhabitants—and shortly afterwards he was nominated to the treasurership of that District during which he had as much as $60,000 in his house, without a bar or shutter to the window. In those times, he said, before the law had power to reach so far, quarrelling was unheard of—in fact the law brought disputes, and not disputes the law.

This evening the rooms of Mr. Longworth were thrown open for another of those soirées, so called, intended to be held every Monday evening during the season. Dancing and conversation were the occupation of the evening. The large hall of the house was well-adapted for the former recreation and was used exclusively therefor. At this party (perhaps from Mr. Longworth Jr. and Miss Longworth being more of that class than our host of the previous evening) I noticed a greater number than before, of the class I have elsewhere denominated the Intellectual. The sensible plan of breaking up early was not departed from at this entertainment, with which everyone seemed pleased.

Cincinnati in 1841.

The quay of the Ohio at this city is a steep slope of the bank of some extent, very much resembling the beach at Seacombe at half tide, from Parry's Hotel to the High Seacombe Hotel [*on the mouth of the River Mersey*]. In front of this quay is a street with a long line of shops, stored with goods most likely to be required by travellers and sailors. Nothing can appear more desolate than the appearance of this city just now. The river is completely frozen over—there is but one solitary steamer hemmed in by the ice, and the only relief to the eye is the large number of skaters who are flitting to and fro with varied degrees of grace.

The cold is most intense, and the thermometer is sometimes at zero in the night, and the sun has forgotten to shine for many days. All Cincinnatians agree in saying that the present season is almost unprecedented for its constancy of unpleasant weather. During one whole year, I think it was 1838, the closest observation showed that there were but very few days the sun did not shine for some hours at least. I think a real American would languish in England, where we have as many cloudy days as sunshiny days. Like the Greek islander taken to the Vale of Tempe, who said "All this is fair, but the sea, where is it?" The American would exclaim "All thus is fair, but the sun, where is it?"

Tuesday 21 Jan Spent the afternoon with Mr. Greene, whose name has appeared in this journal more than once. No one situated as I am can be in Mr. Greene's society many minutes without acquiring information. Mr. G. is a man of considerable natural talent, evidently enlarged by extensive reading, and though fond of a rather dogmatic manner in argument, yet never halting one moment when convinced of error, to confess it. A favorite argument between himself and John V. is the late United States Bank, which the former defends with a spirit only equalled by the latter in his attack. The question is still unsettled by the belligerents, however. [*This, the second Bank of the United States, set up in 1816, was closed down in 1836 after a controversial existence, leaving the federal government with no control over the monetary system.*]

Wednesday 22 Jan The river has broken up and commenced rising. The immense masses of ice, resembling a mer de glâce are floating down with a majestic movement. Navigation will not be resumed, however until the river is somewhat clear of this rather dangerous impediment.

Thursday 3 February The Ohio now presents a very different scene to that of the date of my last entry. The ice has disappeared and the water has risen more than 20 feet above the lowest water mark. The scene viewed from the upper deck of one of the steamboats is one of the utmost animation. The sun is shining brightly over the whole quay. More than 20 steamers are landing sugar, molasses, coffee or a hundred other articles—or taking in pork or whiskey or flour or some other native commodity for shipment down the river. The wharf is covered with moving drays laden or empty, and no one, save myself, seems unemployed.

Thursday 10 Feb Every evening for the last week, the sun has set with a glory which each successive night seems to exceed. From the classic summit of Mount Ida I have beheld the thousand changes of the sky during the final hour. My companion has generally been an agreeable one—either my cousin Virginia [*RCR later obliterated the following names*] or a young artist named Cranch whose early days were spent in Rome, Florence and Naples. He is a good painter, and though not a poet has a true taste therefor. I have taken many a ramble with him and discoursed of the sunny skies, "the clear blue Heaven of Italy."

He has told me many a time that these western sunsets are superior in beauty to any he ever saw in that lovely land. The charm there is said to be the perfect purity of the atmosphere. This is also seen here, two evenings out of seven, but there is wanting in this country a certain thin mist, which rises in Italy at sundown, and which produces the so-often described appearance of golden dust. I may make a feeble attempt to portray the sunset of this evening, as seen from Mt. Ida.

The whole eastern and southern sky is deeply tinged with light purple. The zenith, now covered with the light fleecy clouds called "mackerel's scales," presents the appearance of a sea of fire, wave after wave meeting the eye in endless succession. A few minutes and this has vanished, the sun has gone behind a cloud—whose borders throughout its whole extent are lit with golden fire. Three minutes and the sun emerges, and for an equal space the former scene is renewed. And now succeeds that bluish green which few painters have attempted to draw. The whole west is tinged with this lovely color, and for more than an hour after the sun has departed it continues to pervade the sky. The bed of the Ohio reflects it most faithfully, and the course of the winding stream opposite may be detected in the vividness of the color. This description is indeed feeble, as truly all must be to describe these glories of sun and cloud.

[*After that entry the* Journal *fell silent for two or three weeks, and RCR's private diary for MPH told the reason why:*]

Wednesday 12 Feb. 1840 I fear, Mary, I am about to lose a friend—one whom I hoped I should have added to the list of those worthy to bear that name. He is yet young, but 23, and yet the bed of sickness on which he is now laid will be the couch of death! Two years since he commenced business as a merchant of this city and but a few months ago the firm of which he is a partner built a new steam boat, one of the finest on the Western waters. This afternoon I was down on the quay to see her depart on her second voyage to New Orleans. Not a breath was stirring this lovely afternoon—the slant rays of the setting sun fell upon the boat crowded with passengers, and on the quay equally crowded with spectators. Flags were hoisted at each end of the vessel, and a band of musicians was playing on the wharf—and many a one envied the owner of so noble a vessel.

The boat was detained more than an hour, until the sun had set behind the western hills. Very few knew the cause of the delay. It was to take down the last accounts of Mr. Clarke's illness to his partner in New Orleans. Alas, his sun was to go down at early morn! Night after night I lay at his side, sleeping the sleep of health, unless roused by him for a draught of water, which he was too weak to reach himself. He suffered intensely, but never murmured. It was not until yesterday that his life was thought to be in danger—and today all hope has been given up.

[*Augustus Clarke died on 14 February, leaving a wife of only eleven months, and a baby not yet a month old. A postmortem showed that he died of an abscess on the brain. Two weeks later RCR was preparing to set off in the next stage of his travels, to the South, of which, he confided to MPH "I have many horrors, which doubtless are nearly all without foundation." In this he echoed Miss Martineau, who wrote that she had "rather dreaded the visit to New Orleans, and went more from a sense of duty than from inclination."*]

[?] Mar I succeeded this afternoon in arranging a party to visit the opposite side of the river where I was to tread for the first time on slave soil. An hour's ramble brought us to the head of Mount Beulah upon which we had a delightful ramble, and from which is certainly to be found the finest view of the city. My artist friend was of the party and was in a perfect rapture with some of the views obtained from the lovely eminence.

I have spent this day in farewell calls on my friends in the city—whose hospitality I shall ever laud. And as for the hated duty of packing up, at least so I shall ever regard it until I go through that operation previously to turning homeward.

7

Steamboat

Cincinnati to New Orleans, by steamboat, 1650 miles

Thursday 5 Mar Boarded the "Queen of the West" this evening at 8 o'clock, the hour fixed for her departure therefrom. It was, however, ten before we were fairly under weigh. The evening was very fine with the moon in her first quarter, and the river as smooth as a millpond. My "compagnon du voyage" to New Orleans was a young man from New York, light and agreeable. The evening passed pleasantly in the cabin, Mr. Longworth, Jr. and his society is always acceptable, and his sister, being of the party as far as Louisville, whither they were going to the marriage of the belle of that city to a Swedish baron.

The first night on board a steam voyage no one sleeps well—and my case was no exception. Boz has discovered that the peculiarity of a steamer that wherever your berth is, the machinery appears to be under your bed. Before 10 o'clock in the morning we were taking a stroll through the streets of Louisville. Two or three of the streets are wider than any in Cincinnati, but the general air and appearance of the city, without reference at all to the situation, are inferior, I think, to her rival, "the Queen."

There was too little water over the falls to render the attempt to pass over, a safe one, and at 12 o'clock we were ready to enter the canal—our list of passengers being not more than 7 or 8. A rival boat, the "Independence," which left Cincinnati an hour before us, grounded most carelessly at the entrance to the canal, and kept us two hours, which rather annoyed our captain, who was bent on making an extraordinary passage to New Orleans. Our progress through the canal was most tediously slow—a mile an hour being the maximum speed. Fortunately it is but two miles in extent.

There are two locks of about 7 or 8 feet each at the present time, varying of course with the height of the river. This canal cost the enormous sum of $500,000. To pay interest thereon the charges are proportionate. Steamers pay at the rate of 60 cents per ton. The amount paid by the "Queen of the West" would be about $200. The works at the locks seemed at a superficial glance ill-constructed, and the most wretched contrivance for a drawbridge I have ever seen, save at the end of some old cyclopedia—or other ancient book. A tablet in the lock shows that the canal was completed in 1826. In passing the second gate the "Independence" again detained us an hour by injuring her yawl and rudder—so that it was past four before we were fairly in the stream again.

Our energetic captain's first care was to wood, as night was coming on, and it is a long time since I have seen so animated an operation. There was not a man, apparently, who did not participate in the desire to overtake the "Independence"—now three or four miles ahead of us. The owner of this vessel was on board her, and several bets that she would beat the "Queen" had been offered, and many taken up. The place that we stopped at was in Illinois forestland, partly cleared up round a log hut where the wood-seller lived, but elsewhere presenting a gloomy impenetrable appearance, filled up the back part of the scene. In the foreground was the steamer—a large flat boat on either side of her and 50 busy hands engaged in each, throwing the wooden logs on to her deck. There were but few unemployed, passengers and sailors, cooks and stewards, firemen and enginemen, clerk and captain. The old adage of "too many cooks" &c. would not apply here, as there was room for everyone to work.

In 20 minutes we had taken on 23½ cords [*3000 cu. ft.*] of firewood, an operation generally taking ¾ of an hour. The outside boat was dropped astern, the larboard engine was started. the bell rang, and in two minutes we were again at full speed. During the night we passed the junction of the great rivers [*the Ohio and the Mississippi*] so that I missed the sight at this time.

Saturday 7 Mar Came on deck this morning just as we came in sight of a most lovely group of islands, and in five minutes the vessel was "on her winding way" between two of them. The passage which we took is called technically "a shoot," and many that we navigated in this way have been unknown since the great flood of 1828, which only exceeded the present one by ten feet. During the whole of the day there was no end to the beauty of the distant prospect which constantly resembled the scenery of the English Lakes, of course on a much larger scale. It is now twelve years since the river has been seen to such advantage. Usually the banks are 10 to 15 feet high, the sides thereof being composed of brown or red clay—anything but pleasing to the sight. Now there is no bank at all, and the forests for hundreds, and perhaps thousands of miles are under water.

After breakfast this morning we heard what we thought was low thunder, and I remarked it to the captain. "No," said he, directing our attention to the bank, "it is the river breaking down the banks." It was a fearful sight, though appearances assured us that there were no dwellings near. Shrub after shrub, sward after sward, disappeared before the wild rush of the great waters, and a long line of white sarge stretching for miles alone told where the extreme edge of the land had been.

At 6 o'clock in the evening we passed the "Independence" while she was wooding, but being obliged to do the same shortly afterwards, everyone expected that she would regain her situation. The excitement became intense and the energy in taking on supplies was doubled. The wood at this particular place was on an island formed by the overflow, and the log hut was situated behind a small lake which the river had made, across which the men had to come in a slight canoe. I never recollect a scene of such entire desolation. The miserable appearance of the hovel, the slight space behind which the leafless trees showed their bare branches, the blackened and withered trunks in the foreground—the desolate pool in front would have looked wretched under a bright sun at midday, but seen in the evening's gloom, with the wind which had freshened up whistling through the trees, it produced an effect on my mind of the most mournful kind, and I was glad when I heard the bell sounded, and then the sharp ring of the pilot's signal to the engineman.

As we were swinging round the captain showed us the boilers of the "Buckeye" which exploded at this place. It lay on the bank half in water, just where it was projected last year, when the explosion happened. No signs of the "Independence" manifested themselves, although many an eye was looking astern for the bright glare of her boiler fires. But just as we were retiring someone called out that she was visible, and we hastened on deck and saw the light plainly. One of the pilots however discovered some slight peculiarity about her fires (for these men seem to know the smallest trifles) which enabled him to state that it was not the "Independence," but the "Wm. French" of Louisville. The "Independence" never appeared again until we saw her in New Orleans, where she arrived 8 or 10 hours after us. During the night the "Wm. French" came within 50 yards of our stern, and would certainly have passed us had she not to stop to deliver the Mail, being the boat employed by the Post Office.

Sunday 8 Mar All morning we were passing through the shoots. [. . .] Moored at the bank on one of these, now useless from the high stage of the waters, we found a steam boat built for the purpose of raising the "snags," which are the greatest dangers in these waters. These snag boats, which are employed by the general [*Federal*] government are built on the principle of the cigar vessels, with the paddles on the outside, and a "purchase wheel" of immense size in the centre.

At 11 o'clock we stopped at Memphis, the first break of forest land since we left Louisville. This place is built on land that even at high water is 40 feet higher than the river. Here we found the "Monarch" steamer which started two days before us, delayed by some accident which had happened to her rudder during the previous night. Several boats were moored to the shore, receiving cotton on to their already well-loaded decks and guards. Several Negroes were engaged in tumbling these bales over the bluff, and checking their descent by a thick rope noosed on to the bale. The appearance of a steamboat loaded with cotton to the amount of from 1500 to 2000 bales is most singular. They appear to be almost a moving warehouse of that article. Every space in the vessel is used—tunnels and doors being left in the piling for the very necessary purpose of communicating the different parts with each other.

A few miles below Memphis we passed Commerce, a city built by a Tennessee bank, which certainly is a bad speculation at present, as it is more than two feet under water. We passed several jokes about this place, such as "the banks being obliged to give way"; "water rising in the commerce market," which certainly is an anomaly, as it is "*not at all in demand*"—to which a witty friend of mine afterwards added that "the notes of the Commerce Bank had watermarks to distinguish them."

From Memphis to Vicksburg 250 miles, there is no place on either side of the river on which a city could be raised until levees are constructed. The evening of the day tempted one to an hour's walk on the hurricane deck. The crescent moon, though not very large, was bright enough to eclipse many of the lesser lights, and dim that of others. Our boat is one of the very few whose escape pipes are constructed so that the steam is sent at once upwards, or projected into the paddle boxes. During the whole voyage the latter plan was used, which rendered the promenade much pleasanter as the steam of course condenses and blows everywhere about the deck, and not only stains the clothes but imparts an unpleasant odour to the air.

I had not been in my berth long when we hit a floating log, with a violence that made the vessel quiver again. The moment before I heard the engine bell for the starboard side violently pulled by the pilot, who had seen the log, but too late to avoid it. Notwithstanding the improbability from the high state of the water, yet I thought it might be a snag, and in ½ a minute I had inflated and hung up my life preserver, and was out upon the gallery. Here I found already two or three of the passengers, like myself, come out to discover the obstruction. A loud crash under the paddle in another moment explained that is was a large floating log which merely carried away a board or two from the wheel.

We passed through an immense quantity of this driftwood on the passage, but the vigilance of the pilots enabled them generally to avoid collision with these very large trunks—which, though they do no immediate damage of any consequence to the boat, yet jar her very much in a way sure to tell after a while.

Monday 9 Mar At three o'clock this afternoon we came in sight of Walnut Hills, one of the range on which Vicksburg is built. We had however first to traverse a bend of 12 miles in the river. A canal might easily, and with slight expense, be cut across about ½ a mile of country, and thus save the distance above stated, but the proposition was hailed by the Vicksburg inhabitants (the trade of whose city would it would lessen if not destroy) with such terrific threats that the subject has never been seriously contemplated. It is quite possible however that the river might do that much itself nolens volens as it is often changing its channel, and the extremely flat country over this ½ mile and the shortness of the distance offer great inducements to the fickle stream!

At four o'clock Vicksburg was visible. The distant appearance of this place from the boat was certainly very beautiful. The town is built on the side of the hill, and the white houses rise above one another in terraces. The town at a distance, for neatness, however, I found to be a very different thing from the town on landing. The streets were unpaved and anything but even, large mud heaps and deep chasms being everywhere visible on looking up the avenues. The houses on the wharf were flooded to the first storey—and one of them—constructed of wood, was propped up on all sides. As we approached, our stern struck this half-floating tenement, and the rush of the people standing on the wharf boats told us they were apprehensive of its descent. The people in the interior, however, continued their smoking and drinking, whether from ignorance of the danger or foolhardihood I do not know.

The moment we touched the landing a man leapt on board and told one of the passengers that we were in fact an hour too late to see the fight, as Haynes and Turton had been having it out with pistols. The duel took place opposite to Vicksburg. Both parties escaped without injury, and then came back in the same skiff, very likely the best friends in the world!

Tuesday 10 Mar We have now fairly bid winter and spring, even, farewell. All bears the aspect of summer, and the wild flowers at the place we wooded grew in rich profusion. This change is almost magical. Four days ago and the smallest buds only were visible, which produced no effect to alleviate the bare appearance of the forest. Now the banks are covered with the richest foliage. Early in the afternoon of this lovely day we passed Baton Rouge, a pretty-looking French settlement, and from this place to New Orleans on both sides of the river there seemed to be one continuous village. The whole banks of the river are lined with sugar plantations, some of the planters' houses being very neat in their appearance, and the Negroes' huts generally painted white and built regularly.

On mounting the hurricane deck for my evening promenade I saw what can only be surpassed by the burning of the prairie, and by that, only in extent. This was the burning of the sugar stubble previous to planting. The largest of these fiery fields was about 3 miles in length and of considerable breadth. After passing it, it yet remained in sight for an hour, and I never saw anything so grand in one respect as these fiery lakes. The flames seemed to shoot and fork into the air—each rivalling the other in brilliancy.

At ¼ before 10 o'clock the gallant bark was moored at New Orleans, having made the passage in 4 days 23 hours and a half, including five hours' detention at Louisville. This is by some hours the shortest passage ever made between the two places. The distance is said to be 1550 miles—by far the greatest part, say 1400 miles, is uninhabited forest land.

[*RCR told MPH that he was unable to find a bed in New Orleans that night, except at expensive hotels, so he slept on board the "Queen."*]

8

New Orleans

Wednesday 11 Mar After an early breakfast I sallied forth after Mure. I soon found him. He was as cordial as ever and was fortunate enough under his guidance, to book myself a resident at the same boarding house with him, before 11 o'clock. Our host and hostess are French people, and by the specimen of our dinner today, have a very pleasant house. Coffee after dinner was served round in small cups without cream. I shall ever laud this delightful custom. It has a good tendency too, I should conceive, of checking the consumption of wine. [*Two weeks later RCR reported to MPH that he was "very well situated with this French couple, who served what you may truly call coffee, not the imitations produced in Wesley Place or Blackburne Terrace* [in Liverpool], *but the real "Simon Pure." Besides having it at breakfast it is sent into our rooms in the morning, and we drink it after dinner. Mure is my only associate: we are always together, and if it were not for him I should be truly miserable.*]

    Thursday 12 Mar The first thing upon which the eye of a stranger rests is the St. Charles Hotel. This imposing structure has a front of much greater extent than Astor House in New York. A portico of double Corinthian columns with side wings ornaments the front. The whole structure however is said to be of less capacity than Astor House. The erection cost upwards of $750,000. Nearly opposite the St. Charles, and of a capacity scarcely inferior, is the Verandah Hotel, so called from a wide spreading portico which surrounds the whole building on two sides. I dined at this place today with Mr. Stevens, a very pleasant man to whom Charles introduced me, and who treated me in every respect as a long-known friend would have done. The dining hall is ornamented with the most elaborate devices in plaster of Paris, and three handsome glass chandeliers give light in the evening.

    The dinner was of the same description as those given at the American and Astor House in New York. Soup finished, some one at the bottom of the room gives a sign for the waiters all to take certain places previously agreed upon by them. Another signal, and away fly the covers, with a noise like the upsetting of a cart of bar iron. I was totally unprepared for it, and started up just as if I had found the roof falling in. Not more than about 300 persons dine here at 3 o'clock, another dinner being always prepared at four for the ladies' table, at which single gentlemen are admitted on being introduced and paying $5 a month extra.

After dinner we went to the French theatre. The interior arrangement is somewhat different from the English. A room of four or five benches cushioned off is situated behind the orchestra occupying of course part of the pit. It is called the parquette, and the price of admission is the highest in the house. The prompter stands with his head just elevated above the floor of the stage, in the centre of the footlights. A raised kind of cover conceals him from the audience. The performances being in French I could not understand much of it. There were some good repartees, if one might judge by the roars of laughter which followed the remarks of some of the performers. A foreigner has some advantage with French people—they use so much action to add force to what they say that a person may often know, with the slightest key, what the parties at the distant end of the room were saying. This may be easily conceived, and from this fact I derived some benefit.

Returning from the theatre we passed a large, well-lighted gambling house. All the windows were open and the confusion of voices within was not a little amusing. "Rouge, un, deux, trois—faro noir, c'n'est pas—vous avez perdu. Je n'ai pas—Mettre votre argent—gentilhommes." These amidst roars of laughter, and occasionally, after a momentary pause during which I suppose the ball was revolving, met our ears in the street below.

Independently, however, of the French, there seems to be a gambling spirit amongst southerners generally. There are lotteries continually offered, sanctioned by the State Legislature. The largest now in course of drawing here has landed property prizes said to be worth $2,000,000—probably worth at least half that sum. The chances for the first prizes of $500,000 each, and of course for hundreds of thousands of blanks, is to be had, as the advertisers state, at the moderate charge of $20, and "may gain any of the above."

I went to the Rotunda of the St. Charles Exchange this morning to see the operation of drawing. Two large wheels with glazed sides are placed on each side of the notary appointed to superintend. In one wheel are the numbers, and in the other are the prizes and blanks. A little boy is stationed at each to hand the tickets out. "Number 4080" shouts the clerk. "Blank," "4098"—"Blank," "8104"—"Blank," "124009"—"Blank," "8411"—"One share in the Gas Bank"—which being interpreted means "Nothing." Ten more blanks, and then came another share in the gas bank, and so on.

Monday 13 Mar I went today with an English friend, Mr. Butterfield, to an auction of Negroes. The sale took place in the large bar room of one of the minor hotels. I never saw collected together so many plain-looking and ill-featured men. There were sundry paintings in the room. The largest and most conspicuous for several reasons were those of our Saviour and George Washington. Alas! where were the doctrines and precepts of the former? Was this the liberty the latter achieved for his land? The eye of superstition might have fancied a frown on his illustrious brow for the traffic carried on in the room beneath.

The sale soon commenced. The first negro was named Jem. "Now gentlemen," said the seller, "what will you pay for this likely hand?—$500, 500 bid, 10, 20, 30, 50, 600—going for $600—10, 20, yours for 620, sir. There's your master, you rascal! That good-looking man over there." The buyer turned his quid over in his mouth, and his ugly features relaxed into a smile at the auctioneer's joke.

"Now gentlemen, here's a boy Tom, aged 18, likely fellow. How much wood can you cut in a day, you rascal?" "Much as anyone, massa." "Ah!, so I thought. Gentlemen, I will start him at $500". Several buyers here approached and examined his ankles and wrists. "All sound, gents., warranted so by the articles of sale, free of all vices and maladies named in the law. Sold for no fault. What will you say?" He was sold for $645.

"Now, gentlemen, here is the third lot—a slave aged 32 consigned from the country for sale. Nothing said about him, either for or against. What will you say, gentlemen? Give me a bid. What shall I say? I know there are some in this room who wish to prevent me selling slaves by auction, because it is so against their interests, but I do not mind them. Gentlemen, give me a bid—say $200." (On examination a serious defect was discovered above this negro's right ankle, and he was sold for $220.)

"Now, gentlemen, here is a family I have been ordered to sell without reserve. What will you say for them? Man 32, woman 30, child 6, what will you say, $1100?—for you, sir, at $1250."

This poster, measuring 15″ × 10″, is inserted in *Recollections*.

"Here is a lot I do not wish to separate—a woman aged 28, and her son 13. Turn your grinning face to those gentlemen, Charles. What will you say for them? Guaranteed against all faults. What, no bid, gentlemen?" Pause of one minute. "Then I must separate them. I'll sell the boy first. No bid, gentlemen? Then get down. Get up, Fanny. What will you say for the woman, gentlemen?" (I thought I could detect a tear.) "No bid, gentlemen? Down, Fanny, they'll not bid. . . . There's another sale of slaves tomorrow, and I'll sell them then". [. . .]

If a man had shut his eyes during the sale or rather withdrawn from his senses the ideas connected with the form or shape of his species, he might have fancied that the buyers were inspecting a horse, as they examined the bones and felt the flesh of the boys, before giving the nod, which would complete the bargain, and give the Devil another smile at this branch of his favorite traffic.

[*After those first impressions of New Orleans, there were no more entries in the journal until:*] Saturday 28 Mar The Legislature intending to break up this evening, I went to the House of Assembly. The hall of representatives is divided by columns into a semi-circle, and presents a handsome appearance. There are about 60 members in all. Over the Speaker's chair is a fine, full-length portrait of Chief Justice Marshall. [*John Marshall (1755–1835), the fourth Chief Justice of the United States, whose judgments helped shape the structure of federal government.*] The senate chamber is a very small room, as there are but 17 members to accommodate. When I entered the latter the member for New Orleans was speaking in French, in a very low tone, and very deliberately. In a short time his voice became louder and his utterances more rapid, and in ten minutes he was evidently in the full tide of eloquence. His voice waxed still louder, his speech quicker and quicker—his gestures more vehement—his whole face lighted up. I never was so convinced of the power of eloquence, for although he spoke so quick that I could not catch the few words I might otherwise have done, I felt moved to act just as he would do if there had been occasion for it at the time.

From the Senate I went to the House, and having secured a good place in a commodious gallery, running across the hall I witnessed a scene of confusion which it would be impossible fully to describe. As it was the last night of the session the House was required to pass the bills of expenses incurred during the session, and they were now in committee for that purpose. The usual appearances of the lower houses of legislature it would seem, both in this country and England, were not wanting, by the elevation of large numbers of feet on the desks—but I saw something more that the House of Commons would not allow—two members were smoking cigars on that description of seat technically called a southern rocking chair, in the corner of the House.

The clerk read a number of bills which were all passed, until we came to that from the Picayune newspaper office. [*The* New Orleans Picayune *was founded in 1837, and the title survives in the* Times-Picayune. *A picayune was also a Spanish coin worth* $^1/_{16}$ *dollar, and the name of a small town near New Orleans.*]

A member Mr. Chairman, I move that the items be separated.

Clerk Papers to the House $20, Reporting of speeches $130.

A member I move that the last item be expunged.

Another I move that it be reduced to $50.

Another I move that it be paid.

Chairman The last two gentlemen are out of order.

Another member I move that the—

Chairman You're out of order, sir.

Another member Mr. Chairman, there are persons smoking in the House. (a laugh)

Another There's no ladies here. (renewed laughter)

Member No. 1 I withdraw my motion, and move that the yeas and nayes be taken.

Another I second that.

Another Before it is put, Mr. Chairman, allow me to say that the reports of that paper are not worth even its name. (roars of laughter)

Chairman Order, Order. (rap of the hammer)

The yeas and nayes were put. The latter were triumphant, and the poor reporter's bill was annihilated.

A member I move that the Committee dissolve itself.

Another Before it does I move that the House reconsider the vote it has just passed!!

Chairman Gentlemen must take their seats and keep order. (A few went to their seats but many remained standing about.)

A member Does the gentleman from Natchitoches expect to pass this d——d bill through the House?

Chairman Order, order!

(The question for breaking up the Committee was then put, and was then carried amongst loud laughter and whispering.)

A member Mr. Speaker, I move that the House again resolve itself into a committee of the whole. (Roars of laughter)

Speaker Order, order, gentlemen! There is no decorum in the House.

Another member Will the gentlemen explain why he wants the House to go into Committee again?

First member Mr. Speaker, I wish to explain why—.

Speaker Sir, you are out of order.

First member Mr. Speaker, I am desirous of—

Speaker The Chair has decided that you are out of order. If you choose to appeal from the Chair you can.

First member Then I will appeal.

Chairman (with somewhat of a sneer) The gentleman appeals against the decision of the Chair. (the appeal was made and lost) First member I move then that the standing rules of the House be dispensed with, that I may explain to the House why I wish the House to go into Committee. It was seconded and put, amidst laughter, Yeas 2, Nayes 62 (renewed chuckling and laughter) I do believe that the House has lost all—(the rest of the sentence was unheard amidst the confusion).

It was now ½ past 11, and I left the House, tired out with the noise and want of decorum, in which this House is very much below the quiet and more orderly one of Ohio.

Friday 10 April A ride out through the swamps on the Nashville Railroad amply repaid me for the walk in the warm sun to the station. I was agreeably disappointed—thousands of wild flowers adorned each side of the road, and trees of all sizes from the sapling to the giant trunk entirely covered the swamp. One would think little, to look over the surface, so fair and green and beautiful, that the elements and causes of death slumbered below, yet so it is.

Many attempts have been made at different times, chiefly by a joint stock company, to drain the land, but they have hitherto failed or have not been prosecuted with the vigor necessary to make the experiment universally beneficial. A plan was mentioned to me by a French gentleman as having been successfully employed in the swamps in the south of France—on the banks of rivers and streams bearing alluvial deposit, and which would appear without much difficulty might be adopted with the pestilential swamps behind New Orleans, in consequence of Lake Ponchartrain being upon a lower level than the bed of the Mississippi River during the spring months of the year. It is to flood the swamp from the river, allow the water to remain 2 or 3 weeks until it has deposited its alluviant, and then let it run off into

The line behind which I have placed
dots will shew you where the land
once ended and all the islands, (if
such marshy swamps can be called
islands) marked with a star, have
been formed by the vast quantities
of alluvial mud, brought down
and deposited by the waters of the
river. Indeed many have ventured
to assert that the spot upon which
the city of New Orleans stands, 130 miles
from the Gulph of Mexico, was once washed
by the waters of the Gulph itself.

Page of journal written for Rawlins' fiancee.

the lake; the same process to be repeated until a permanent alluvial soil one or two feet in depth is secured.

There are so few sights so characteristic of the unhealthiness of this city as a walk through its cemeteries. The day upon which I visited them was intensely hot; the thermometer stood at 86°, and not a breath stirred the sultry air. I wandered through the deserted grave-yards. Hundreds of thousands of lizards of the chameleon tribe, their hues forever changing, were crawling over the heated tombs. As Moore somewhere says:

> And where the sickening sunlight falls
> Gay lizards glittering on the walls
> Of ruined shrines—busy and bright
> As they were—all alive with light.
> [*Thomas Moore, "Paradise and the Peri"*]

Amongst the graves of many a nation and kindred and tongue, these creatures were the only living inhabitants, and no other moving object met my eye save the millions of dragonflies "with their double wings for hasty flight / And a keen unvarying appetite" enjoying their happy existence under the shadow of the long line of tombs.

The walls of each cemetery are built up into catacombs, many ready to receive the living, but more closed over the dead. Many a poor Roman Catholic is buried here and resting along the ledge of the simple tablet the hand of affection had placed flowers, now faded, alas, or a strip of crepe, or some mark, perchance to show that the living still thought of the dead. But let me not forget one simple tomb in the centre of the ground erected over Marie Angelique, who died at the age of 21. Four glass vases filled with the most lovely flowers evidently renewed daily were placed at the corners of the tomb, and the space between that and the railing was filled with them also. Carefully swept and cleaned from the ruin surrounding the other graves, this one appeared more tended than any, and I could not divest myself of a feeling of intense interest in the death of one so young, and perchance so lovely, whose remains were so faithfully tended. Fancy was busy in guessing who it might be who watched that early grave so constantly. Was it a mother, a sister, a companion, or was it one whose love surpassed even these?

A notice in English and French requests the visitor not to remove the flowers from the graves. Who would, who <u>could</u> be so sacrilegious?

[*There was now another long silence in the Journal, but every Sunday RCR wrote something in his companion diary for MPH:*]

Sunday 5 April Sunday in New Orleans! "You should go to the races today," said a man to me in the morning. "It will be a good day's sport." "Are you going to hear Brough sing at the St. Charles Theatre tonight?" said another. "Will you be going to the Ball next Sunday evening?" said a third, not long ago. These are some of the ways of spending time. The theatres are always open on Sunday, and races and balls are things of course.

Sunday 12 April I have fallen into a regular routine which I should follow at home: breakfast 8, dinner ½ p. 3, and tea at 7. There is little new to write about, my dearest one. I love to write to you on this day of rest. Rest, why should I call it so? It is not a day of rest; many and many an office is as fully employed with business as any other day—bands of militia with the loudest and most unpleasant tones are disturbing the streets—the news rooms are crowded with anxious merchants—drinking is carried on, and everything appears just as it would be on a Monday. [. . .]

Sunday 19 April The hot weather has now fairly commenced, and ice cream, soda water, and all kinds of iced water are becoming quite the rage. You have heard of the celebrated mint julep. This is made by mixing wine with sugar, water and ice, and then placing in the tumbler a few sprigs of mint.

This is quite a favorite beverage, though another entitled by Mure and myself "Ambrosial Nectar" has a large share of public patronage. It is made with wine, sugar, ice and the rind of a lemon. All these things are, as you may well conceive, very refreshing when the thermometer is at 90° in the shade!

Then, everyone is dressed just as waiters or barbers. Let me describe my costume today—a broad-brimmed straw hat, a ribbon round my neck—my shirt collar turned down as low as possible—a white vest and trousers, and a surtout made of blue striped linen !!! I hardly think you would know me, particularly as a southern sun has somewhat bronzed my face.

[*The* Journal *resumed:*]

Tuesday 28 April This was the day appointed for the choosing by ballot election, a mayor, aldermen and councilors for the next year, when three candidates for the first office proposed themselves. One of these, Mr. Freret, the gentleman who was elected, heads a party in New Orleans called the Native American Association, whose object is the repeal of the Naturalization Law, and the exclusion of all foreigners from office of any kind!! Their rabid antipathy to England, if properly represented in their organ (The Native American) is disgusting, and their political economy is of that reckless, selfish and suicidal nature which would suit well the councils of the Emperors of China or Japan, and pass uncriticized, but paraded forth in the columns of a newspaper published in the United States of America, can only excite our pity and surprise!

The City of New Orleans is divided into three municipalities, each governed by its own council elected by the people. The first municipality and the greater part of the third, and generally called the Lower Fauxbourg, consist almost entirely of the French, and is consequently ruled after the Parisian mode, gens d'armes parading the streets at night &c. These gens d'armes sleep in the strangest kinds of cribs imaginable, all huddled together in one enclosure, and reminding you more of the Black Hole of Calcutta than the healthy habitation of men who have the power of leaving the service almost whenever they choose.

A single glance will inform the stranger which is the French and which the English part of the city: the streets of the former are narrow, though the houses look comfortable, and have large balconies which are crowded with ladies and gentlemen in the evening, whilst those of the American municipality are wide and airy, and with one exception all the best buildings are in that part of the city. The exception is the Bank of the Citizens of Louisiana, whose front is the purest white marble, and whose columns are crowned with capitols of bronze, which has an exceedingly beautiful effect.

Further down the French quarter is the Branch Mint erected under General Jackson's administration, but for what good purpose was never made apparent, as the Philadelphia Mint will coin a far greater quantity than the wants of the nation can require, at the expense of [blank] compared with that of New Orleans.

There is little doubt, from all I can learn, that before long the French will be almost unknown in this city as a distinct community. This is owing to the large influx of Americans into the city, whilst the French scarcely increase at all in numbers. A French gentleman mentioned to me his belief that in 6 or 8 years' time the language itself will cease to be spoken, as it is now very generally through the Lower

Fauxbourg. It appears to be extremely desirable that this consummation should be hastened, as the difference in language and habit seems to be the cause of much unpleasant feeling between the French and American inhabitants. [*Miss Martineau had also observed that 'the division between the American and French factions is visible, even in the drawing room. The French complain that the Americans will not speak French, and will not meet their neighbours even halfway in accommodation of speech. The Americans ridicule the toilette practices of the French ladies, their liberal use of rouge and powder. If the French ladies do that to beautify themselves, they do it with great art.*"]

New Orleans to Iberville and back, by steamboat, 180 miles

Saturday 2 May I received an invitation this afternoon from Mrs. Avery to accompany her on a week's visit to Mr. Avery's plantation on the coast [*the banks of the Mississippi*], and I accordingly embarked in the steamer "Persian," one of the finest on the western waters. We had the ladies' cabin to ourselves, our party consisting of Mrs. A., her niece Miss Kate McGavock and myself. We passed the evening in reading and backgammon till 9 o'clock, when our attention was drawn to a steamer puffing and blowing behind us, determined to conquer. We were much amused by the exertions of the firemen who were actively employed in piling wood upon her fires. She manoeuvered for more than an hour to pass us, but as often as she attempted it, the current threw her bows off into the stream, and she fell still further behind. At length she gave it up, crossing to the opposite bank of the river, and we saw no more of her.

I slept little, for there were sundry little holes in the mosquito bar which the little blood-suckers made their way through, in spite of all my endeavors to patch them up, and nothing but the exertions used in warding them off their buzzing attacks induced sleep at last. I rose early, but found my friends already on the guards [*rails*] and we amused ourselves till breakfast time watching this beautiful line of coast—ornamented every few hundreds of yards with lovely cottages and gardens, chiefly the residences of French planters, whose estates, though narrow in front, are of great depth, extending back to the woods some 2 miles distant. It is worthy of note that the French planters bring some inferiority in their planting, and seldom produce such fine crops either in quantity or quality as the Americans.

At 2 o'clock we came up to Success, the name of the plantation we were to visit, and after exchanges and embraces between members of the family I was introduced to Mr. McGavock (Mr. Avery's partner in the estate), Mrs. McG., (Mrs. Avery's sister) and Miss Owen, the governess, whom I found afterwards to be a woman of high intellectual powers. Mrs. Avery's other niece, Miss Martha, I had known before, and she had also been spending some time in New Orleans. A very few minutes enabled me to discover what afterwards was well confirmed, that I was most heartily welcome.

[*The name "Success" does not appear on an 1858 map of the sugar plantations, but it shows the estates of the Averys and the McGavocks. The former was one of the largest in the parish of Iberville, about 30 miles downstream from Baton Rouge.*]

During the five following days we had a complete round of amusement, with more extraordinary hours than I had ever met with. I rose at ½ past 5 and we had breakfast over before 6, rode out on horseback, and lunched at nine on hot sponge cake and claret sangaree, read aloud for two hours, chatted for one, dined at 12 precisely, played chess and backgammon till 3 or 4, rode out in the carriage, down or up the coast until 6, then came tea time, and after tea time a walk on the levée or through the garden; and after that when the darkness closed, and the fire-flies by millions, with their brilliant light, music and songs and recitations followed, and closed the evening at nine. At ½ past everyone in the house was fast asleep.

The morning's amusements were once varied by a ride I took with Mr. McGavock over the estate to the cotton gin, and through the young sugar and corn. Here, hanging on most of the trees I saw a description of [*Spanish*] moss, common in all the southern districts, which when pulled and dried makes a most excellent substitute for horse-hair, and indeed may be considered almost equally good for all practical purposes. It sells for $3 a bale of about 240 pounds. The planter, however, never thinks it worthwhile to cut it, and on estates where the Negroes are well treated the profit goes entirely to them, their time for the cutting being during the period of the day when not working for their "owners"—or when holidays are allowed them.

I went into the Negro quarter on this estate, and though nothing in the world could ever reconcile my mind to the presence or name of Slavery, I was yet pleased to find the conditions of the Negroes much better than I expected. New and commodious cabins were erecting when I was there, and attached to each of them is a piece of garden grounds or place for chickens, a numerous family of which is raised by every Negro, thereby yielding no small sum from the sale of eggs, the greatest part of which, Mrs. Avery told me, she purchased

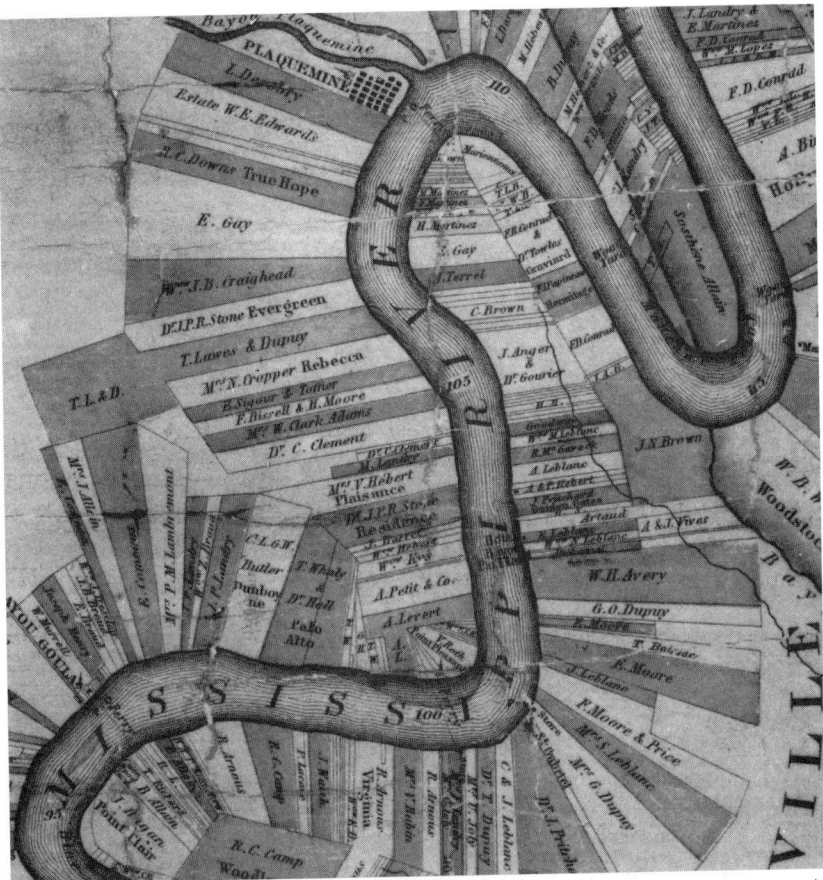

Section of 1858 map of plantations. The Historic New Orleans Collection 1947.
l.i–v (detail).

for use in town, or Mrs. McGavock for use in the home. Besides this
they may realize $3 a bale for moss. They have the use of the cotton
press for pressing it into the requisite size. A keeper of a store down
the coast told me that the Negroes spent $75 at his store during the
previous week. Another amelioration of the Negroes' condition at
Success is in the giving out of the stores. On most estates the food for
the Negro quarter is given out to each head of a family every day, just
before meal time. At Success it is served once a month, so that the
squaw may make what arrangements she chooses in a domestic way.

During sugar-making time the men work night and day, being
relieved by each other as occasion requires. As soon as the sugar is in

cask, as Miss Owen informed me, they have a week's holiday, and forthwith proceed to dress themselves in their best attire, and ornamenting themselves with garlands of flowers, dance round the sugarhouse. They then march in procession to the front of the house, and sing snatches of doggerel in praise of the ladies of the household; and at Christmas time when they have also a week to themselves they enjoy the like festivities.

But the marriages are the most joyful for them. There were two shortly before I arrived at Success. Dancing is the chief amusement of the evening on these occasions. With one exception every laborer's cottage was exceedingly neat and clean, and I amused myself in tossing some of the round little plump babies, with magnificent black eyes like jet, to the delight, mingled evidently with some portion of fear, of the respective mothers. I could not but come to the conclusion that the Negroes at Success were as happy as their relative situation could permit. The standard of happiness must of course be vastly lower in the Negro race than that of free men.

I had many pleasant conversations with Miss Owen, and one on the subject of Slavery. Moral influence with her had overbalanced surrounding circumstances, and I found her opposed to slavery, although her opposition arose more from her opinion of its effects on the white population than on the colored. She had seen many estates during her residence in Tennessee in which State she was born, and she told me that there were few that treated their slaves as well as those at Success. From her and Mrs. McGavock I heard some worse accounts of the effects of slavery, or rather of the treatment of Negroes by dealers in them than I ever heard anywhere else. I considered the way in which this information was given me by ladies as great evidence of candor. Miss Owen I found had never been in a free State. She has a great desire to visit England, and was much interested in my accounts of many places I had seen in my own country.

I must not omit to mention that one evening we spent a few hours at a Dr. Pritchard's, a neighboring planter who cultivates an extensive sugar estate [*shown on the 1858 map*]. The tea table was covered with every imaginable article, suitable and unsuitable for the food of man—fish in every form, from the little thing that was floating in the bayou an hour ago, to the Scotch salmon that was speared in 1839, or perchance before that. Meat, poultry and venison, dressed for everyone's taste, cream cheese, Cheshire cheese and some Dutch peaches, limes and guava jelly, curry and rice, eggs poached and boiled, hard and soft; bread, new and old, hot and cold, butter churned an hour since, dry toast and milk toast, tea, coffee and chocolate, and last, though by no means least, fresh buttermilk, although the last, I confess, fell short of that rich fluid of the same name, which never failed me at breakfast and tea and at dinner, to the entire exclusion of wine, during my week's residence at "Success."

But I must not think of leaving without a few words on sugar-making. When the cane is ready to cut, it is the height of a man on horseback, and as each cane always grows to exactly the same height as the others, the plantation presents a very singular appearance. The cane is conveyed on carts to the sugar-house and is placed on an endless chain receiver which carries it up to the rollers, four in number, through which it is made to pass, the sugar juice being fully squeezed out in one journey. The stubble comes out on the other side mangled and shattered, while the sugar falls into a vat below from which it is conducted into pans, five in number, and boiled— the first of these pans being larger in consequence of the greater quantity of scum issuing from the sugar at first; which scum is then thrown into the next pan, from that into the next and so to the last, where it is thrown away, having by that time become worthless. The sugar when boiled down in the pans, is then taken out, placed upon coolers, and finally put into hogsheads.

The sugar cane, after being cut, will yield two years more without fresh planting. After the first year it is called "rattan," and is supposed to yield much less sugar in quantity, but of a finer quality than the first planting. When the first planting is made it is done by cutting the cane into lengths of about 3 feet, and placing it horizontally in the ground, where from each of the divisions there will spring up a new cane. Some pieces that Mr. McGavock pulled up for me, one of which I brought away, were not more than 3 or 4 inches below the surface.

On the estate at Success is, I suppose, the longest private railway in the south, if not in the States. It extends as far as the bayou, somewhere about 2¼ miles, to the woods in the rear of the plantation, and is used for bringing in wood for shingles and staves, and for household purposes, and for sale to steamboats on the banks of the river, where it commands a price of $3.50 per cord [*128 cubic feet*]. The cost of laying down this railway, exclusive of any reckoning for Negro labor was $2000 per mile, or about $4500. The rails are 5 feet apart and the iron used is of the old kind, half-inch thick, with peg holes for confining it to a continuous length of wood.

The weather during my stay here was intensely hot—though relieved during the day by a pleasant breeze across the water.

On Thursday evening, May 7, as we were returning from a visit to a Dr De Shiel, another neighbor some three miles from "Success," we were aware of the approach of a storm by the commencement of a series of flashes of dazzling lightning, which glared every moment over the bed of the Mississippi, along whose banks we were riding. Strange to say, the horses neither started nor reared as I expected every moment. We quickened their speed, and arrived in time to escape the most fearsome storm I ever witnessed. For more than an hour it thundered and lightned without the slightest intermission, and the concussions of the air which appeared to be right over my head, shook every moment the bed—upon which I was not content to lie until I saw some signs of abatement. The rain meanwhile fell in such torrents that I more than once fancied the river had broken through the levée. For the greatest part of the time the whole planta-tion, from the house to the forest, was lit up by a glare scarcely equalled by the mid-day sun. At length the flashes became less and less vivid, the thunder died away in the distance—the rain ceased, and I———fell asleep—and rose at 5 to pack up, breakfast, and make ready for a departure to the city.

After dinner a fine little colored boy, named Charley, who had been my peculiar attendant, announced that there was a steamboat in sight. My kind friends all came to the brink of the river with me, to make an imposing appearance, as we knew that no steamer would be well content to round-to, for one passenger.

I was obliged to go, to write per packet of the 19th—or I should have been loathe to take them in. The boat that Charley had seen soon approached. She was of the very largest size, loaded with cotton to the very edge of the guards. We thought she was going to pass, so some of our party mounted the wood-pile, from which more con-spicuous elevation they were seen by the boat, which (expecting a dozen at least) after considerable trouble succeeded in coming near the edge—but not near enough to take me on board without the additional necessity of sending out the yawl. I said farewell to my hospitable friends, threw my valise into the boat, jumped in myself, and was pushed off at once—the waiting boatman being apprized that there were no more coming!

The steamboat I was approaching, from its vast size, and the im-mense height to which the cotton was piled, reminded me more of the six houses composing Blackburne Terrace than anything else. Whether the kindness shown me by the family I had just departed from was an additional stimulus to make me think of home, and

Missis.ᵖ Steam boat, laden with Cotton

consequently to make the Terrace a subject of comparison, I will not
pretend to say. My friends may think so if they choose.

Few persons save those who have seen or travelled on them can
have an idea of the vast size and singular appearance of these cotton
boats. Carrying, as they do, the bales in every possible place where
they can be laid, it becomes necessary to leave tunnels for connecting
the different parts of the boat with each other, and as the whole
surface on the top is uncovered, and as one of the many sparks
proceeding through the chimneys from the wood fires below might
ignite a substance so dangerous as cotton, a number of men are kept
constantly watering the upper surface from huge cans, and moreover
two hoses from a pump worked by the engines are in readiness in
case of accident.

This boat, the "Ellen Kirkman," has on board a cargo equal to 3746
bales of Mississippi cotton, which is the utmost she will carry. She is
perhaps the largest boat that ever navigated the western waters, and
at present hauls between New Orleans and Nashville Tennessee.
Owing to the cotton from Tennessee being much more bulky than
that from Mississippi, her cargo, in point of numbers of bales, the
former would be inferior to Mississippi.

As we were rounding-to at the levée in New Orleans to a landing
place, we saw a boat called "The Prairie" which the Capt. of the "Ellen
Kirkman" declared had been blown up by gunpowder, judging from
her appearance. When I landed, I went on board of her, and found
she had passed us as we were mending our boiler in the night, and
that she came from Natchez, Mississippi, and had been wrecked
during the storm of Thursday evening. No language can describe the

smashed appearance which this boat exhibited. The upper cabin was completely blown away—not a vestige of it save the floor and a few sashes from the skylight windows being left. Wood, iron, glass, everything seemed blended in one mass. The machinery was bent and distorted by the falling lumber from above, and altogether the boat presented such an appearance that one who had not seen it might well be forgiven for doubting the account, and one who had, for doubting that wind merely, was the cause of so extraordinary destruction as the one before his eyes.

But the first news that met my eye on entering the Exchange Room was sufficient to dispel whatever doubts I had. A tornado more fierce than ever blew across the face of the earth, as far as any accounts will show, had swept the country contiguous to Natchez and had levelled with the ground almost every house in that devoted city. Two steamboats were totally lost, and it is supposed that nothing could have saved the Prairie from the like fate, but the intrepidity of her engineer who stood by his post and kept the engine at work, which so far retarded the force of the gale, aided by her two anchors, and the effect of some thousands of pieces of lead on her boiler deck—that she drifted but slowly to the other side of the river, and was lodged safely as far as those left on board were concerned.

One young man returning from college to his family in New Orleans was blown overboard in the cabin and was drowned—his body having been found two days afterwards. It is singular that Natchez and the places immediately in its vicinity, only, felt the greatest force of this tornado. Down at "Success" and further south at New Orleans it was far more moderate. As soon as the awful event became known in New Orleans a subscription to the amount of $2000 was raised, and a deputation appointed to convey it to the devoted city.

[*RCR must have arrived back in New Orleans on Saturday 9 May, and he was to remain there for a further three weeks.*]

There are several ways of leaving the din and bustle of the city, and gaining a somewhat purer atmosphere, and I frequently adopted one or the other of them. My first expedition was to a place called Carrolton, situated up the river, three or four miles from the city. The railway cars convey you in a few moments to one of the most beautiful gardens I ever saw. The hotel has a delightful view of the river. As I was standing upon the balcony I observed the singular effect of the sun upon the water falling over the large stern paddle-wheel of a steamboat going up. There are several boats built in this way, chiefly for ascending narrow streams and bayous, where paddles of the ordinary construction would be in the way. These boats, as might be expected, are much slower in their running than those of the ordinary kind.

A very favorite drive out of the city is down by the side of the canal which connects New Orleans with Lake Ponchartrain. The road is formed of shells from which it takes its name, and at its terminus the lake refreshes the eye, and the body too, as more than one delightful bathe would lead me to testify. In the evening this road is used by hundreds of people from the city, in all sorts of carriages and on all kinds of horses. On another occasion Mr. Mure and myself went down to another part of the lake, distant some ten miles from the city. The railway I have elsewhere mentioned, was originally intended to run to Nashville Tennessee distant 800 miles. A great labor has been accomplished certainly in carrying it through the swamp, but it is said to be morally certain that it never will be completed, which is likely, as long as there are such navigable rivers as the Mississippi and the Cumberland. [*It was many years before New Orleans was linked to the north by rail.*]

In twenty minutes after starting we crossed the canal and the shell road, the former being accomplished by a moveable drawbridge, which seems to fill all the duties required, at an expense very much less than an aqueduct or bridge would have required, and without the necessity of making two inclines, if such a thing could have been done through the swamp, which was of course impossible. "Stop at Bath" said the conductor, and a few minutes later we halted in the swamp and I looked out for Bath—which I found to consist of a Chinese pagoda and a log hut, the former a sort of tavern, both situated on a small oasis of dry ground. In ten minutes more we left the woods and came out upon an extensive prairie, many miles in extent covered with long grass and the most glorious wild flowers. The grass grows so swiftly that the engine is necessarily provided with a scythe on each side to mow it down.

The pools on each side of the road are said to abound with alligators, and a diligent searching with both eyes gratified me with the sight of several, some sunning themselves on a log, from which they quickly dropped off, and others with their slimy heads [*a common misconception*] and little eyes just visible above the water. Their length might be about 4 feet, though the conductor told me they were caught more than five, sometimes.

The train left us at a solitary little house called Prairie Cottage, and then continued its way some 10 miles further into the forest again where men are constantly employed cutting wood, which they convey into New Orleans. This forms the profit of the company—as the amount received for passengers, I was told, only paid expenses—and hardly that. The fare for ten miles is 25¢. The great time for passengers is Sunday, when the boat races and pistol matches at Prairie Cottage prove a great attraction.

Friday 28 May I accompanied Mrs. Avery this morning to Rev. Mr. [*Theodore*] Clapp [*pastor of the Congregational Church*] and had a conversation with him of some ½ an hour. The recent escape of Mr. Simmons from Mobile in consequence, as alleged, of his preaching an Abolitionist sermon, brought on the question of Slavery, and Mr. Clapp gave me some of his opinions upon it. I record them in his own words: "In every instance I have an opportunity of observing, I have found education to produce no good result. I do not think the African race were created for self-government, and so long as they remain unmixed with the Anglo-Saxon they will be fit for little else than hewers of wood and drawers of water."

I alluded to the case of Puerto Rico, and asked him if he thought that white labor could not be used with as much or more advantage than black? He entirely coincided with this. I then said that it would be so long before planters could be induced to see that, and the cloud was darkening around the future so fearfully that there seems to be little hope from that feeling. He then said, "My opinions on that point I have rendered firm by the most diligent investigation and thought, and in accordance therewith I believe that another century will see the African race dwindled away to a small and scanty remnant—as the Indians have done—in accordance with that grand scheme of providence which has destined that the Anglo-Saxon race shall be pre-eminent throughout the earth."

I was just about to ask Mr. Clapp how he reconciled this opinion with the continuing increase of the Negro population, whose numbers—it is well known—increase in greater proportion with less chance of death from ordinary causes in childhood than the Anglo Saxon race, when Mrs. Avery rose, and though I was asked to call again, yet I know I should not have the time. [*He might have benefited from a longer exposure to this man. According to a 1988* Dictionary of Louisiana Biography *the chief attractions for visitors to New Orleans were the French Opera, the American Theater and "Parson" Clapp's church, where a typical (segregated) congregation would include liberal-minded whites and free blacks, together with visiting planter-merchants and professional men. A*

Yale-educated New Englander, he had been appointed pastor to the First Presbyterian Church of New Orleans in 1822, holding strict Calvinistic views and being opposed to slavery. But in course of time his views changed, rejecting much accepted religious dogma, and moving to a moderate pro-slavery stance. He maintained closer personal and intellectual ties with Roman Catholic priests and Jewish rabbis than with his Protestant colleagues. For the reasons that he explained to Rawlins, on the question of slavery he believed that the South needed an orderly caste system in the light of the African's supposed racial inferiority. Mrs. Avery brought the meeting to a close before the young visitor could debate that issue.]

[*Rawlins was now preparing to leave New Orleans without having committed to his diary any report of his business activities. It was only in his* Recollections *that he recalled that "in conjunction with William Mure, whom I had long known in Liverpool, I invested the £5,000 received by Bill of Exchange from Mr. de Saussure in cotton and wheat, watching the market to make cheap purchases."*]

That this question of slavery is an intricate and exceedingly difficult one, every person who has beheld slavery will allow. The Abolition Party in the North have beyond all doubt greatly retarded the cause they wish to advance. They have made the slave holder more jealous of allowing his slave the slightest taste of liberty—fearful lest he should love it too well. When a slave has a kind Master I can well conceive that he is perfectly happy according to his standard of happiness—and merely informing him that he ought to be free, without giving him the means of freeing himself—is only making him miserable.

According to the Constitution of the United States, the general government has no more power to legislate for any one of the Slave States in this matter than England's government would have. The movement must therefore come from the State itself—yet who would dare to moot it? A bold man, verily, for he would hold his life in his hand. Even if his own State were favorable to a change, the vengeance of surrounding ones would be aroused, and a feeling of that kind, once created, would never die in the South and South Western States.

With regard to the question of abolition, though there are many exceptions of course, it is to be feared that the vast mass of the African race, as they at present exist are without intelligence [*RCR uses the word in the sense of "knowledge" rather than mental ability*], utterly devoid of any forethought, and without education, if liberated would perish in thousands. Yet, propose education, and the idea would be received with horror by the slave-holder. He too knows that "knowledge is power"—and like the genie in the fairy tale, that slave would find his chains "huge to the eye, but brittle in the grasp." No—it appears to be that the more the candid observer studies this subject, the more he will long for the annihilation of the curse—and the more he wishes, the more difficulties he will see crowding around— until he is almost driven away from hope itself, and could almost doubt the strength of his faith in "the eternal progress of truth."

The most deplorable feature in the South is the disregard of law, which so continually manifests itself. No opportunity for displaying the constant desire which would appear to exist, of superseding the law by popular demonstration, shows in stronger light than the question I have lately been alluding to. On one occasion, when the Rev. G. F. Simmons preached an Abolition sermon at Mobile, the newspapers there and at New Orleans openly advocated violation of the law. The Mobile paper, in language couched thus: "We have in Alabama no printed law for the punishment of such crimes, and if the people do not take the matter into their own hands what protection have we against the doctrines of the Abolitionists?"

But it is not only on this question that a desire to break the law displays itself. The practice is universally adopted among a certain class of wearing concealed weapons, so the South West affords irresistible temptations to break the law, when anger occasions their use. The most horrid murders may be committed in this way: the murderer is perhaps arrested, angry words are proved, and the verdict is "justifiable homicide." While I was in New Orleans a young man of some 22 years of age, with whom I was brought in contact, named [*blank*] shot another man at a political dinner. He was arrested: "angry words" were proved. The surgeon stated that the man was not in immediate danger, a small bail was demanded, and B. was liberated. The next morning the man died, and B. took a boat and went up the river, and on landing at Somerville I saw him. He came on board with a swaggering air and conversed with some young men he knew. I afterwards saw him at the Salt House in Louisville, where he was staying. If any vigilance had been used to arrest him it would evidently been successful.

These instances come under my own cognizance, and during my residence in New Orleans there were numerous street fights with knives or pistols—one of them early in the day between two cotton brokers, in which the injured party probably dared not appeal to the law. This practice of carrying concealed weapons is so common that save with one exception, viz. in the theatre, you cannot enter any public place of amusement without a rigid examination of your person to discover them. When found by the officers of the city a fine of $20 is imposed for the offence.

Alas! in the southern country it is not only that the people are everywhere disposed to take the law into their own hands, but the law itself, which in older countries is lynx-eyed—is here either slumbering, if really strong enough, or weak and ineffectual. Sooner than live under a state of society which prevails throughout the southern country at the present time, I would hail with joy the despotism of the Autocrat of Russia!

There is one excellent feature about New Orleans that certainly should not be left unrecorded, and that is the unbounded liberality of the residents towards the poor and sick. It really is a noble trait, and redeems many a dark spot, in my opinion.

The situation of New Orleans, rendering it a point of attraction for foreigners, it is seldom that charity is needed for native Americans— and I was told that nearly at all times 80 out of 100 inhabitants of the hospital are foreigners. At the time that Natchez was so awfully visited, not only were $2000 raised and sent up in less than two days afterwards, that a further sum, scarcely less than the first, was collected during the following week.

These are things which it is a real pleasure to place upon record, and well may we express our heartfelt wish that they will stand forth bright and enduring upon the pages of the Book of Life!

[*Miss Martineau's verdict on New Orleans, after a stay of ten days, had been that she had learnt much that had been useful in helping her to interpret some things which met her observation both previously and subsequently. "But my strongest impression is that whilst it affords an instructive study, and yields some enjoyment to a stranger, it is the last place in which men are gathered together where one who prizes his humanity would wish to live."*]

9

New Orleans to Washington

Via Cincinnati by steamboat (1650 miles)

The morning of the 2nd June was intensely hot—the thermometer above 90° in the shade. It was the day I had fixed for my departure, in the same boat that had conveyed me down. She was advertised to start at 10, and at 11 I had my luggage on board, and had time to observe the confusion and bustle of many who had left everything to the last moment. Dozens of small skiffs, loaded to the water's edge with oranges, bananas, melons and pineapples, giving an exceedingly foreign aspect to the scene were crowding round the boat to dispose of some of the contents. The levée was crowded with produce. It is one of the busiest scenes in the morning that perhaps could be seen in any part of the world.

At ½ p. 12 the 8th or 9th warning bell was tolled, and we backed out into the stream. In two hours the dome of the St. Charles Exchange and the towers of the new cathedral and the Cottar Press had become invisible, and by the time I had my state-room to my satisfaction dinner was ready. I found the table laid out the whole length of the cabin, but still insufficient for the large numbers. We continued to increase, too, as we took in some 4 or 5 passengers for every one we landed, and for many nights the cabin was literally covered with beds. Natchez was passed at dusk, so that little could be seen of the fearful devastation with which that devoted city was visited.

The routine of a steamboat voyage is much the same at all times, and I have described this. But few incidents occurred. We had our share of Mississipians, gamblers and squalling children—a fearful storm one night, and a floating log the next. We passed the junction of the great rivers in the day time, and saw Grand Cairo, a speculation which many a Cockney was taken in, from finding Mr. Nicholas Biddle's name at the head of the Share list [*he was president of the second U.S. Bank*], and which has but recently been submerged from the overflowing waters—to which accident from its low situation it will always be liable.

Most true indeed were the French in calling the Ohio "la belle rivière." Its high banks crowned with foliage, with here and there the grey mountain limestone peeping forth to vary the view, and its constant windings, constitute its chief beauties—and the eye must be pampered indeed which could fancy it monotonous. The salutation of a shot, and the hoisting of the colors were proposed when we arrived at North Bend, the residence of General Harrison, but finding that he was gone to Fort Meigo the compliment was dispensed with. Though not exactly a log cabin, it is a plain-looking farmhouse, pleasantly situated for the view, and well shaded by trees.

On Wednesday 10 June, at 12 o'clock, being 7 days and 23 hours from New Orleans we landed at Cincinnati, and I found myself once again amongst the best of friends. In the afternoon of this very beautiful day Mrs. Stetson called in her carriage for Mrs. Vaughan and Virginia to go with her on a visit to the Lane Seminary, and I was asked to accompany them. This seminary is a theological one, built, and chiefly at present supported by, voluntary contributions. It has fallen off very much during the last few years, owing to the introduction by the Principal, Dr Beecher, and others, of Abolition principles!!! It is said to be somewhat recovering its lost ground just now. Every year the directors hold an examination, at which anyone may be present. After this, a collation is spread in the wood, and music and songs fill up an hour or two. This was the anniversary, and though we were too late for the exercises and amusements, we passed an hour or two very pleasantly looking over an extensive and valuable library of about 10,000 volumes collected by Prof. Stowe, chiefly in Europe at an extremely small expense, owning to the very judicious way in which this gentleman executed the duty assigned to him. [*Calvin Ellis Stowe also ensured that his name went down in history by marrying the principal's daughter Harriet Beecher who later achieved world fame with her* Uncle Tom's Cabin.]

Monday 15 June The semiannual examination of the Common Schools of Cincinnati having again come round, I went with John to one of the schools and was much interested by the answers returned by the girls in history and geography, many of which I secretly confessed ignorance concerning. The questions were not put regularly from the book but varied by the master or visitor.

When I left Cincinnati in March exertions were being made to rescind part of the city provisions by which the property of free Negroes amounting in value to about $60,000 was taxed, whilst they were not allowed to send any colored children to the Schools. I was very glad to find that the Reform had been accomplished—and that though free colored persons were still taxed it was for the erection and maintenance of their own schools.

Tuesday 16 June Today J. V. took me to the Type Foundry of Mr. Guilford. Mr. G. took me through the foundry and explained the working of the most beautiful ingenious piece of machinery for the making of types, by which 40 lbs. per diem can be struck off. It is the invention of Mr. G's partner and is said to be unknown out of Cincinnati. [. . .]

Wednesday 17 June This morning I again said goodbye to Cincinnati for a while, and took my passage in the "Boston" for Pittsburgh, Penn.

Cincinnati to Pittsburgh by river, 465 miles

[*Rawlins spent the next few days in pleasant conversation with fellow passengers and admiring the scenery along the Ohio river. They called at Wheeling, Va. where he*] took the opportunity of ascending the steep hill behind the city, population 10,000, [as] I was told by an intelligent little boy who came up while I was seated on the hill. I asked him if there were any public schools? He said No. "Any good schools of any kind?" "Why there is only one school of any kind, but they say it ain't worth anything."

At 8 o'clock we left for Pittsburgh. The river seemed to increase in beauty as we advanced—lofty banks on either side, clothed with wood, with here and there a town on the Ohio shore, varying the view, kept our attention constantly alive—and when a sudden bend in the river brought us in sight of Pittsburgh at five o'clock in the afternoon I could hardly repress an exclamation of surprise at its beauty. No smoke spoiled the cleanness of the atmosphere for it was a day of rest for the artisan.

After securing a place in the canal for 9 in the evening I sallied forth for a walk through the town. [. . .] Pittsburgh is surrounded by hills on each side and was the site of Fort Duquesne where Washington was so providentially saved from the rifle bullets of the old Indian chief. [. . .]

Pittsburgh to Harrisburg by canal and railway, 311 miles

At half past nine in the evening we were fairly on our way eastwards in a more comfortable boat than I found on the Erie canal. The morning rose bright and beauteous of Monday 22 June and the whole day we passed the most beautiful scenery of its kind I had not yet seen. Our course for some time lay along the banks of the Allegheny, into which the canal occasionally enters—the water being dammed up below. This slack water navigation must have saved a great deal of expense.

On the route I met Mr. C. L. Schlatten, chief engineer for the state of Pennsylvania who gave me a great amount of information. He stated that had this work been constructed again steam navigation would have been employed and the whole of the rivers would have been converted into slack water, and engineers are now surveying two or three rivers in Kentucky with that objective in view. About 4 o'clock in the afternoon, on turning a bend in the canal we found ourselves in a deep valley without any apparent outlet save over the lofty hills. Presently we discerned a tunnel through which we vanished. It is 908 feet in length, the whole distance being through limestone hewed rough without being faced save a few yards from the end.

Before five in the following morning we left the canal boat and entered the cars of the celebrated Portage Railway, one of the greatest triumphs of the skill of man perhaps the world has ever seen, but the energetic Americans would have attempted. While we were waiting for the engine I had time to observe two contrivances for the safe conveyances of goods from Philadelphia to Pittsburgh. The first consists in having canal boats constructed in four divisions capable of being placed on four railway cars, thus:

Pittsburg Eastward. Johnston & Hollidaysbg
placed on four railway cars
thus.

The goods are loaded in Philadel-
phia in these boxes as they
may be called — whence they
proceed by canal to Holliday-
burgh. Here by a simple contri-
vance they are unscrewed from
each other & placed upon the
carriages — carried over the
mountain — launched into the
canal at Johnston — Screwed
together & thus continue their
voyage to Pittsburgh — The
other contrivance is to invert
this order of things. Carriage
bodies are filled with ~~wh~~
goods & conveyed by Railway
110 miles to Harrisburgh. Here

The goods are loaded in Philadelphia in these boxes as they may be called, whence they proceed by canal to Hollidaysburg. Here by a simple contrivance they are unscrewed from each other and placed upon the carriages, carried over the mountain and launched into the canal at Johnston, screwed together, and thus continue their voyage to Pittsburgh.

The other contrivance is to invert the order of things. Carriage bodies are filled with goods and conveyed by railway 110 miles to Harrisburgh. Here they are taken off the wheels and placed on canal boats to convey them to Hollidaysburg where they are hoisted out and conveyed over the mountains, and again consigned to the canal.

At five o'clock the engine was attached, and conveyed us along a winding level of five miles to the foot of the first incline, which rises about 1 foot in 15. A safety stage was hooked on behind the last car, a signal was given, and we almost instantly gained a speed of 9 miles per hour, which was maintained until we reached the summit.

Here I learnt that all the inclines on this side of the mountain are worked by 35 horsepower engines, whilst those on the other side being (the greater weight of goods being conveyed westward) were 60s, both high pressure. Proceeding a short distance by horsepower we passed through a tunnel 900 feet in length, and a engine then being attached we travelled a level of 17 miles at a good speed, now winding around the base of a cliff and anon crossing some wide torrent rushing to the depth of the river beneath.

At the foot of the third incline we breakfasted, and never did I enjoy a half past six breakfast so much as this one on the Allegheny Mountains. The fifth incline surmounted we reached our highest elevation viz. 2382 ft above the tide water. A series of levels and inclines similar to the others conducted us again to the canal.

I might however allude to one of the inclines on the east side. It is almost fearful to look down as it is so very steep. The actual elevation attained is 307 feet and its whole length is 3116. It therefore falls nearly one foot in ten. It is impossible to suppress ones admiration at this stupendous work—seeing that it was completed more than 7 years ago when practice had not advanced engineering so much—and that its cost did not exceed $47000 a mile.

When entering the canal boat we found the time consumed in crossing the mountains—a distance of 36 miles was only 3½ hours including stoppages, giving an average speed while in motion of 12 miles per hour. The same distance up and down similar hills would have taken a stage a day to perform, at least.

On the eastern division of the canal there is the same beauty and variety of scenery which forms such a pleasing a feature of the western. The locks are pleasanter to pass through as they are wooden, cased with masonry—which I was informed by Mr. Schlatter was much cheaper and durable than mortared stone. He gave me information on many subjects, most particularly connected with his profession.

Thursday 25 June This morning I was roused at 4 o'clock and found it necessary to dress in a very few seconds to secure a seat in the stage, which had already been waiting some time for the canal passengers. We had arrived at Harrisburg during the night, but the steward had overslept himself.

Harrisburg is a neat-looking place, reminding me in some respects of Cincinnati. The House of Assembly of Pennsylvania is here. On leaving the city we crossed the river by a very long bridge, in two parts, in consequence of an island in the centre. The bridge for the railway which is a little below is 4972 feet in length.

I should have mentioned a situation of great beauty which we passed in the canal last evening. It is at the junction of the Juniata with the Susquehanna: the latter is dammed up and the canal boat crosses the whole breadth of it. The bridge for the road, and for the horses attached to the boat, is a most beautiful structure on 13 arches of 300 feet span, and is therefore upwards of 2600 feet in length. The sun was setting as we crossed, and the sound of a key bugle, well played by the steersman, gave a charm to that hour I shall not forget.

Harrisburg to York, by stage, 25 miles

From Harrisburg to York is 25 miles, which we accomplished by stage in 3½ hours over a roughish road. This said York is a neat little town reminding one somewhat of Prescott [*near Liverpool*].

York to Baltimore, by railway, 80 miles

At ½ past 10 I booked a place for Baltimore on the Baltimore and Susquehanna Railway, and found the cars very comfortable—one being like a parlor, the seat being all round the sides, and the other being in three divisions—the first a closed car for gentlemen, the middle an open space for smoking, and the third car for ladies, fitted up very handsomely with dressing room, mirrors, &c. &c.

These cars are about 25 to 30 feet in length and are supported on 8 wheels, four at each end, which distributes the weight very equally. The carriage is set on a moveable circle, which enables it to pass over curves of great radius [*he means short radius*] without the slightest

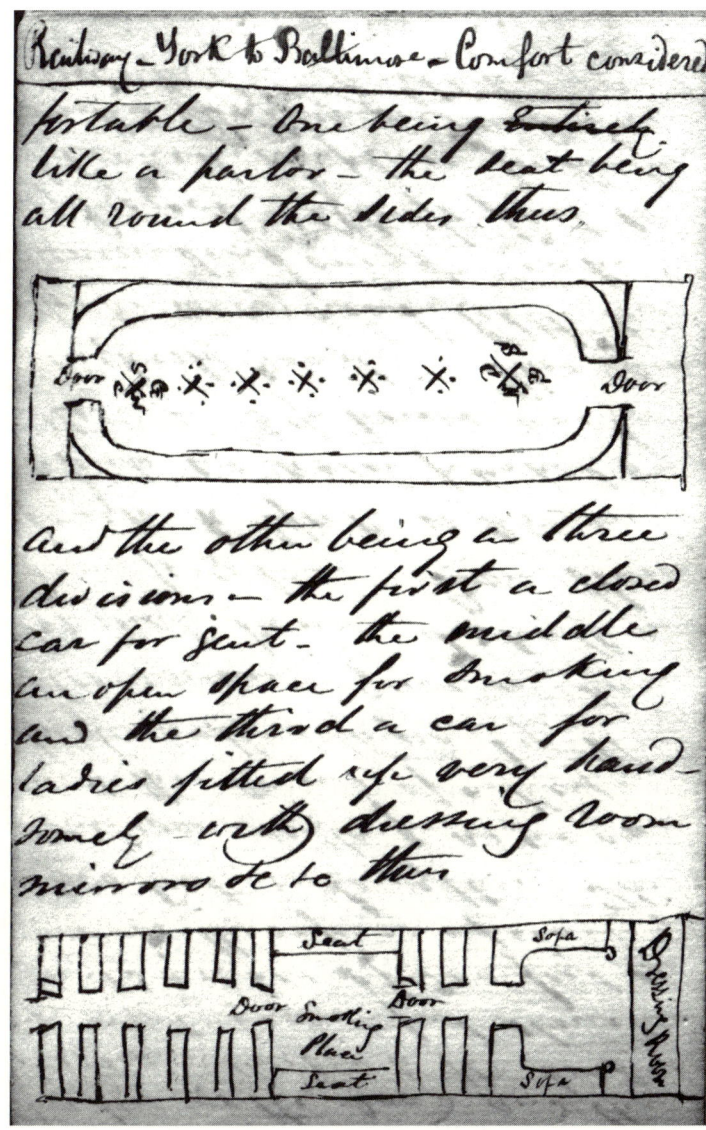

Railway - York to Baltimore - Comfort considered portable - One being entirely like a parlor - the seat being all round the sides thus.

And the other being a three divisions - the first a closed car for gent - the middle an open space for smoking and the third a car for ladies fitted up very handsomely - with dressing room mirrors &c &c thus.

strain to wheels or axles. The Baltimore and York railway has only one track at present. There is room, however, left for another and there are several turn-off places. The curves are so excessive that at no point during the whole distance was the road straight for half a mile!

An accident having detained the train from Baltimore, that we should have met at a point exactly halfway, obliged us to proceed with great caution for the next 30 miles, keeping the deafening whistle employed the whole time incessantly to avoid a collision, which without such a precaution might easily take place round some of the curves. It may be well to remark that the road is necessarily a winding one from the hilly nature of the country through which it is carried. It was four o'clock when we arrived in Baltimore, two hours beyond the usual time. In a very short time I had discovered the residence of some very kind friends Mr. and Mrs. Fowler. They were very cordial, and after a ramble I returned there to tea. We spent 3 or 4 hours and then went to the Washington Botanical Exhibition room of Mr. Frost, a very successful horticulturalist. Half the beauties in Baltimore seemed to be there on the same motive, too to see that queer flower, a night blooming [*in pencil "cereus"*].

Baltimore to Washington, by railway, 40 miles

Friday 26 June Having again partaken of the hospitality of my friends at breakfast I entered the railway carriages of the Washington line at 9 o'clock, and was most agreeably surprised at finding therein my friend Dr. Gibson, whom I found in excellent health, and in as fine spirits as when I left him in the autumn. There is nothing of interest on the road, but I passed a very pleasant time talking with the Dr. on old scenes and incidents of our passage.

At ½ past 11 the 40 miles were passed, and the Dr. and I once more found ourselves in Gadsby's Hotel in Washington. After registering my name I went to the Capitol. This magnificent building is in the Corinthian style of architecture, ornamented with some beautiful bas reliefs. The principal front looks away from the city. On ascending the long flight of steps, two noble colossal statuaries of white marble strike the eye, the one to the right, that of War, the one to the left that of Peace. Mars stern and commanding, "a truncheon in his hand," and "lovely peace with plenty crowned."

After surveying these I entered the Rotunda, where four large pictures at once enchained my attention for a considerable period. The subjects are:

The Declaration of Independence
The Surrender of Cornwallis (1781)
The Resignation of Washington (1783)
The Surrender of Burgoyne (1772)

They are all painted by one man—a soldier artist, once aide-de-camp to Washington, Col. Trumbull, and bear such internal evidence of truth that the beholder is almost constrained to forget everything else in looking at them. There are four niches yet to be filled, and four artists are now engaged on their respective pictures. The subjects are:

The Landing of Columbus

The Landing of the Pilgrims

The Baptism of Pocahontas

The Scene between Boon and the Indians

After gazing at a fine bronze statue of the iron-hearted Jefferson—whose very name seems to cause a thrill of admiration, I went into the Senate Chamber. It is a splendid room, fitted up at great cost, but with much taste. The members all have separate desks and large armchairs of the most beautiful mahogany, and the fronts of the Clerk's and Speaker's desks are of the same material. The Vice-President of the U.S. occupies the latter post.

There was nothing of interest going on, so I went across to the House of Representatives. It likewise is built in a semi-circle, spectators' galleries running all around. The difference between the two Houses was at once perceptible. The spectators retained their hats on the place for which they were designed, and the members had their feet on the desks—for which they were not designed. Mr. Biddle was defending the U.S. Bank with considerable energy. He seems a very good speaker.

[*In his companion diary RCR wrote:*]

Here, dearest Mary, at the seat of Government, I have visited both Houses of Congress—a Senate, to which each of the twenty-six Confederated States of the Union sends two members, and a House of Representatives to which every district of the country having about 10,000 inhabitants sends one member. The number of members of the Senate is therefore 52 [*the admission of Arkansas in 1836 and Michigan, the twenty-sixth State in 1837, had preserved the balance between slave and free states.*], and the number of members of the House of Representatives about 220. In the Senate they are very orderly and dignified. [. . .] not so in the House. There they do pretty much as they like. [. . .]

In the afternoon I rode out with Dr. Gibson to obtain a view of the neighborhood. It turned out misty and damp, however, which rendered it somewhat less pleasant than it might otherwise have been. Washington is certainly very beautifully situated for a city. It is surrounded by rising grounds, and the windings of the Potomac add much to the variety of the view. But as yet it is but the skeleton of a city. It has been laid out to be perhaps 20 times larger than it is at present.

Saturday 27 June I called this morning, and presented the introduction given me by Mr. Guilford of Cincinnati to the Hon. John Davis, Senator for Mass. We conversed for some time on the restrictions on the Suffrage, which remain in so much force in so many of the States, and he defended it on the grounds of the imperfections of the Naturalization Law, which was so framed that it could be continually violated with impunity. He repudiated the idea that it arose from any want of faith—but arose sincerely from a desire to prevent the improper admission of voters on to the seats for those States.

From Mr. Davis I joined Dr. Gibson and Dr. Gunnell, and we proceeded to the White House. A footman out of livery opened the door and pointed to the stairs. At the door of an antechamber there was a black servant who said the President would see us. We entered a room somewhat resembling a library with a green baize table in the corner at which the President was reading. He rose at once, and when I was introduced he shook hands and offered seats to our party. A desultory conversation ensued, chiefly respecting the Virginia Springs, but the President made scarcely a remark about England, as I partly expected he would.

After we had been there about 20 minutes, other visitors entered, and we came away. Mr. Van Buren is a man of very gentlemanly appearance and manners. In height he is about 5 feet 6 inches, rather stoutly inclined, his hair quite white and not very abundant. He observed the same courtesies when we retired as on our entrance.

We then went into the reception room and grand entertainment room below. The former is a small oval apartment, very beautifully furnished, however, and the latter a most splendid room 94 feet by 45. Eight costly mirrors of great size, resting upon cabinets, are placed round the room, and add to the brilliancy of the general effect.

In the afternoon I again visited the Capitol. The Sub-Treasury Bill was still before the House. [*This was Van Buren's Bill to sever all links between the government and the banks. It was repealed in 1841 by the next Administration.*] Last night a rabid stump orator was addressing the House—tonight a prosy old man in spectacles. Query, which is the worst? I then called upon Judge Cranch, and presented my letter from his son (the artist). Here I spent a most delightful evening, Judge and Mrs. C. being both exceedingly kind. Their daughter Miss Margaret did not come in until late. Here I met with several gentlemen, Mr. Greenleaf (Mrs. Cranch's brother), formerly consul at Amsterdam, Bishop Chase, Bishop of Illinois, a venerable old man with a purple or black velvet cap on his head, and Mr. Fanquinet, an artist—a native of the Netherlands, at present painting a room in the Capitol. Mr. Cranch kindly asked me on parting to call again.

Monday 29 June A member of the House of Representatives (Dr Duncan of Ohio, I understood), occupied the House the greater part of the day. The House at present is in committee on the famous Sub-Treasury Bill. Mr. Duncan spoke very loudly but the hall is so big that I could not hear him the few times that I went in, and it struck me, however, from his manner, to be a sort of stump speech. He wore no neck-cloth and had his vest apart

> To catch Heaven's blessed Breeze
> For burning thoughts were in his head
> And his bosom was ill at ease!
> [*Thomas Hood, "The Dream of Eugene Aram"*]

In the Senate I heard read the communications from the English envoy to the Secretary of State for the United States relative to the Maine Boundary, together with a message from the President to the Senate recommending surveys to be entered on immediately by competent persons, and congratulating on the earnest desire evidently manifest by H.B.M's. [*Her Britannic Majesty's*] government for a pacific arrangement of this long-pending dispute.[*This concerned the northern boundary of Maine with New Brunswick, and therefore the frontier between the U.S. and Canada, which had been in contention since 1783. A compromise was reached in 1842 in which Maine and New Brunswick each gave up about 5000 square miles, but it was not until 1910 that the State of Maine accepted terms from the Federal Government for their loss of territory.*] The evening I spent very pleasantly at the house of Mrs. Childs, to whom Mrs. Stetson had sent a letter by me.

Tuesday 30 June Today is an era in my life. I have seen the Declaration of Independence, and I have called on, and presented my letters of introduction, and conversed with Henry Clay and John Quincy Adams. The declaration is kept in a mahogany case in the Department of State, and some of the signatures are almost illegible from the fading of the ink. It is written on parchment, and bears marks of having been rolled up very tightly. Above it in the same case is George Washington's commission as Commander-in-Chief, dated June 1775 and signed by John Hancock. In the same apartment are the following treaties:

First with France, signed Louis 16. 1778
Second " " "　　　Buonaparte. 1803
Third " " "　　　　　Louis 18 1822
Fourth " " "　　　Louis Phillippe 1831
First with England "　George III 1784
Second " " "　　　George P.R. 1814

and also treaties with Bernadotte Alexander, Don Pedro, Frederic William of Prussia. Both Louis sign nearly the same hand, thus:

Accompanying each treaty is the Seal of State enclosed generally in a silver box 4 or 5 inches in diameter, and running through the seals are worked silken cords and tassels—some of great beauty. In a glass case in a corner of this very interesting room are two splendid trifles—one mounted most gorgeously with gold and the other with silver. They were presents from the Bey of Tunis. In a glass-fronted cabinet are more swords and sabres, the presents received by ambassadors, which the diplomatic laws of the U.S. forbid them to accept.

From this interesting chamber I went to the house of Mr. Adams, and presented the letter from Mr. Cranch. Mr. Adams must be an old man now; his head is almost entirely bald, and what hair he still has would rival snow for whiteness. His head is therefore fully developed, and I am sure would make a fine study for a phrenologist. I was too fully on my guard against occupying the time of Congressmen to remain here long, or at the residence of Mr. Clay, where I called with my letter from Mr. Greene. I was delighted with Mr. Clay's manner. It is dignified yet cordial, and his smile is so peculiarly placid—nay, I may almost say beautiful, that it is difficult to imagine that he ever could be so stern as circumstances have often proved him to be. Mr. Clay is tall and rather slight, his hair thin and grey, his eyes small and his mouth so wide as to give the spectator a constant smile.

When I first entered the Senate I was struck with Mr. Calhoun's appearance. He is very tall and slender, but particularly narrow across the shoulders, with a slight stoop. His complexion is dark and sallowish, his hair abundant, something between white and grey. I expected to find Mr. Benton of Missouri a coarse, vulgar working man, but he is far otherwise—indeed many would suppose him the best looking man in the Senate. In person he is stout and well-proportioned, and in mind he is considered the leading man on the administration side. Mr. Webster is absent, so that I lose sight of him at this time.

The evening of this day of feasting I spent at Judge Cranch's, after a pleasant stroll round the Capitol grounds with Miss Margaret and another young lady staying with her, Miss Read. I found the former pretty, very pleasing, and highly intellectual and the latter sang and played some beautiful ballads.

Wednesday 1 July A morning spent in the Senate is always interesting—though perhaps not always instructive. I entered rather early on this occasion, and found the Senate at prayers. The members all stood, and seemed to listen with attention, very different from the other House, where I was told they write and talk during the service. Prayers over, and the minutes of the previous day are read. The petitions are then received. After these, reports from standing and special committees are given in, and the Senate then takes up the Orders of the Day.

The first question which came before the House was the canal round the Falls of Ohio. Three plans were proposed to do away with the present monopoly, which in five years causes boats to pay more than half the original cost in tolls, while the concern is yielding 17 per cent profit over and above a certain sum set aside for repairs. The first plan was to buy up the remainder of the stock, as the U.S. already owns a third, or about $250,000. To this it was objected that the general government would then be owning an expensive property, under the surveillance of the government of Kentucky, which might at any time defeat the grand effect in view, viz., the passage of boats through the canal free. The objector to this first plan proposed that the money to be expended should be devoted to reducing the waters of the rapids to a narrow channel which might be made deep enough for all stage of the water. Objection was offered to this plan by Mr. Crittenden from Kentucky, who quoted witnesses to prove that if such alterations were made in the bed of the river at the Falls it would cause a great decline in the medium height of the water from Louisville upwards.

The third plan was to make an opposition canal on the Indiana shore. At this point it was proposed to adjourn the bill sine die, which was done to make way for one of more pressing importance, regarding the collection of duties on imported goods.

This arose out of a singular train of circumstance. A Yorkshireman sent out his son to New York as his agent, and sent out a large quantity of dry goods, which were all invoiced at least 30 percent below what they ought to have been. The former's failure, and the consequent necessity, which from the interwoven state of his affairs existed, of producing some of his son's letters, brought the whole affair. I heard no part of the bill read but the 7th clause, which provided that no importing merchant should be allowed to appear as a witness. Mr. Clay rose, and defended this clause, though he acknowledged it would be an infraction of the common law, which, however, he stated was practically unrecognized by the

States in aggregate, though followed by all of them in their own codes.

Mr. Clay's gestures are exceedingly graceful, more so than any speaker I ever listened to, save Brougham. His voice on this occasion was not clear and melodious as in conversation. I in vain endeavored to account for it.

[*RCR told MPH that he had today heard "the greatest man in the political field. [. . .] His name is Clay, and he occupies a very commanding situation in the Senate. Even members of entirely opposite politics look up to him and acknowledge his talents."*]

When he sat down, Mr. Calhoun arose, and spoke against the clause—he thought that the Senate, if it should pass that clause would strike a blow at the business of importing merchants, and he had no idea of making a sweeping suspicion against the whole body of them because of the rogueries of a few. He contended that "shirts and drawers if of worsted (though ready made)" did not come under the title of "ready-made clothing," which pays 50 per cent duty, but under the title of hosiery at 25 per cent. So in fact it had been decided by the Supreme Court, that though the Collector, who was the defendant in 30 cases, all of which he lost, now stated that he lost them because of the prejudices of the witnesses called, who, though not interested in the event of that particular trial, yet were generally from such a trial forming a precedent for themselves.

Mr. Calhoun further argued that the Supreme Court having decided that the articles he had alluded to ought be admitted at 25 percent, it would be unfair to alter it now, as relying upon that decision. He understood that merchants had sent large orders to England. The discussion of this question was postponed at Mr. Calhoun's request, who was called away to see a friend who had been taken dangerously ill. Mr. Calhoun's manner of speaking pleased me much, it is exceedingly firm. He raises himself to the full of his height, which is about six feet, when he approaches a climax. No man, from the depth of his voice and the sternness of his countenance, common even in repose, could be much more capable of uttering withering sentences than himself. His face is strongly marked with lines of extraordinary firmness.

At the house of Mrs. Childs last evening, I was introduced to Mr. [*Franklin*] Pierce, the Senator from New Hampshire. [*He was the son of a former governor of his State, and in 1852 was to become the youngest president of the Union.*] He promised to show me a rare room in the

Capitol in the morning. This was no less than the depository of the last uniform which George Washington wore in the Revolutionary War. It is carefully kept locked up in a glass case, secure from the pilfering hands which once did much to despoil it. [. . .]

From this interesting place I went to call on Mr. Tillinghast, Representative from Rhode Island. I presented my letter from Mr. Greene, and during an engagement Mr. T. had in the house. [. . .] I spent an hour examining Napoleon and American medals. [. . .] I then went to the Senate and again saw Mr. Pierce, who called out Mr. Calhoun and introduced me to him. There is an anteroom to the Senate for members to see their friends in, well furnished with recesses and sofas. Mr. C. remained with me here some time, conversing on sundry matters, chiefly relating to improved means of travelling in both countries by steamboats and railways. Mr. C.'s manner is much pleasanter in conversation than I should have supposed from his speaking. There are few men who have made so important a figure in American political history as Mr. Calhoun. Of him as of a much younger but equally ardent spirit, Mr. Pitt, it may well be said, "this man, like the oak, faced the tempest." He stands at the present moment utterly alone. To be sure, he leans to the Administration, but he is scarcely more feared by the Whigs than he is doubted by the party he has now espoused.

As you look down from the gallery upon the firm muscles of his face, worn, it might seem, from deep thought, the conviction is irresistible that you see a man who has made some great false step, which no power can ever bring him to confess or to retract, come what will, come what may—his pride is indomitable. "Not to confess an error" is a motto on every line of his countenance. I give these remarks on Mr. C. just as they struck me, irresistibly, whenever I looked at him. [. . .]

[*On this visit to Washington RCR had been received by the most important men in American politics, missing only Daniel Webster, who was not available. Miss Martineau had met them all socially, and remembered "Mr. Clay sitting upright on the sofa, his snuffbox ever in his hand, who would discourse for many an hour in his soft, deliberate tone, on any one of the great subjects of American policy which we might happen to start. Mr. Webster, leaning back at his ease, telling stories, cracking jokes, shaking the sofa with burst after burst of laughter, or smoothly discoursing to the perfect felicity of the logical part of one's constitution, would illuminate an evening now and then. Mr. Calhoun, the cast-iron man, who looks as if he had never been born, and never could be extinguished, would come in sometimes to keep our understandings upon a painful stretch for a short while, and then leave us to take to pieces his close, rapid, theoretical illustrated talk, and see what we could make of it. Our active-minded genial friend Judge Story found time to visit us frequently— sometimes with the aged Chief Justice Marshall. [. . .] Mr. Webster speaks seldom in the Senate, and when he does it is generally on some constitutional question, where his reasoning powers and knowledge are brought into play, and where his authority is considered so high, that he has the glorious satisfaction of knowing that he is listened as an oracle by the assemblage of the first men in the country."]*

Washington to Mount Vernon and back, by carriage, 24 miles

<u>Friday 3 July</u> I left the wharf at Washington at 9 A.M. and after a very pleasant sail of a few minutes' duration landed at Alexandria 2 or 3 miles further down on the opposite side of the Potomac. A coach was waiting on the wharf, and in a short time I was on my way to Mount Vernon. A ride of nine miles brought us to the outer gate, flanked on each side by a ruined lodge. In ten minutes the house was in view, and on presenting the letter for Mrs. Washington, given me by Judge Cranch, the doors were opened, though Mrs. W. had left home for several days. The present Mrs. Washington is the widow of George Washington's grandnephew, but is connected with the family by actual relationship. In her portrait, which hangs in the dining room, I noticed many lines of likeness to her illustrious predecessor.

In the hall of this now sacred mansion is the ponderous Key of the Bastille. From the hall we passed through a small parlor and thence into the summer room, a lofty apartment in which there is a most beautiful piece of sculpture, viz. a marble mantelpiece presented to Geo. Washington by John Vaughan's brother (of Philadelphia). This was a favorite room of Washington's during the summer, and is now as well as all other parts of the house in precisely the same state as when he died. [. . .]

The library is the next room, and completing the basement storey. It commands a most beautiful view of the winding shores of the Potomac, almost always enlivened by the sails of the greatest whiteness. Here in this very room, counselled perhaps by some of these mouldering tomes did this great being imbibe those principles of virtue whose influence has procured for him a title far more noble than all the courtly trappings of courtly favor, that of "the most incorruptible of patriots."

From the Library it was meet that I should wander away to the old tomb, the spot in which the remains lay for many years after his death. The most lovely trees bend over the tomb as if to mourn the loss of the departed being. The scene is wild enough now. No hand of care has been stretched forth to tend it, and the long grass which grows tall and rank in the dense forest shade obscures the lovely wild flowers that cannot spring so high. Yet, oh! who will not say that there is more of interest here, though the remains have gone, than in that brick-red vault, erected without taste, and left to fare as it may with the trodden clay and sand right up to the iron bars. I grieved deeply at what I saw here, and it required that gaze to be fixed within to divest oneself of a feeling almost of anger. [*Miss Nartineau wrote in similar vein five years earlier. She thought the tomb should either be restored or destroyed.*]

There, behind that gate, are the remains of one, a single day of whose life was worth the whole existence of Alexander or Napoleon, whose lightest action would outweigh as the small dust of the balance, the noblest of their still-famed achievements. Oh! illustrious being! how bright thy glorious example. While time shall last, as century after century of the world's history shall unfold new prospects, and tell of the continued progress of our species, will that example still be exhibited, that character still shown, as a bright and enduring model—the wonder and admiration of the world!

My most delightful recollections in the East I think I shall always find, will be connected with the family of Judge Cranch at Washington. I called this evening to take my leave. They have been exceedingly kind to me during my stay. When I came away the old gentlemen came out with me and blessed me fervently and bade me Godspeed through life. I shall never forget the kindness of his manner on this occasion as long as I live.

Saturday 4 July Early morning of this glorious anniversary was ushered in by the ringing of bells and the firing of many guns. I grieve to find the day is to be desecrated by political demonstrations.

I walked up in the morning to the city of Georgetown—a sort of continuation of Washington, but much neater and more compact. From the heights of Georgetown a most beautiful view of the coast of the opposite side of the river, as well as the river itself is obtained.

10
Back to Cincinnati

[From this point on RCR abandoned the strict diary format, and I have interpolated dates in brackets, to give some indication of the passage of time.]

[4 July] Before four in the afternoon I had called upon my friends and was on my way to Baltimore, on the most expensive railway I ever travelled on. The road is very level, there being two or three inclines not more than 20 or 30 feet to the mile. At Baltimore I made my home the hospitable residence of Mrs. Fowler. With this pleasant family I spent Saturday evening, Sunday and Monday. During my residence in the city I visited the Cathedral. Here I fell into conversation with one of the officers of the church. From him I learnt what was afterwards confirmed, that the Catholics in this city are 30 percent of the whole population nearly, being 30,000 out of 100,000. They have eight churches besides the cathedral, a large seminary, a nunnery and some school houses, which latter are open to children of all denominations. It is not in this respect alone that the Roman Catholics set an example to other professing Christians.

The most imposing monument is that to George Washington. It is a plain column surmounted by a colossal statue and from its summit (some 150 feet) a most extensive view is obtained of the city and surrounding country on all sides. The upper part of Baltimore is very regularly built, and marble of dazzling whiteness, taken from quarries in the neighborhood, is used for steps, and occasionally for fronts, although the general material is a very expensive kind of brick which costs $20 per thousand. It is certainly well made, and looks more like red stone than brick.

Next to New Orleans, from the statements I heard, Baltimore must be one of the most gambling cities in the Union. I was told that all the public functionaries gambled more or less. I accompanied John Fowler out into the country on Sunday afternoon, and on our way out we passed taverns where he showed me a round building used for a

140

cock pit, and gambling tables, in which latter purpose it was then being employed.

Baltimore to Winchester, by railway, 112 miles

With a desire to linger still longer if possible, I took leave of my friends in Baltimore on Tuesday 7 July and was soon in one of the carriages of the Baltimore and Ohio railway. This road is intended to be carried to the Ohio River, and is one of the most beautiful I ever travelled upon. Instead of avoiding, as most roads of this kind do, the most beautiful parts of the country, it seems to have sought them out. For more than 50 miles it winds round the banks of small streams whose steep sides are clothed with wood.

At four o'clock in the afternoon we came in sight of Harper's Ferry. Now, wherever I had been I had heard the beauty of this place extolled. It is called "the beautiful place of Virginia." I was not prepared therefore to be disappointed, but I was so in many respects. A dirty little town is the most conspicuous object in the scene, and that most unromantic, anti-poetic of all sights, an iron railroad, occupies no small share of the view. I think I can say I have seen more than one place in Virginia in the States, that I think much more beautiful than the far-famed Harper's Ferry.

The same evening I went on to Winchester, 112 miles from Baltimore, drawn by one of Berry's engines. The hotel was unusually crowded, and as there is no solitude for a stranger so great as a crowded hotel, I retired early and was roused at ½ past 3, to take the stage for Staunton, the geographical centre of the State of Virginia [*until 1863 when West Virginia was created as a separate state.*]

Winchester to Staunton, by stage, 92 miles

It was too dark to see my only fellow-passenger but he greeted me pleasantly. After some time we took up an old woman, feeble and very full of sorrow. She told us some of her afflictions. She knew deeply how "sharper than a serpent's tooth it is to have a thankless child" [*Shakespeare*, King Lear]. My other fellow traveller turned out a gentlemanly, well-informed young man and I was amazed to find that his residence was one of the wildest parts of the State of Mississippi. [. . .] He gave me a very interesting account of the convocation of about 10,000 Indians and 1000 or so more of whites, the former selling their lands, and the latter wishing to purchase. The Indians had each had their mile square allotted to them by government, and as they sold it at a good price to the new settlers, they were able to appear in the most gorgeous dresses imaginable. The whites, out of compliment to them, all dressed in blanket coats, some bright purple, others a brilliant blue, other fiery red. There could hardly be conceived a more singular assemblage than this presented, from the immense variety of dress and colors worn by those composing it. It took place in 1835, I believe, and was the last, in all probability the very last, fine collection of red men in the eastern part of the continent of N. America.

All day our road lay through the finest mountain scenery in the distance I have ever seen, up the centre of the great valley of Virginia, bounded on either side by ranges of lofty hills their tops occasionally hidden by vast rolling masses of clouds. [*The Blue Ridge Mountains to the left, and the Appalachians to the right. Interstate 81 now follows this line.*] Neglect is visible to even the unobservant eye all along this beautiful valley, and so lovely does the land look, that to the uninitiated mind this would be a mystery, but alas, "the trail of the serpent is over all." Slavery and its effects (those effects themselves partly unexplained) are written on every village we pass through. The wooden houses are unpainted and rickety, and utterly destitute of neat and cleanly appearance. No little garden ornaments to the front, which comes at once upon the street by ill-constructed wooden stairs. To this we observed, few, very few, exceptions. How different to the little thriving places in Ohio!

We halted for the night [*8 July*] at a dirty little inn in Harrisonburgh [*about 75 miles from Winchester*]. No mirror, no soap, no towel, and no water. "Here's 6¼ cents" (¹⁄₁₆ of a dollar) addressed to a little Negro girl, brought me the latter two. It is not the custom in Virginia to give soap at all, and as she said there was only one mirror in the house, and that was "in the top of master's shaving box," I did without the first.

At four in the morning [*9 July*] we resumed our journey. The same glorious scenery as that of yesterday appears in the distance on each side of our path. We have had a drawback in the nature of the road. It is a perfectly new one all the way to Staunton, and is made of Macadamized stones. It is easy to conceive what a constant and deafening din was caused by the stage driving over a road in such a condition as this.

We arrived at Staunton about mid-day and at once discovered that this pretty little town was in commotion from some cause or other.

Groups of well-dressed people were marching up and down the streets, bands were playing lively airs, banners streaming aloft. The windows were crowded with gay onlookers—in short everything bore the appearance of a day of general rejoicing. Our landlord soon solved the mystery by informing us that it was the day appointed for laying the foundation stone of a new asylum for the deaf, dumb and blind, and that an oration was to be pronounced by the "celebrated Mr. McDonnell," to commence almost immediately. I did not happen to have heard of the celebrated Mr. McDonnell, but went at once with my fellow passenger (Mr. Carruthers) and listened with some pleasure to a studied and tolerably well delivered address of some hour and a half long. In the middle of this address, how, I know not, he managed to bring in the opium trade, and took occasion to censure in no very measured terms, the conduct of the East India Company.

A concert of music was announced for the evening. We attended, and were somewhat pleased. The blind, however, hardly acquitted themselves as I expected, though one boy played upon the violin with much ease—and, as I understood, execution. He certainly made, to my ear and discernment, most eloquent music.

At ½ past six in the morning on the 10th July a small party consisting of myself and two Carruthers—one my fellow passenger, and the other a relation he had quite accidentally met, was on its way to Wayer's cave. Our road lay, for the chief part of the 17 miles, through the most beautiful woods, which long before our arrival, and still more on our return, we were to have as a shelter from the heat of the sun.

On arriving at the cave we found two young men and their sister just about to enter. We joined them, of course. The young men were both wags, and served to enliven our party even more than it had been before.

My journey through this cave was one of the most singular expeditions I have ever had. It reminded me, though indeed in an extremely remote and minor way, of my visit to Termination Rock. Each of our party was furnished with a candle placed in a socket and shaded from the eyes by a semi-circular reflector. Our woollen-coated friends having become turncoats, and everyone having tucked their trousers into their boots, we set out in regular march with the guide of course at the head. In this cave there are an immense number of stalactites and stalagmites, indeed the whole interior is composed of them. They have assumed every imaginary form, and names descriptive or as seen to be descriptive of these formations have been given to them. Thus we have Solomon's temple, the Tower of Babel, the Mammoth Oyster, Mahomet's Coffin, Jacob's sideboard, Paganini's Statue, Frozen Niagara, the Spread Eagle, and Jacob's bake oven.

There are several large chambers in the cave, of which the Washington Hall so called from a huge stalactite statue of the "Pater Patriae" is perhaps the largest. The Ballroom however is very extensive, and on one side, from the thinness of the stalactite drapery (too natural to be considered stone) there is a spot where the loudest tones of the most melodious drum can be provided by the application of a hand or foot. A little way from the drum is a tambourine, and above these a set of panpipes. Once every year there is a ball in this immense room on which occasion the whole cave is lit up with one or two thousand candles. It is easy to conceive that the sight would be most magnificent.

Our road back to Staunton lay again through the woods, and was exceedingly pleasant.

Staunton to Natural Bridge, by stage, 50 miles

At four o'clock on the following morning our stage left Staunton, and when daylight fully revealed my fellow passengers I found them to consist of a phrenological lecturer, Dr. Wooster from New Orleans, a young lawyer who had just finished his studies at the University of Virginia, Mr. Minor, and some others. From the time of leaving Staunton until we parted with him, the Dr. was forever poking his phrenology at us, and lecturing apparently upon its beauty and truth, but really upon the great advantage it would be for us to pay him $2 for an examination. My other fellow passenger Mr. Minor, I found to be a pleasant and well-informed young man.

At Lexington [*30 miles on*] where we stopped to dine, and where the Virginian Military Institution is erected, I parted with my acquaintance of the last four days. [. . .]

We halted within two miles of the Natural Bridge, on the lovely evening of the 11th July, and on the following morning the stage drove to this wonder of the world. It was Sunday, but I little expected to have a sermon preached to me through the medium of the eye. My expectations had been raised, ever since, many years back, I found a picture of the bridge in turning over some old cyclopedia, and since then the descriptions of more recent travellers had left their glowing accounts upon my mind. I was therefore prepared for disappointment, and took my first view of this extraordinary bridge with some such feelings. But at my first view of what I shall call its sister wonder Niagara, I had no such feelings now, as I took my first view from the rocks above. Beneath was a yawning canyon, the very bottom of which was hidden from the overhanging nature of the rocks upon which I lay.

After viewing the bridge from above, we went below, and only then realized the full magnitude of this stupendous piece of Nature's architecture. No adequate conception can be formed of this vast gorge. To the eye of the beholder even, it seems perfectly miraculous that the force of rushing waters could have caused the scene before him. Yet such has obviously been the case. The lofty arch and the vast rocks which form the sides of the chasm are limestone; and loose earth that must once have existed there has evidently been carried away by some mighty torrent. In the very centre of the arch, by one of the extraordinary chances of Nature which we occasionally see, is an expanded eagle apparently carved out of the limestone—so exactly that I still have doubts whether some daring fellow had not contrived, some time or other, to reach the place with a mallet and chisel!

Natural Bridge to Fincastle, by stage, 26 miles

We spent all morning in roaming about under the bridge, and then moved on a few miles further for our resting place for the day, the little town of Buchanan. Buchanan and Pattonsburg are two little towns, one on each side of St. James's River [*a tributary of the Shenandoah*]. I patronized the former, and about six in the evening commenced the ascent of a mountain called Purgatory from its long and rocky sides, in company with my fellow passenger the young Virginian. An hour and three quarters of the most laborious climbing brought us to the summit, whence the view far more than repaid us for our labor. Right beneath us, to the east, in a narrow lovely valley, lay the two towns we had left, while beyond range after range of mountains bounded the prospect, the dark and rugged peaks of Otter towering above all, 4800 feet [*actually 3875*] in height. To the west we had a valley of almost illimitable extent bounded by the Blue Ridge, so named doubtlessly from the precise appearance, so visible on this occasion from the effects of the departed sun. Utterly forgetful of everything but the imposing prospect before us we sat gazing at the distant peaks of the great valley we had left the day before, in which Point Lookout stood highest. From this spot, it is said, the red men looked down the valley with their eagle eyes for the fires of the pale races "long time ago." We watched this peak until it almost faded into the hue of the mists beneath, and only then thought of our descent.

We had delayed so long, and the sides of the mountain so rugged that I more than once thought we should have to make our bed upon the mountain. We had at least the prospect of food, for thousands and thousands of huckleberries grew around at our service. Nothing daunted, however, at our occasional failures in finding the road, we pressed on, and soon after nine arrived safely at our inn in good spirits, though I was rather damp from having made a somerset [*sic*] into a mountain brook when leaning over to obtain a draught of water!

We were duly aroused at four in the morning [*13 July*], rather stiff, and entered the coach, which only waited for our proper persons to make up the full number of nine inside. One of these was a colored woman. Not the slightest objection was made in my hearing, though I have seen a colored person turned outside in a free state, to do what he could not, ride in the face of an atmosphere not exceeding 8°.

We reached Fincastle at breakfast, and were obliged to remain there until the following morning, where at two o'clock my companion of the last three days entered the Lynchburg stage, and I the one for the White Sulphur Springs [*RCR was now heading west, over the Appalachian Mountains on a road that later became Route 113*], and we whirled away on our separate routes.

Fincastle to White Sulphur Springs, by stage, 50 miles

We reached the head of the first mountain in time to see the sun rise over the valley beneath. I have seen sunrise itself more beautiful, but never before from so glorious a situation. It surpassed all previous experience, and did I not fear that I might have to recall the word, I should say this surely must exceed in beauty and grandeur anything I shall ever see.

All morning we were ascending a hill called Seven Mile Mountain. It is that number of miles to its summit, and five down on the other side. Down these roads the horses run at an easy speed, and the coach, instead of being left to the chance of the wheelers [*the pair between the shafts*] holding it back, is provided with a brake (worked by the driver's foot) which presses at pleasure on both hind wheels; and is quite effectual in all cases, except that of horses running off, an event generally unlikely to occur, as the coaches have seldom less than nine passengers with at least one trunk to each, and often more. The skill of the drivers in descending the exceedingly steep declivities upon this route I admired very much. Sometimes the corners to be turned are often at very acute angles to the road upon which the coach is running. To avoid being whirled into the pine forest "a thousand feet in depth below," it is therefore necessary to come to a dead stand before coming to the turn, an object, as everyone knows, not very easily attained with a heavy lumbering stage.

About three in the afternoon, after a day spent I might say amongst the mountains, we halted to dine at the Sweet Springs, situated in a valley of great beauty. These springs are of a powerfully tonic nature, and when tired of the various sulphur springs, visitors come here to recruit so that the crowd does not commence till the close of the season at the other springs. Would that language were inexhaustible! At least that terms for expressing admiration for the sublime were more numerous. I would then enlarge upon the lovely mountain road that leads from this place.

Just as the sun was setting we arrived at the White Sulphur Springs, shut out from the world by lofty hills, with the pretty white cottages peering through the woods, and forming altogether one of the prettiest views I ever saw.

On the morning [15 July] following our arrival I found out the family of Judge Brooke, and presented my letter from Charles. My welcome from Mrs. B. perfectly astounded me. Charles had evidently left a good impression behind him, but I fear I can only act the part of showing him to more advantage. [. . .]

Judge B. is a very pleasant man. He is now 76, but he is more erect than I am, and more youthful in his gait than many men at 50. Having been an officer in the Revolutionary War he can discourse upon those glorious times of old with the accuracy and fervor which an eye witness only can possess. I listened with great delight to his account of La Fayette, under whom he served, and he made my bosom burn again with instances of that disinterested being's generosity.

[*Judge Brooke seems to have been the proprietor of this resort hotel, at which the guests were accommodated in cabins, and at meal times were called to assemble in a large dining room by the ringing of a bell. At that time there were 350 guests there, but in some seasons there could be as many as 700. The poor exchange rate between States was apparently keeping Southerners away. A man from Mississippi said he had paid 60 percent for his Virginian funds. RCR had intended to continue his journey immediately, but changed his mind and stayed a week at White Sulphur Springs, relaxing, walking, making new friends.*]

White Sulphur Springs to Guyandot, by stage, 159 miles

Pursuing my journey westward [*22 July*], I found as I expected that there was "nobody with me at sea—but myself." It was quite dark, and my stock of songs to the time of every rut, and the astonishment of the driver outside, was nearly exhausted when I arrived at the top of the Great Sual [*?*] mountain. The piercing wind howled round the closed-up coach when we stopped, and before I reached the door of the wooden tenement, called tavern, by a winding path, I was shivering with cold not unlike December. The house was built in good old Virginia style, with wide chimney nooks, and never did I pile log on blazing log with such zest and satisfaction as on this bitter evening in July. I made the very rafters ring as well I might, 3000 feet above the valley below. I sat and slept, then supped and slept again. Then I stumbled up to my room, and piled blanket upon blanket on the bed above as I had done log upon log in the fire below.

In due time came sleep, and then nightmare, heavy blankets or heavy supper, which I know not, and then sound sleep again. The grim landlord entered with a lantern at two o'clock and told me, as they always do, by the way, in such cases, that the coach was waiting for me.

About 10 o'clock we arrived at the Hawk's Nest, a fitting after-piece for the Natural Bridge. As everyone knows, it is rocky platform surrounding an almost perpendicular precipice of 1300 feet in height at the very foot of which, apparently, in a narrow valley, the river dashed foamingly along. The view is truly magnificent, and it would take long to satisfy the eye of the beholder with its rugged grandeur. I did, as everyone does, try to throw a stone into the water, and failed, as everyone does, without David's sling, from the really great distance of the water!

I answered the driver's signal horn with reluctance, and walked the few dozen yards full of wonder and admiration, but alas! the stage was empty, and the road, a limestone one. Now cram a man as full of sentiment as one of Bulwer's novels, and put him alone in a stage, and he will lose every atom, as grunt after grunt, groan after groan will do their work, until he is as bare as a pork curer. 'Twas so with me. In minutes I had forgotten the Hawk's Nest, and was thinking of the "nice" eggs and milk I had for breakfast.

The whole scenery of the western part of Virginia is exceedingly beautiful. [. . .] and through such scenery our course lay all day, as indeed through many days. In the evening it lay along the banks of the navigable Kanawha, celebrated for its salt works. [. . .] But alas the road was still rough, and the stage still empty. [. . .] and when the coach stopped, it stopped me in the middle of "Rory O'More" [snore!]. Nine o'clock to bed, and 2 or 4 o'clock to rise, is the stage custom in Virginia, and I became used to it soon.

We did not leave Charleston, however, until 6 o'clock the following morning, as no one woke up the driver so he could not rouse the hotel, and the hotel could not rouse me. Just so, if there had not been a maiden all forlorn, to milk the cow with the crumpled horn, that delightful series of incidents told in the tale of the House that Jack built, never could have transpired. The first change of horses was at our breakfasting place, and if there was any other place, I would say avoid "Major" Clarkson's, but as it is Hobson's choice [take it or leave it] you must be content with sour bread, pie-crust, rye coffee, no eggs, and all other wants and superfluities to match.

At four o'clock on Friday 24 July I arrived at Guyandot on the Ohio River, and at six had the satisfaction of seeing a wee boat coming down. In ten minutes I was on my way to Cincinnati in a little stern-wheel cockle-shell called the "Odessa" [160 miles].

Three weeks more were spent with an increasing regard for the people, and liking for the city of Cincinnati and I am quite sure, if I could look just so far into the future as to tell me I should not return, it would be with a very melancholy feeling that I should say adieu to more than one. During my stay here on this occasion I had every opportunity of seeing the neighborhood of the city, through the kindness of Mr. Stetson, whose horse were always at my disposal. [In Recollections he recalls the many excursions he made under the guidance of Mr. Charles Stetson ("a light-hearted laughing good souled man") and his ever kind wife, and the hours spent in their hospitable house—"a sort of rendezvous for all the intellectual society of the City".]

Miss Martineau has mentioned the scenery of the little Miami in one of her books, and has certainly given no exaggerated account of its beauty. I cannot say merely that it is equal to the Vale of Clwyd [North Wales]—that would be doubtful praise—it far surpasses it, and not the least superiority it possesses is in the distant view of the meandering Ohio. Mr. J.H. Perkins and myself ascended the hill to obtain this view. The hill is called Jusculum and is covered with vineyards. The grapes though not ripe hung around in profusion. [. . .]

There is no end to the glorious views to be obtained of and about Cincinnati. My opinion was continually changing as to which was the most beautiful, but I finally awarded the palm to the prospect from the farm of our cousin John V.'s, distant some three miles on a hill commanding the whole valley.

Cincinnati to Oxford and back, by carriage, 74 miles

Monday 10 August This morning a party consisting of Mr. Perkins, Mr. Stetson and myself was arranged to go over to Oxford to be present at some part of the Commencement, as it is called, of the Miami University. We had a pleasant jaunt in Mr. Stetson's wagon, remaining for the night in the pretty little town of Hamilton, and completing the distance, 35 miles, on the following morning. [. . .]

Connected with the University is one of the grossest and unpardonable instances of mismanagement I have ever met with. When the State of Ohio was surveyed, two townships of land were granted [*a survey township being a plot six miles square*] for two universities, one in the eastern and the other in the western part of the State. In 1820 Miami University was founded, and the board of managers immediately leased out the whole township under perpetual lease. Now there are two kinds of perpetual lease, one subject to revaluation every stated number of years, and the other not. This sapient board of trustees, not being able to see beyond their mere nose tips, leased away on the latter principle the whole of this beautiful land for $5000 a year, which in spite of the hardness of the times is now worth $50,000. The same kind of blunder has been committed in Ohio with regard to the school lands. The general government provided for the education of the masses by granting land, but almost every section has been managed as the Miami township was. Had this not been the case there would not be a tax of ¼ percent existing in Cincinnati.

The road from Oxford eastward is surrounded by rich lands for a mile or two, when comes the interminable forest. We had a most delightful trip, taking our leisure in reaching our good city of Cincinnati on Wednesday afternoon, 12 August.

Were I to take up my pen at the head of this page I know not where or when I should stop in speaking of friends in this city and the many kind words received this morning of Monday 17 August. I will not attempt the task, pleasing as it might appear. Most sincerely do I hope to be able to show substantially the gratitude I feel for the many kindnesses showered upon me. I leave the place with regret—and it is with no vanity that I write it—nor yet relying on the parting re-marks of almost every friend—but I know that there are very few who will not remember one, who will regard a place in their memories as no small treasure.

[*Before leaving RCR wrote in his other book, "You will wonder when you hear of my staying so long in Cincinnati—whether I have any good reason, or rather, dearest Mary, you will wonder what that reason is, for your love for me will tell you that I would not return to Cincinnati, much less remain there, prolonging my absence from thee, without a very excellent reason for doing so. And a good one I have too, which I will explain to you when you ask for it, if not before."*

On the face of it, Rawlins' third visit to Cincinnati was an unnecessary detour in his itinerary, but it was evidently premeditated. It was not until his later Recollections *that he revealed that he was so impressed with Cincinnati that he would like to settle there if Mary would be willing. This final three-week visit was an opportunity to talk things over with John Vaughan and family.*]

11

To Canada

<u>Cincinnati to Sandusky, by stage and railway, 214 miles</u>

> 'Twere long to hear, and vain to tell
> The various chances that befell
> Myself and baggage upon the way
> From Cincinnati to Sandusky!!
> [*Possibly adapted from William Combe's "The Death Blow"*]

Suffice it therefore to say that the said Sandusky [*on the shores of Lake Erie*] was reached after passing some fine prairies of considerable extent, and travelling the last 16 miles on the only railway in Ohio.

Sandusky to Niagara, by steamer and rly, 263 miles

In Sandusky Bay I found the splendid steamer "Erie" on which at five o'clock I found myself dashing along over the clear waters of the Lake at some 12 knots. Were I a poet, philosopher or sage with time on hand I would write folios upon steamboats, describe their advantages, touch lightly on their dangers, and wind up my panegyric, which for language should not be surpassed, and yet for <u>truth</u> too shall not be surpassed, when compared with stages, railways, canals or even private conveyances.

This particular steamboat has the reputation of being one of the finest on the lakes. She carries about 500 tons of goods. One or two of the high pressure boats carry some 800. This trade on the lakes is increasing of course every year. More than 50 large class steamers arrive at and depart from Buffalo, besides an immense number of schooners, many brigs, and one ship, the only one, I believe, on these waters at present.

We reached the thriving city of Buffalo on <u>Wednesday morning 19 August</u> at six o'clock, and here took place a scene I never saw equal-

152

led before. No porters from hotels, no agents of conveyances, by a very excellent regulation, are allowed to come on board. A stage and two canal boats were all starting in about an hour, and there was an agent with a hoarse throat from each. There were also posters from three principal hotels. The moment the boat came within pistol shot they began, and soon drowned the sense, if not the words. Now and then you could catch half a sentence of each, producing a sort of ludicrous cross-hearing. "Fare by canal $4, breakfast on board now," said one man, but before he had finished another lean unwashed artificer cut off his tale with "baggage for the Mansion House." All these things however were adjusted at last, as other and weightier things have been and shall be. Those who wished to go by canal now went by canal, but whether any did "breakfast on"—"baggage for the Mansion House"—I do not know. I for one did not. Nay, verily, on something more digestible, not to say better tasted, tea and toast, which, being duly swallowed, the railway train was reached, and before 12 o'clock I was in the Post Office at Niagara, watching eagerly the distribution of the letters the train brought, including New York dispatches. Never did I receive "Nothing for Rollings" from any postmaster so sourly. I felt my temper curdling up my blood. The antidote was at hand.

In ten minutes I had tossed my temper into the rapids, and was lying on the rocks over the Great Fall. It was almost impossible, from the circumstances, that my present visit would offer me the intense delight which I felt in November. I am only too happy to think that not one impression has been effaced. [. . .]

Niagara to Oswego, by railway and steamer, 150 miles

From the Falls you are conveyed to Lewiston by railway. An hour and a half was to elapse before the good steamer "St Lawrence" was to sail down Lake Ontario, and I used it to ascend to Brock's Monument on the opposite side of the shore. [. . .] At six our boat unmoored and we were soon on the bosom of Ontario. From the upper deck I witnessed the gathering of a storm just after sunset. Strange and unnatural, with a deeper red than I ever saw before the sun went down. Wind and rain then freshened up, and before 11 o'clock, with everything as snug as it could be in a long, narrow boat, we scudded along before it, and when we landed at 6, it was as peaceful a Sunday morning [23 August] as one could well wish, and the lake showed but small sign of its agitation of the night before.

Oswego to Kingston, steamer, 60 miles

It was necessary for me to cross the lake to Kingston to take the boat for the St. Lawrence, so at eight I turned my back upon the little village port of Oswego, and was once more in Her Majesty's dominions, and better than that in a more comfortable room than I had witnessed for a very long period. Just as I had my home-writing materials in order, the soldiery came out of church, and forming into companies, marched to their barracks preceded by a full band of music. [. . .]

In the neighborhood of Kingston is a very extensive fort and arsenal called Fort Henry, and more than half of the guests at the little inn at which I sojourned were officers attached to the regiments stationed there. It sounded very "strange to mine ear" to hear a Tory and a Reformer discussing English politics at dinner, after a dead silence of eleven months on those points, and a substitution of Sub-Treasury, Hard Cider, Log Cabins, Tip and Tyler, and all the other names which the parties in the United States are known.

On Monday morning I witnessed the turning out of the artillery, with guns, ammunition &c. Contrary to my expectations, however, they only made a parade through the town and returned to the barracks at Fort Henry.

Kingston to Dickinson's Landing, steamer, 110 miles

At one o'clock I was on my way down the Lake and all afternoon was passing the "Thousand Islands." This scenery is indeed strange and fascinating. Occasionally it would seem that the steamboat's onward course is suspended, but in a moment just room enough for her width is discovered between two islands. This occurred more than once, affording the most possible variety to this charming river. It was almost dark when we arrived at Prescott, but the windmill one mile below the village, the scene of the battle between the patriots and Royalists, was quite visible.

[*The young British colony was in a state of unrest. In 1791 it had been divided into two provinces separated by the Niagara river: the French-speaking Lower Canada and the English-speaking Upper Canada populated by British loyalists. After the war of 1812 between Britain and the United States, many English-speaking settlers moved into Lower Canada, and in 1837 a few French Canadians led by Louis Papineau took up arms hoping to establish a French republic on the St. Lawrence. He was captured and charged with treason but escaped to the States. In the same year William Lyon Mackenzie led a similar abortive revolt in Upper Canada, and in 1838 the Earl of Durham was sent as governor-general of both Canadas to advise on a new constitution. The Act of Union was passed while Rawlins was there.]*

About nine o'clock I observed great bustling on deck—the sailors were covering the cabin skylights with the boat's flags, the wheel was unshipped, and the ordinary tiller was substituted, and all preparation, I found, was making to shoot the rapids of Galoop. In five minutes we were in the middle of them, foaming and dashing around. Every now and then, some sudden sweep of the water made the boat shake again to her very centre. For more than 20 minutes we seemed to fly past a dark and sombre forest, just barely visible on the banks in the evening gloom. At ten o'clock we had safely passed the rapids and were in smooth waters again. Since the Canadas have been settled, boats built for the purpose have descended not only these rapids, but the far more dangerous ones of Loungue Sault and St. Louis, at the rate of 27 miles per hour, but five years ago the idea of steamboats shooting the Galoop would have been scouted as worse than madness.

Dickinson's Landing to Cornwall, by stage, 12 miles

I did not sleep much, and at two o'clock on a cold bright starlit morning, we were roused to disembark and see our luggage safely packed on the stages, which were waiting to convey us 12 miles round the great rapids of Longue Sault. It was quite dark, save a few misty lanterns, and those who had much luggage were obliged to use all diligence. One of the passengers, the Honorable Mr. Justice Somebody, of 5 Lansdown Terrace, Cheltenham, England, or rather he was going on a visit to some relation there in the "Arcadia" from Halifax. Besides his wife and daughter, a nurse and a baby and 23 trunks, van-boxes, workboxes &c. &c., besides coats, cloaks, umbrellas, sticks &c. &c. The boxes were numbered, one upwards, and so that no mistake might be made as to the dignity of the owner, every package large and small had a comprehensive sized card upon it with "the Honorable Mr. Justice Somebody, Lansdowne Terrace" and all the rest of it at full length.

Three stages and wagons were sufficient to convey us the 12 miles, but the ride was over a bad road in a small stage, and I sat opposite an officer whose sword would strike my leg at every jolt. He was anxious to take it off his belt, but he was fat, and had no room, and I was obliged to endure it, as well as many worse things. At five we reached Cornwall where a splendid steamboat, the "Highlander" was waiting for us.

Cornwall to Montreal, steamer and stage, 90 miles

I turned in again, and had the necessary remainder of my sleep quantum. At nine o'clock we again took stage to the head of the Coteau du Lac rapids, and had a pleasant ride on the top with a Rev. Mr. Lindsay, an Oxford Tract Divine, of Upper Canada. Our Canadian driver wore long jackboots reaching to his hips, but poor protection, he told me, in some of his winter drives.

We again took steamboat at the mouth of the Ottawa, up which the Hudson Bay Company's boats proceed every year to their trapping. We again returned to the stage mode of conveyance at the head of the rapids called the Cascades of St. Louis, and after nine miles travelling we approached Montreal. Two miles from the city we passed the great stores and offices of the Hudson's Bay company, and presently afterwards the residence of the famous Papineau.

The approach to the city is exceedingly beautiful. The road, before entering the city, crosses the brow of a hill from which there is a most extensive prospect of Montreal, the river St. Lawrence, and its beautiful islands, and the mountains in the distance. There are several spires visible, but exceeding all other erections in height and extent is the great Catholic Cathedral, said to be capable of holding 10,000 persons.

Montreal to Quebec, steamer, 170 miles

In half an hour after arriving in Montreal I was again on the St. Lawrence in a second rate sort of steamer, called the "Canadian Eagle."

Wednesday 26 August The river from Montreal to Quebec seems to be one continuous village. It is a noble stream, the St. Lawrence, some two miles or so in width, and occasionally widening into a lake of many miles. At 12 o'clock I caught the first glimpse of the distant Cape Diamond, and in half an hour we were moored beneath its lofty summit. The Spanish caliche is the vehicle in universal use by the poorest and richest in Lower Canada, and the streets of Quebec swarm with them. I jumped with my trunk into one of these, and shortly found myself in a very pleasant inn within the walls. Lunch was over when I entered the dining room, but some half dozen officers were sitting round the table. Their conversation was made up of two products, oaths and nonsense, and I could not help thinking if an American reader of [Captain] Marryat's Diary had been sitting in my place he would have been more astonished than I was.

My first expedition was over to the Falls of Montmorency. The road lies through one continuous village. There were many crosses, made of rough wood and painted, by the road, and more than one little chapel and pointed-roofed church on the way. [. . .] The Falls are well worthy of a visit. The whole height is more than 200 feet, and the deep narrow chasm into which the snow-white water falls seems a vast depth beneath your feet. [. . .]

Below the Falls is perhaps the largest sawing mill in the world. There are 24 water wheels of small size in constant operation, but there is water enough in the river to turn a thousand such. The wealthy proprietor Mr. Paterson has purchased the land on both sides of the river, and thus secured the whole of this very valuable rainwater power. The appearance of the Fall in winter, when the spray freezes and forms a huge cone ⅔ of the height of the fall itself, must be singularly pleasing and novel.

The road from Montmorency to Quebec abounds in the most beautiful views of the city and river—at one point, about four miles from the city, Quebec looks like a silver mountain, as it is built on the side of a hill and every spire and almost every roof within its precincts are covered with metal plates. This is one of the most singular appearances I ever saw.

The dining hour in Quebec is six o'clock. How delightful, I felt, to be once more at an English dinner table, to have a pause now and then, time to lay down my knife and fork, and take a piece of bread, and then how pleasing to sit between two, and opposite three, who hand you everything within their reach. So different from the perfect selfishness to which I seldom, if ever, met with an exception, at a public table in the States.

There are some places that we see, and have an instinctive sort of opinion concerning, that there can be no such other in the world, and just such a view is that from the North Platform of the Battery at Quebec. Its beauty, and the magnificence of the range over which the eye passes, are indeed beyond compare. Right beneath your feet are the tall ships amongst which may be immediately detected by her trim rigging and square yards, the well-ordered ship of war.

Far to the northwest is the broad bosom of the St. Lawrence, divided some way down by the fertile island of Orleans, until it is lost in the distance among the dark mountains of Tourment. To the north is the river St. Charles, and beyond it a plain, covered with villages extending for miles and miles before the almost unlimited gaze—it too bounded in the distance by long ranges of lofty hills. Behind you, crowning the summit of Cape Diamond is the frowning bastion of the Citadel, with the iron mouth of a 48-pounder just visible above the edge.

The citizens of Quebec are indebted to a destructive fire for this magnificent platform, for upon its site stood the Governor's residence, the castle of St. Louis, which was burnt in 1834. When Earl Durham was governor he had the House of Assembly converted into a residence. Through this building I was taken by a Mr. Lindsay, to whom I was introduced by his brother the Rev. Mr. Lindsay. Mr. L. was exceedingly kind in going about with me and showing me everything worthy of attention that his time would allow.

In the hall of the House of Assembly is a likeness of Louis Papineau. The countenance is thoughtful and the eyes dark and intellectual.

After inspecting the Governor's quarters, Mr. Lindsay, who is secretary to the Council (which with the Governor are the present lawmakers of Canada), offered to use his influence in obtaining a pass for us to see the Citadel. He however prepared us for disappointment, as the rules are so exceedingly strict just now in consequence of the connivance of some of the citizens in the escape of two patriots, Theller and Dodge, from the Citadel in October last. Mr. Lindsay first took us to the office of the Commisariat and introduced us to Capt. Finden, an exceedingly gentlemanly and obliging officer, who immediately donned his cap and promised his influence with the Brigadier-General.

Forth we all sallied, and after some delay Capt. Finden joined us with the pass and offered to accompany us, and in fact would take no denial, though the day was exceedingly warm and the walk to the Citadel rather a tiring one. As he very kindly remarked, his one walk might save us two, as after all they might not admit us even with the pass, without an officer to show that we had come by the pass rightly.

This Capt. Finden told us many little matters about Quebec, and the strict surveillance kept up at night in the Citadel. Being in the Commisariat his person is unknown to the Grenadier and Coldstream Guards who are stationed at the fort, and when returning from dining a few nights previously with some brother officers in the barracks inside the Citadel, he was challenged no less than 14 times, each time being, in spite of his officer's dress, compelled to give the watchword and counter-watchword.

We approached the fortification by an angular road guarded at each turn by 28-pounders, as some of the gates are. I give this as a rude sketch of the Fortress.

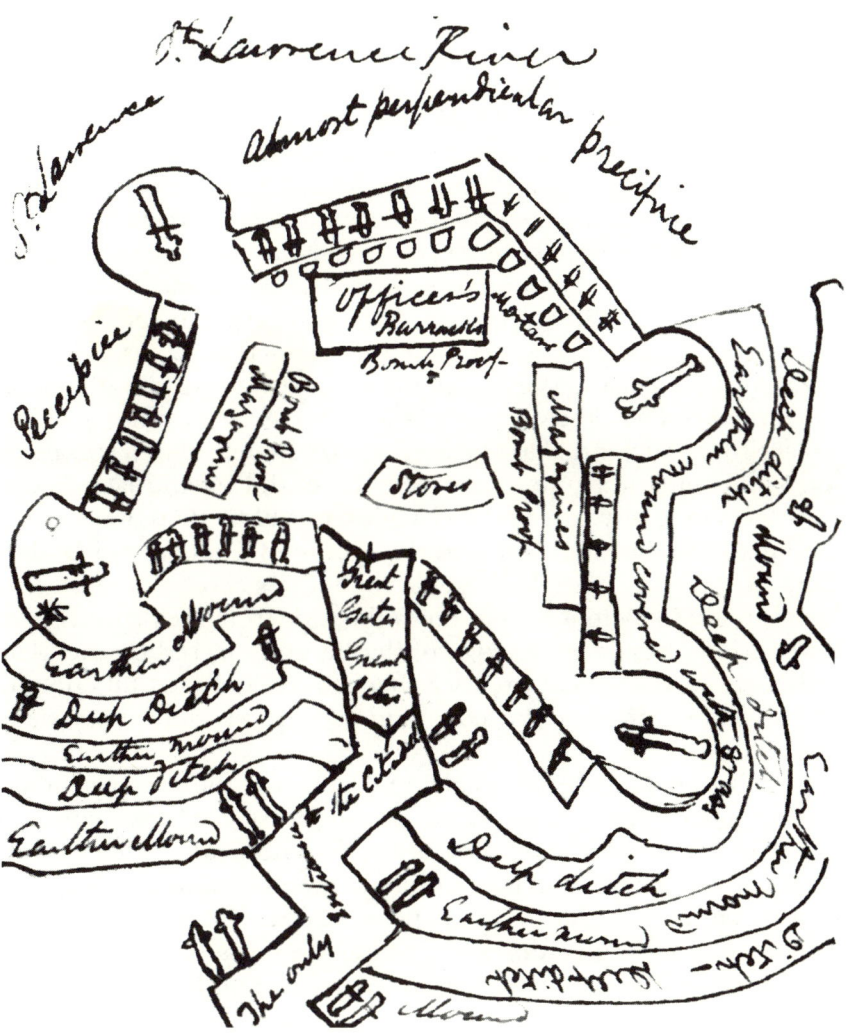

From the Citadel I walked out from the well-protected gate of St. Louis to the Plains of Abraham. A short column with the single inscription "Here Wolfe died victorious" marks the spot where he fell. Returning to the city I passed one of the Martello towers of which there are four, as additional protection to this already well-defended city. Each tower is about 40 feet in height, 120 feet in circumference, and mounts 2 or 3 field pieces, which would easily sweep the whole country beyond the Plains of Abraham. Beneath the Citadel on the other side of the city is the monument to the memory of Wolfe and Montcalm. There are two inscriptions in Latin, though the first one would be enough, as it is short and appropriate. For the benefit of a better translation I give it entire: "Mortum Virtus Communem Famam Historica Monumentum Posteritas Dedit."

Besides the Citadel and the Martello towers, Quebec is protected by a stupendous range of batteries inside the line of the walls. To the south and west there is the Dallhousie Curtain, mounting 5 guns, and away to the north, guarding the approach to the city from the water, is first, the Grand Battery of 14 or 15 28-pounders, second, the St. Charles Battery of 3 28-pounders, third, the Montcalm Battery of 3 more 28's, fourth, the 1st Nunnery Fort, and fifth, the 2nd Nunnery Fort. At each of the five gates, which are named St. Louis, St. John, the Palace, Hope, and Prescot, there is a guard house with in one or two instances a block tower, and a sally port to each. I cannot imagine a place so well defended as Quebec, and yet strange as it may appear, the inhabitants were more alarmed there, during the late disturbances, than in any part of the Canadas. It is likely there were many disaffected in the city, as indeed the escape of Thellon and Dodge from the Citadel showed. These daring fellows chose one dark and stormy night in October to cut down the rope from the flagstaff, and lower themselves over the edge of the Bastion marked on the plan with a star, to the top of the rocks beneath. It looks fearful enough when you stretch over the edge and see the precipice they went down.

Not the least interesting sight in Quebec is the great Catholic Church. On each side as you enter are two very small chapels containing altars and confessionals and at the far end is what is called the Vestibule—in which as in the church there were lamps burning continually before the altar. This chapel is built in the form of a cross, with deep recesses on either side forming the cross—and containing each an altar. The principal altar in the great church is gaudy in the extreme.

Four massy beams, richly gilded, springing from the end and sides of the ellipse forming the extreme part of the church, meet in the centre and support the carved and gilded emblems, the Cross and the Crown of Thorn.

This church, like most of the Catholic churches in the country is never closed, and when I was in there were 20 or 30 people in different pews praying and dropping their beads.

Quebec to Montreal, by steamer, 170 miles

I returned from Quebec with even more love for the St. Lawrence than before. Every turn in this river shows the two spires of a Catholic church—all built in the same way with high pointed cross—painted red, and two spires covered with tin.

Three miles below Montreal the river becomes narrow, and exceedingly swift. This part is called St. Mary's current, and before steam was in use, ships and brigs coming to Montreal were towed up it by several yokes of oxen on a towpath bank. I rose early on the morning following my arrival to visit the great French cathedral, said to be one of the largest single interiors in the world and capable of seating 10,000 people. This stupendous structure towers above all others in the city.

There are two towers in front, completed only to the height of the roof. The whole if ever finished will present much the same appearance as the views of the cathedral at Rheims. On entering the church I witnessed a most imposing scene. The funeral service was being conducted by a priest and a great number of attendants. In the broad centre aisle on a platform about 3 feet high with steps on all sides lay the coffin covered with a black pall, fringed with white and surrounded on all sides by wax candles, numbering about 100, placed on the steps. I walked up to the grand altar and witnessed the greater part of this extraordinary service. The principal priest stood at the altar with his back to the people and read certain prayers to which responses were said by a choir of four boys on each side of the railed-in space which is about the same size as many churches I have been in.

Within about six feet of the railing with their backs to the people were three priests robed in black and wearing high conical black hats with no brim. At certain parts of the service they rose and simultaneously doffed them. Alternating in this way they continued during the entire service, while a fourth, seated on a cushion, seemed to sit abstractedly throughout. In a short time two little boys entered with censers of incense which soon diffused their odour through the church.

All then knelt down, the church was darkened, the priest took off his girdle and key, and having knelt three times opened the door over the altar and took out the emblems, held them aloft. This, I presumed, was the Elevation of the Host. The priest, with the assistance of his attendants who held up his long sweeping robes carried a golden vase of holy water to a woman sitting within the railing of the altar. I suppose she was the widow of the deceased. This done a procession was formed . . . The gates of the altar were thrown open and in regular order they proceeded down the aisle and surrounded the coffin. At this point I came away.

12

Back to New York

To Saratoga Springs, steamer, stage and railway, 222 miles

At nine o'clock [A.M.] I entered a steamboat to cross the river to La Prairie. I understood this boat was a very powerful one, and soon saw the necessity of it, for we were presently in a very strong rapid, which are so common in the St. Lawrence. For four or five minutes in the swiftest part we barely did more, with a very powerful engine, than what sailors call "holding our own." In an hour we reached La Prairie, and were immediately conveyed 17 miles by railway, over rather barren land to St. John's [*St. Jean*], the head of navigation on Lake Champlain, and the place where a very powerful little fort of ours is erected. I went through the barracks—extensive erections, which including the making of the bricks—was completed in four months from the date of commencement.

At this place I saw for the first time the pontoons for constructing bridges across streams. Over a stream ¼ mile wide a bridge may be constructed in 25 minutes. These pontoons are made of tin, and being watertight, and in different sections, would not sink or be destroyed if struck by a cannon ball. Those intended to convey the cannon across are about 2½ feet in diameter, and those for the troops 1½. Two of the large, and four of the small pontoons, with the planks and ropes necessary, are conveyed upon each wagon, and at this fort it is part of the military practice to run these wagons down to the water also, as if in regular battle, and practise making these bridges.

The steamboats on Lake Champlain are the finest for internal accommodation I have ever travelled on in the United States. The good boat "Whitehall" on this occasion landed us at Ticonderoga Fort at 10 o'clock at night, where we found persons waiting to receive ourselves and baggage. Our voyage down Lake Champlain had been pleasant. [. . .] Plattsburg was the only place of interest, the scene of

163

a very decided victory over the British by land and water. Burlington is a neat looking town in Vermont, where the State University is erected. It gave me the first prospect of a New England village.

There are few points on Lake Champlain that have not some associations connecting them with the late War, which are never to me very pleasing—not, I can safely say, because British arms were seldom successful, and were eventually beaten off, but because I feel, as everyone must, that it was a sort of civil war. I can revisit scenes connected with the Revolution with the same fervor and delight that the most ardent American could testify. With such feelings I visited Ticonderoga Fort, compelled to yield in 1775 to a mere handful of men, headed by that sturdy old Puritan, who took possession, as he said, marching up the gateway, "in the name of the great Jehovah and the Continental Congress". The fort affords a pleasing view of the Lake, besides its intrinsic attraction. A subterranean passage which connected it to the lake, and doubtless used during war, has recently caved in.

I spent a wet Sunday [*30 Aug.*] at this place [*waiting for the Lake George steamer*], and shall remember it as a consequence, though the following morning presented one of those transitions from a wet to a fine day so common in some parts of the country.

The passage of Lake George has been praised by everyone. I presume I must follow in the track, though to confess the truth I consider the scenery of most of the English Lakes to be equally fine. [. . .] There is but one steamboat on Lake George, built in the form and resemblance of a canoe, with such overhanging guards that the very passage from one side of the boat of two men in company would cause it to careen slightly. "Keep still, or the boilers will certainly blow up," said a Mississippi captain. "Keep still or we shall make no progress" said our captain. But as we had the whole of a Whig convention on board the order was not very well observed, and we only arrived at Caldwell, at the head of the Lake, before dark.

[Tuesday] 1 Sept The little village was all astir this morning. It was the gathering place of the convention, previously to going over to Glens Falls, the trysting tree for all good Whigs on this occasion. All kinds of conveyances were being prepared and were already on their way when I arrived. They had all departed when our ship set out, and I derived no small amusement from observing the various kinds of equipage for transporting the admirers of Gen. Harrison. The most original and amusing was a long board, about 10 feet in length laid upon the axles of four wheels—upon which board 9 or 10 persons were very comfortably seated. This mode of riding on a board for two people, the seats being placed upon the board, I was told, was common in many parts of the country, and it is by far the easiest mode of proceeding over the ground.

I intend some day to devote a few pages to the consideration of politics and political influences in the United States, so I shall banish the Grand Convention on this occasion, and betake myself to Glens Falls, about half a mile below the village to which they give their name.

There is something very singular about Glens falls, and they possess more interest than they otherwise would, by being the scene of Alice and Cora's hiding place from the Indians in Cooper's novel The Last of the Mohicans. The cave may be entered from beneath, but with all due submission I would venture to assert that it would be both cold and damp for anyone to hide in, and certainly exceedingly so, for such fragile flowers as Cora and Alice are represented to be.

Wed 2 Sept Saratoga Springs present quite a feature I should think in American society and manners, and I was only sorry on occasion of my visit there that I had not an opportunity of being admitted behind the scenes. The hotel at which I dined was the largest there, and at dinner there were some 2 or 300 people there bearing on their faces and manners the hauteur and aristocratic dignity (so called) for which the New Yorkers are everywhere pretty well known. I do think as a general rule, to which there are doubtless many exceptions, that the New York people are the least pleasant of all the dwellers in the northern States. I have had the very questionable pleasure of being with two of them for some days, and not the smallest part of my amusement was to hear criticisms upon grammar fulminated against the New Englanders by one of them, whilst all the while he was murdering the President's English in the vilest manner possible.

Saratoga Springs are very different from the White Sulphur Springs in Virginia. The former are at a village where there are a dozen hotels. You may therefore be as comfortably accommodated as you please, and do as you please without interfering with anyone, or attracting the notice of anyone. At the White Sulphur Springs you can do nothing that is not known to everyone in two hours afterwards. Just as well as if it was regularly printed in some "Morning Herald" of nonsense and scandal.

The waters of Saratoga are numerous—there is the Congress

Spring, the Iodine Spring and half a dozen others, at which people seem to be incessantly drinking; and besides this the hotels have large vases in some places set aside for that purpose, filled with water from the different springs.

The scene at the railway when a train comes in is one of great amusement and bustle. The arrangements are excellent. Each porter has a stand awarded to him, and over his head is painted the name of the hotel whence he comes. They are, I believe, not allowed to elicit patronage, so that all the annoyance of jostling and pushing so common in many places is avoided.

People at Saratoga are driven to all kinds of amusement to pass away the time, for there is very little scenery about to entice the walkers or riders. Among other matters of the same stamp is a circular railway with cars of a peculiar contrivance for propelling yourself by turning a handle. This is a sign of the wearisomeness which devotees of fashion must wade through.

Saratoga Springs to New York, railway and steamboat, 173 miles

The railway from Saratoga is good, but the want of another track obliged us to wait at the Mineral Springs of Ballston for half an hour, without the advantage of being able to visit the springs, as the arrival of the other train might be at any moment. I was put down at the little village of Waterford [*near the confluence of the Hudson and Mohawk rivers*], as I intended to visit the Falls of the Mohawk. A walk of 2 or 3 miles brought me to the spot just as the sun had set. The falls are very beautiful, as well as the general scenery of the river, but for mass of water, all save the unchanged and unchanging Niagara, should be visited in the spring of the year. The Falls of the Mohawk are well worth a long walk. It was late when I found myself at Troy, and my fatigue, for I rambled much this day, sent me to rest.

The Hudson River has long been celebrated for its steamboats, but one recently built, which conveyed me down on this occasion out-Herods Herod. She is 294 feet long, 61 feet beam extreme breadth, and 9 feet 6 inches deep. She is propelled by two bell-crank engines, 44 inch cylinders, 10 feet stroke, and called 100 horsepower each. This is probably overrated, as there seems to be no fixed rule for ascertaining the power of engines, as laid down by Boulton and Watt [*British steam engine pioneers*] or any other engineer. Her cabins, from the peculiar arrangement, extend the whole distance from stem to stern, and are therefore about 280 feet long. She is called the "Troy," and is said to be the longest steamboat afloat on any waters.

The city of Troy looks very pretty from certain points. On one side there is a lofty hill rising abruptly, to which the classical citizens have given the name of Mount Ida. The long bridges across the Hudson give a singular appearance to the river at this place. Albany, some six miles distant, and Troy, are rivals, and with a far better chance of fair competition than many other rival cities—Cincinnati and Louisville, for instance, though Cincinnati can hardly be said to compete even with Louisville. The latter is rather beneath its notice. Troy is a great place for the manufacture of stage coaches which may be found in all parts of the United States. We stayed but a few moments at Albany. The scene of the late dreadful accident, from the giving way of the bridge, is within sight of the wharf.

At ½ past 10 the steamer left me at Catskill to take me to the Mountain House [*which RCR had missed on his journey* up *the Hudson*]. Our road lay through meadows and green knolls to the foot of the mountain, and then the toilsome ascent began. I had but one horse, and that none of the best. It required all my stoicism to avoid taking a peep at the angles of the road but I refrained until fairly on the platform [*an overhanging rock in front of the hotel*], and then burst upon my astonished gaze a view of fairyland—a view which no evidence of positive senses could convince me for some moments was real. I gazed upon it in a sort of charmed dream. From this place, the vast plain, bounded only by the distant mountains of Vermont, is seen as it would be from a balloon, with the Hudson winding through it, in apparent breadth not wider than a canal.

To the north, its white buildings contrasting with the forest, lies the city of Albany, to the east are the Green Mountains of Vermont, and the rich fields of Massachusetts and Connecticut; nor is that the whole, for those far distant peaks just visible in the purple haze of the horizon belong only to New Hampshire. I was forever reminded of Martin's picture of Moses viewing the Promised Land. Miss Martineau says she would sooner have missed the Hawks Nest, the Natural Bridge, and even Niagara than this. To the two former I answer "yes" also, nay, to the latter, too, had I not visited Niagara alone and made every spot almost holy in my thoughts.

At sunset on the day of my arrival [*3 Sept*], I walked over to the Falls of the Kaaterskill [*the Dutch for Catskill*]. No scene of wild grandeur and beauty has moved me more than this. The dark, overhanging

rocks of this narrow mountain gorge, the sombre pine trees, the utter
loneliness of the place, seemingly increased as the light faded away—
have left an impression which time will scarcely efface. The falls are
260 feet in all, the water, of which there is a mere handful, descending in two leaps, 180 and 50 feet respectively, situated 2200 feet above
the Hudson. In the depths of winter these falls present a singular
appearance of a frozen torrent, and would surely repay a visit even at
that season. [. . .]

   I walked over the next morning with a pleasant young man. [. . .]
and spent the rest of the day ascending the two highest peaks within
one range accompanied by my new acquaintance. The sublime view
from the mountain is, of course, sunrise. I did not see it quite early
enough, as the man whom I trusted to call me did not perform his
promise before half past four. I was soon out upon the platform, and
though I did not see the first lighting up of the earth, I saw the
bringing out of objects as the sunlight fell upon them. [. . .] In the
afternoon I spent the time until our departure in rambling over the
South Mountains. On the way down, the spot where Rip Van Winkle
fell asleep is pointed out, and a small shanty is built at the place, with
a picture of Rip just waking amongst the giant oaks, and exclaiming
"Oh! that flagon, that wretched flagon—what excuse shall I make to
Dame Van Winkle?"

We found the little town of Catskill in commotion from that now very common occurrence, a convention, and the various modes of conveyance, and the grotesque appearance of some of the characters who were coming away kept our stage load in good humor until we arrived at the village. "The Swallow," one of the very best boats on the Hudson, conveyed us down in a very short space of time. At some periods we must have realized a speed of more than 20 miles an hour. The motion on the bow of this light-built vessel, when at this tremendous speed, is of the most singular kind. It keeps the person standing in a perpetually dancing motion, like the room told by Cowper, [?] which

> when you went in
> you were forced to begin
> a minuet pace
> with an air and a grace.

No person can travel on the Hudson boats without being struck with the admirable arrangements for landing passengers and receiving them, combining extraordinary celerity with the greatest safety. A certain number of men are appointed to jump ashore and carry the luggage in—others hold a four-foot wide plank in the air ready to put down—others stand with lanthorns on each side—others have hands and arms ready to guide ladies over the plank. In short there is the most perfect order and regularity imaginable—and for my own part I could never praise these excellent arrangements sufficiently.

In due time I arrived at New York, but as I saw nothing worthy of note that is new to my readers, I will say nothing about my two days' stay.

13

Rhode Island and Massachussetts

[Saturday 5 Sept] At 6 o'clock I was on my way up Long Island Sound in a crowded but comfortable steamer, provided, as they all are now, with Francis lifeboats [*Joseph Francis, a New York pioneer of lifeboat design*] at 2 in the morning. Passengers for Boston land here and take the railroad all the rest of the way. When I rose at 6, I found we had lost almost all our numbers. At 8 I landed at the pretty-looking seaport town of Newport, Rhode Island. The Island is about 12 miles long and 3 broad, and gave its name to the whole State.

I rode over to Oakland, the residence of Dr. Channing early this Sunday morning 6 Sept., hoping to hear him preach at the little church at Portsmouth, in the neighborhood, in which I was disappointed. Dr. and Mrs. C. received me most kindly. The situation is a most lovely one, and the day was such a one as would show its beauty to the greatest advantage. A large party of friends, some from Boston and others from Philadelphia were staying at Oakland, but went early. Dr. Channing's appearance is somewhat singular, short in stature, slightly made, his hair is slightly grey. When in repose his look is not highly intellectual—but the moment he speaks there is a change, and he becomes quite animated. His voice (perhaps from his present indisposition) is very low, and he generally speaks very deliberately. His remarks, even the most casual ones, seem to be made in just the most choice and appropriate language possible. [*William Ellery Channing (1780–1842), uncle of William H. Channing of Cincinnati, was one of the leaders of religious thought in America. Miss Martineau said of him "of all the public characters of the United States, the one in whom the English feel the most interest."*]

The conversation turned upon the ordinary topics of the day. He seemed extremely surprised at the supineness of dissenters on all occasions when energy of even an ordinary character would enable them to take a decided stand against what Dr. C. said he had no other

term to name it by than the "insolence of the Church of England."
He thought that its ascendancy over the State was increasing every
day. I asked Dr. C. if he had any reason to change any part of his views
on slavery since writing his book. [*This had been published in September
1835, whilst Miss Martineau was staying with the Channings, and had been
branded as "incendiary" in Congress.*] He said not. He said he thought
the agitation in England would have its good effect, but he deplored
the cause which Mr. O'Connell had thought proper to pursue in
speaking of the United States of America as he had done.

Dr. Channing criticized the talents and character of many leading
men in both countries without any of the reserve that I should have
expected. He spoke of Mr. Emerson [*Ralph Waldo Emerson (1803–
1882)*], Mr. Brownson [*Orestes Augustus Brownson (1803–1876), whom
RCR was to meet later*] and other noted men here. His opinion of Mr.
George Combe [*George Combe (1788–1858), Scottish phrenologist, who
visited America in 1838–1840*] is very high. Of Mr. Carlyle he spoke as
almost everyone else does. He made many enquiries about Messrs.
Martineau and Thom. He seemed much interested in the writings of
Rev. D. Thom, who had sent him some of his books for perusal. He
had thought it right, he said, in acknowledging them, to condemn
the spirit of some passages, in which he considered the opinions of
others were remarked upon in rather an un-Christian manner.

After the conversation had continued an hour or so, Dr. Channing
said I must excuse him for a while, as he made it a point of duty to
support by his presence the minister of a little chapel in the neighborhood. The Dr. would not allow me to accompany him, and I
thought what a proof it was that the accusation made by his oppo-
nents of spiritual pride contained not a shadow of truth. [*Miss Martineau wrote in* Retrospect *that Channing's manner of speaking, and his
writing, might sometimes give that impression, but that was misplaced.*]

On the Dr.'s return we resumed our conversation. He was unwell at
this time, and though the day was warm, and he was well wrapped-up,
he complained of the cold. At times he covered his eyes and continued to pour forth for many minutes the most eloquent remarks
upon the Constitution of the United States I ever listened to. I valued
at the time, and far more since, the privilege I enjoyed then, and I
only wished that someone more worthy than myself could have the
same advantages. Dr. Channing's son and daughter are I think clever,
but I think I never had such difficulty in drawing out someone of my
own age as I did with Mr. Wm. Channing.

Newport to Providence, carriage and steamer, 34 miles

Late in the evening I returned to Newport, and when I called for some letters on the following morning at seven o'clock, on my way to Boston I found the young people almost all absent from the breakfast table, and the Dr. notwithstanding his indisposition, already down. This morning ride over the island was one of the pleasantest I ever enjoyed. The road lies right over the ridge, or highest part, and commands beautiful views of the Atlantic on one side and Narragansett Bay on the other. The sail up the latter in a pretty little steamer I found no less pleasant than the ride. We reached Providence about 11 o'clock. This place is at once a monument to bigotry and true faith in God's protection. When Roger Williams was expelled for heresy in 1636 from the colony of Massachusetts he set out from there firm in the consciousness of the truth of his principles, and having wandered thus far through the wilderness, here took up his abode, and in gratitude called it "Providence."

Providence to Boston, by railway, 40 miles

Were I commencing my travels just now I should probably describe the passage on the railway from Providence to Boston, but as one sees more of a country, the propensity to enlarge upon, or even mention trifles decreases. [. . .]

My visit to Boston at this time [*6 Sept.*] was unfortunate for many reasons, as in three days more a convention of Whigs was to be held, and those who intended to enter into the gaieties were too busy to attend to strangers, and those who did not had flown into the country to be clear of the din and bustle of politics. Amongst the former were the Hon. J. Chapman, the Hon. D. Webster, Mr. Henry Lea and others, and amongst the latter the Rev. Messrs. Bartol, Pierpont, Cranch and Ripley, Dr. Binney, Professor Ticknow and other eminent individuals, to whose acquaintance I was furnished with introductions.

After a ramble through the streets of Boston I took the omnibus out to Cambridge, and was once more enjoying the society of the Rev. William Channing, the nephew, who happened to be visiting Harvard. He took me to the Universities and showed me the library of 50,000 volumes, for which a fine Gothic Hall has recently been completed at a cost of $60,000. For this express purpose the sum was bequeathed by a Mr. Gore after whom the erection will be named.

[*According to a history of its first 350 years by Kenneth E. Carpenter, published by the Library in 1986, Gore Hall was opened in 1841. No reference was made to its benefactor.*] After spending some time examining rare books and portraits, Mr. Channing took me over to Mount Auburn. Everyone speaks in terms of such glowing eulogy of this cemetery, that I shall doubtless be thought singular in dissenting from the praise so lavishly bestowed upon its beauty. To my mind Laurel Hill at Philadelphia possesses greater advantages than even those of Mount Auburn, wild and beautiful as it is. [. . .]

From one mound in the cemetery, a view of Boston, five miles distant is obtained. "This spot," said Mr. Channing, "was my favorite one when a boy for reading and thought. Oh, if this ground could speak," he continued, his dark black eyes lighting with the fire within, "of how many hours it could tell, of how many doubts removed, of how many dark shadows driven from the soul, of how many warnings from the past, and hopes for the future."

We turned away from the spot, and were soon on the way to Waltham. I shall never forget that afternoon. After a long pause, when the glories of the setting sun were lighting the beautiful village of Waltham, and when I thought Mr. Channing had taken one of those fits of melancholy or perhaps mere abstraction, which I had often before observed, the slant rays of light striking the village church, drew an almost simultaneous remark from both of us. From that moment, for 2 or 3 miles of our journey, he seemed to have unlocked the door of his mind. He spoke of the necessity of obtaining an entire victory over selfishness, of our Saviour's life, works and mission, and of the glories of the world to come—in a strain of the most fervid eloquence I ever heard from the lips of man. Never before, in society or the pulpit, had I heard him speak with so much warmth. He seemed like one inspired. [. . .]

We returned to Cambridge, and the evening was pleasantly passed. [. . .] I walked over to Boston by the light of a nearly full moon. The view of the city was most lovely, crossing the long bridge of nearly ¾ of a mile sometime about midnight, when the only sound that fell upon my ear was the faint huzza of some members of the political party, who were to keep high revelry on the morrow.

Thursday 10 Sep. The man who was not awake before five this morning must be cousin-german [*a first cousin*] to the Seven Shepherds [*the "Seven sleepers" of Ephesus*]. Verily he must be more somnolent than Christopher Sly of Tinkering memory [?]. I threw up my window at six and beheld crowds hurrying along below with ribbons flying, and pantaloons of the most unspotted whiteness, towards the grand scene of action—the great mustering-place for the procession, the Common of Boston. To this place I also went, having discovered my old acquaintance Chas. Hubbard, and his cousin John ditto, and having been introduced to the pleasant mansion of Mrs. Hawes, passed the morning with satisfaction.

[*Politics apart, the main topic of conversation was money-raising to complete the Bunker Hill Monument, on which work had been halted four years earlier, when it had reached only one third of its intended height. The next day RCR took an outing to Nahant, and returned to Boston to find that the delegations had vanished and that the city had returned to its "auld heigh-ho" of steady and sober gravity.*]

Boston to Lowell and back, by railway, 52 miles

Saturday 12 Sep. The factories of Lowell are quoted everywhere and are pointed to by New Englanders with proud satisfaction, and if the erection of 30 mills in a pleasant situation, where there is fine water power, the employment of capital of $10,000,000, and the labor of 8,500 inhabitants are the sources of satisfaction, the New Englander has cause to be proud.

"All this is well, or is not well," but the great evil of the factory system as it exists at the present moment in England, exists in moral Massachusetts; and if the testimony of Mr. Brownson, who for a long period superintended the factories at Canton (Mass.), is to be received, there is a state of things in existence, whose catalogue might well make the moralist a mourner. At Canton, Mr B. assured me, in 6 cases out of 10, the women employed were mothers before they were wives!

The work people are paid monthly, the girls $2 for that period, and the men 80¢ per day, and they are all boarded by the different companies. The directors erect houses near the mills, and put tenants into them, who pay their rent by boarding a certain number of the work people. The fare is said to be moderately good. The long hours of work surprised me, being 13 per diem. Half an hour only is allowed for dinner, but in 20 minutes the girls are generally found at the mill, assembled in groups, talking till the bell rings. Forget all these things, and a visit to Lowell is both gratifying and profitable.

I joined a large party, amongst whom were the Averys of New Orleans, and we were shown through every part of the mills and works, save the engraving shop. There are about 7 factories employed in the manufacture of cotton, 5 in that of wool, 3 in carpets, besides print works, saw mills &c &c. The consumption of cotton in the course of one year in New England factories is not more than that of [*obliterated*] weeks in England. To protect this, a tariff was made to oppress 18,000,000 people, for of course every man who paid the additional amount of Customs duty to the importer's price of his cotton cloth <u>was</u> oppressed, and was paying the price of his oppression to encourage the northern manufacturers.

Oh! a most disinterested cry indeed was that of the rich capitalists of the north when they had nought else to do with their money, "Let us be independent of England, for in case of a war with the old country, what should we do for shirts!" And the cry was heard by the unthinking and echoed and wanted not for echoers, too, among the wise and the great; and the tariff was imposed. In two years its period will have expired, and the cry will be heard again. Let us hope that echo will this time answer "What!"

One of the most beautiful specimens of Yankee ingenuity I ever saw was exhibited to us at Lowell—a machine for making cards for cotton spinning. The work required to be done is so various that watching the machine in operation seems to induce a belief in its positive intelligence. Here also we saw a machine for winding catgut on whip-stocks, by the most singular combination of rollers I ever saw. These rollers were fixed on a moveable circle carried round by water power, and not only revolved on their own axles in a kind of sun-and-planet motion, but also on the axles of the neighboring rollers, which seemed to give way at their approach, and drop into the hand of the attendant who stood ready to receive them. The whip-stock remained stationary in the centre.

Objectors to Mr. Owen's system of community will tell its supporters to go to Lowell, with a knowledge deeper than the surface, and be cured. But Lowell is no fair specimen of living in community—for one fact puts it completely out of the pale of Mr. Owen's or anyone else's community system, and that is, that the workers have no power or direction in the management of the household in which they live.

The immense saving which it is known is effected by the owners of the Lowell factories by providing for their work-people on so extensive a scale might give any one qualified to enquire into the subject some useful hints as to the expediency of erecting large buildings in the manufacturing towns, well divided off for families, and having one common hall and dining table. Upon reflecting upon this subject one cannot help mourning that the eye of a mind like Robert Owen's should have been so jaundiced as not to foresee, and guard against, the evil of a system of almost universally allowed practicability becoming mingled beyond separation, with a set of dogmas upon religion and morals—an error which has startled the great mass of the Christian world, and has kept them, as it will ever do, as long as the connection exists, from enquiring into what is really useful, and undoubtedly worthy of esteem.

[*A contemporary commentary on an historic experiment! The town of Lowell was named after Francis Cabot Lowell, who introduced the power loom there in 1814, and was incorporated in 1836. The corporation developed this community system along the lines of Robert Owen's (1771–1858) pioneering work in England and Scotland. RCR had met Owen at a reception in Liverpool in 1838, and heard a first-hand account of his views on socialism. As RCR perceived, Owen had alienated religious and other leaders, who might otherwise have supported his liberal views on the organization of society, by rejecting their articles of faith.*]

Monday 14 Sep. Amongst the other acquaintance I numbered in Boston I remembered that of Dr. Walter Channing,(Dr. Wm. C.'s brother) and his daughter. The Dr. took me this morning in his chaise to see the hospital. It is much the same, I presume, as other institutions. Everything seemed very neat, and the ventilation, and the means of preventing noise, and facilitating the escape of patients in case of fire, had evidently been well carried out. [. . .] From the hospital Dr. C. took me to the State Prison of Massachusetts, whose superintendent appeared to be very confident of its superiority over the Eastern Penitentiary at Philadelphia. There is no punishment here but the shower bath, which he told us never failed in subduing the most determined. The water is allowed to run on until they yield and cry "Peccavi" [*I have sinned*].

[*At this point RCR interjects that his notes on Boston, which I have already abridged, "seem interminable," but that he must introduce his "listeners or readers, as the case may be," to Mr. Stephen Perkins, brother of J. H. Perkins of Cincinnati, and keen horticulturalist.*]

The Americans have the reputation, I believe, of maintaining a less expensive navy than ours, without that miserable and miscalled economy which forms so lamentable a feature in the payment of almost all their civil officers. The true secret seems to lie partly in their acting on the fact that ships rot quicker in the water than they do on well-protected stocks. At all the Navy yards I believe, and for the one at

Boston I can vouch, there are at least two 84-gun ships so far completed that three months would place them ready for commission. The navy yard at Boston is kept in excellent order; there is a graving dock here for repairing ships, but as the tide does not rise more than 10 feet, some 12 feet of water have to be pumped out by steam power. The operation usually occupies 5 or 6 hours.

My last day in Boston was one of the most interesting. In the morning Mr. Channing called and took me to Chelsea, a village on the other side of the bay. Our design was a visit to the Rev. Orestes Brownson, now president of the Chelsea hospital. Mr. Brownson at present occupies so prominent a position on the Democratic side of politics, by the editorship of the Boston Quarterly Review, that mere curiosity, I confess, to see him, occupied a very large portion of my desire.

A pleasant walk and sail [*across the Mystic River*] brought us to the hospital, and we were at once shown up to Mr. B.'s study. He rose when we entered, displaying the most studious looking exterior I had ever seen. His whole suit, once black, had degenerated into a russet brown, and a pair of ungainly feet in black cotton stockings had hastily been thrust into corresponding shoes. If he had a shirt on, it was not visible. All this I secured at a glance. He commenced conversing at once with Mr. Channing, and there I sat for two or three hours, listening to these master spirits, only uttering a word or two when either made a remark or put a question to me out of compliment. Towards the end of our interview, Mr. Channing rose to choose some books from Mr. B.'s library, and I asked him a few questions upon leading topics. In a few moments I found he had no confidence in Mr. Van Buren personally. He regards him as a mere politician. "Were he to be proposed as Governor of the State of Massachusetts," said Mr. B., "I would rather lose my hand than vote for him. I contend for Mr. Van Buren because he is the proposed candidate of a party who are fully committed in questions I deem of vital importance."

Mr. Brownson is believed to have injured his party in the South by an article in which he so truly asserted that the whole tendency of the Democratic Party was against slavery. I alluded to the question, and asked his opinion as to the jurisdiction of Congress over the District of Columbia. He (in common with Mr. Quincy Adams and others) is of the opinion that Congress has no power. The cession from Virginia and Maryland especially states "that the rights of property as then existing shall be respected." The same doubtful language occurs in the cession of the promontory of Chelsea for the purpose of erecting a hospital for U.S. seamen. This cession was made by Massachusetts to the general government.

At the last State election, votes from Chelsea and from Charleston, which is under the same circumstances, were reprised at the Massachusetts polls, on the grounds of the said districts being out of the State. This case was referred to the Supreme Court of the United States, which has not yet decided upon the matter.

I talked to Mr. Brownson about Carlyle, as I do with all New England people, not because I know much about him but because it seems quite apparent that the largest acknowledgement of his power has come from this quarter of the world. Mr. Brownson was the first person who expressed anything like a doubtful opinion of Mr. Carlyle. I pointed out to him passages in the opening chapters of Sartor Resartus which have always appeared to me like a truckling to obtain an admission into Fraser's Magazine. I found Mr. Brownson had noticed the passage, but only viewed it as somewhat of an anomaly in Mr. Carlyle.

To my amazement, I found that he thought that Sir E. L. Bulwer's mind was of higher order than Mr Carlyle's. [*Edward L. Bulwer (1803– 1873), first baron Lytton, better known as Edward Bulwer-Lytton, novelist and politician.*] He referred me to the Quarterly for April for more views on the subject from his own hand, intimating that he meant at some future occasion to follow the question up in a still closer examination of both. Upon my producing the second paper issued by the Land Redemption Society, and finding that I was somewhat interested in the subject, indirectly if not directly, he offered to read to us, and invited our criticisms upon an article upon that subject designed to appear in the forthcoming number of his Review.

The article is well and forcibly written, and when at some future day I shall read it I shall be at no loss to trace some alterations which the less fiery spirit of Mr. Channing, by calm argument and logical persuasion prompted or proposed.

As we returned from the hospital and were on our way back to Boston, I thought if I ever wanted a renewal of faith in democracy, one hour with this extraordinary man would make it stronger than ever.

14

The White Mountains

Boston to Portland, Maine, steamer, 120 miles

Friday 18 Sep At seven o'clock I left Boston in a crank-built steam-boat for Portland in Maine. The Americans do not understand navigation for sea-going boats. They never think of placing the machinery below deck—it would diminish profits by taking space from the decks below to put the engines in the hold. As a natural consequence a paltry puff of wind sent the Capt. into Cape Ann Harbor at 11 o'clock in the evening, and there we lay, not daring to venture into a sea a Mersey ferry boat would have laughed at. For the first time for a considerable period my equanimity was destroyed. The storm without was at least equalled by the storm within, for I knew that to be too late for the stage on Saturday, was another word for waiting in the little town of Portland till Tuesday.

All turned out exactly as I feared. We did not reach Portland until 8 o'clock in the evening, and I booked myself with the worst grace possible for two days' stay, with the pleasant consciousness of being so destitute of provision for contingencies as to have reprised several letters of introduction to Portland, because I did not expect to remain more than an hour or two there. Could anything have been more unfortunate?

[*RCR's annoyance is understandable: the sole purpose of his journey north was to visit the White Mountains, and if possible, to climb its highest peak, Mt. Washington, not to be outdone by Miss Martineau, who had also made the ascent; in ten days' time he was due to sail home from New York.*]

Monday evening 20 Sep I answer my question of Saturday evening in the affirmative, if not in the best of spirits, certainly in none of the worst. The weather has been fine, and I consoled myself with the idea that it might have been wet and thus kept me confined to the dull

179

hotel. As it was I saw a good deal of this pretty town with willow-lined streets and neat houses.

Portland to Conway N.H., stage, 62 miles

At seven on Tuesday morning I found myself on the box beside an attentive and well-informed driver, one of the few fat ones, by the way, I ever saw. I wonder Capt. Marryat has not remarked this fact, as a very striking result of a democratic government, the extreme leanness of the coach drivers! A short period only served to inform me that the driver was the proprietor of the line of stages himself. In all the north part of New England I found upon enquiry the drivers either owned the lines altogether, or have exclusive management of them, buying and selling the horses as they choose, and in fact having equal control, whether owners or not. This evidently was the reason why there was such a respectable-looking set of drivers on all the roads where I had the opportunity of observing.

The ride from Portland in Maine to Conway [*just inside the New Hampshire boundary, 60 miles northeast of Portland*] is not likely to impress a stranger with the fertility of the Boundary State. About four in the afternoon we passed the dividing line between Maine and New Hampshire—an upright granite block with "Me." on one side and "N.H." on the other serves to mark the spot.

[*RCR spent the night at the Petawquet House in Conway, where the Chinese proprietors could not make bread (Miss Martineau had also found it inedible), but he enjoyed a plentiful dish of "Irish praties" cooked the way "only only known to Paddies."*]

Conway to the Notch in the White Mts. stage, 60 miles

From seven in the morning until 10 we were winding through a lovely valley, with many a smiling farm on either side of us. At 10 we came to our first view of the Notch in the White Mountains. Mount Washington himself, whose snow-capped summit I watched all yesterday on the road from Portland, was now hidden by the lofty ridge which forms one of the walls of the Notch. In two hours [. . .] we arrived at the solitary dwelling, once known as the residence of the unfortunate Willeys [*a family of six who were killed by an avalanche in 1826*].

At 2 o'clock the coach left me at a lonely cottage at the end of the Notch occupied by Thomas Crawford. The afternoon was cloudy, not promising much for the morrow, but I told Crawford that as my time was limited I would try the ascent of Mount Washington at all events on the following morning at 6 o'clock. I then walked down to the Notch to take another and longer view of the Silver Cascade.

[*That evening of Wednesday 23 September he wrote in his other diary: "Five miles from the nearest habitation, in a little inn in the very heart of the wild mountains of New Hampshire, your friend is now reposing—it is 8 o'clock in the evening, and there is a blazing fire of logs burning in a fine chimney nook. I intend to ascend the White Mountain tomorrow early."*]

By the feeble glow of a misty lamp I dressed at five on Thursday morning to ascend Mount Washington. Before six, Thomas Crawford and myself mounted on shaggy ponies named respectively Belle and Arabian were on our way. A dense cloud overhung the valley, but my determination was unshaken—I had resolved, if Crawford would accompany me, to reach the summit and take a chance on the view. I never pitied hard-worked brutes more than I did those two ponies during the long toilsome ascent of Bald Hill some 3000 feet in height, and the first attained on the way to Washington. The higher we rose the more rare the mist became, and when we emerged from the forest on the summit of Bald Hill, what was my joy to behold the bare peak of Mount Washington, rising clear and distinct into the blue sky. [. . .] The cold here became severe and every pool between the rocks was well covered with ice. We journeyed on, the mist gradually rolling off on either side of us, until passing the summit of Mount Franklin, I saw my guide's attention riveted by something, and turning my head I saw a rainbow of remarkable form and appearance. When I introduced Crawford to these pages I ought to have said that he is no common guide. [*He had pioneered a footpath to the summit in 1821 which was later widened to create a bridle path and given Crawford's name.*] He is a man of real information and in his rough way a true lover of nature, in the midst of whose wild grandeur he has lived from his boyhood. "Man and boy," said he, "I have known these hills for 30 years, yet I have never made so remarkable ascent as this. Look there!" Two thousand feet beneath us lay the even unbroken masses of white clouds for hundreds of miles, white as snow in the sunbeam—no land was discernible.

To the left the mist was rolling up the side of the mountain and immediately dissipating in that magical manner which everyone must have noticed about mornings on the mountains. On the face of the mist was the remarkable rainbow I have just alluded to. It seemed to be of the most vivid colors and to be perfectly circular, save where broken by the eye and body of the observer and his horse. We compared notes, and we agreed that it appeared to both of us as if the shadow of our whole figure were reflected on the middle of an otherwise perfect circle. I leave it to the skilled in optics to account for this very remarkable appearance. [*As an erstwhile physicist I can offer an explanation: an observer on a pinnacle could see a complete rainbow, mostly below eye level, if the sun were at an elevation of not more than 40°, and his shadow, falling on the bank of mist, would reach to its center.*]

At ¼ before nine we reached the base of Mount Washington, some 800 feet from the summit. To the highest point there has been the same kind of rough bridle path, which to my utter amazement has been threaded all morning by our sure-footed ponies. I declined trusting myself on the frozen snow, even with Arabian, so we tied our Navagansetts to a huge stone, and commenced clambering over the vast masses of rock. The labor was great, and I was glad to accept Crawford's offer to take my coat on his arm. On all sides of us were the most beautiful formations of ice I had ever beheld—I never raised my eyes from the rocks which lay in our course until we stood upon the summit, the highest point of land east of the Rocky Mountains. Crawford, directing my attention to the north showed me one of the highlands which form the boundary of Maine, the subject of the present controversy between England and the United States. [. . .] Crawford repeated the assertion he had made on Mount Monroe. He had never seen a view like this. To the east and southeast lay the vast ocean of clouds—far beyond which the Atlantic at Portland marked the horizon which bounded our vision. As we watched some of the nearer masses rolled away and showed us as through a rent in a curtain the valley beyond Conway—while the dark peaks of two or three neighboring mountains just raised above the clouds, irresistibly represented to my mind huge rocks rising above the bed of the ocean itself.

We looked long at this stupendous scene—evidently enjoyed too by my guide who frequently exclaimed as if involuntarily "This is indeed wonderful—wonderful."

Casting my eye round over the vast valley to the west—perfectly clear save for a few floating clouds—two or three thousand feet below us was shown the distant range of the Green Mountains and to the south-west the far peak of Mount Monadnock rising clear and

distinct on the very edge of the half dreamy horizon. Oh! Here was a sight "to keep the heart from sinking, and the soul from sleep". Above, about, everywhere, was a world of wonder, of grandeur, of glory I never saw equalled before. [. . .]

Notch to Concord, New Hampshire, by stage, 105 miles

Before one o'clock we were again at the Notch House, after the most fatiguing ride I ever experienced. The afternoon was a fit one to follow the morning. I spent it journeying through the Notch once more. When the Mountain came in sight it was covered with cloud, which only cleared away as the last rays of the golden sun were tingeing the horizon.

[*That is all RCR says about the descent of nine miles of steep mountainside, after which he spent the night at the little inn in Conway.*]

From Conway I journeyed from north to south along the shores [of Lake Winnipesaukee . . .] and passed through a Shaker village. [. . .] Late in the evening [*of 25 September*] we reached Concord, and I found out my friend Mr. Pierce, the senator from New Hampshire who had been so kind to me in Washington. He pressed me with real warmth to remain the next day with him, but my time was limited and I was obliged to refuse it. [. . .]

Understanding I was going to Claremont, he took me to the residence of Judge Gilchrist, before whom he had been pleading a case all day, and introduced me as an intending passenger for the following morning. While we were talking, the sheriff came with a message from the jury who were locked up upon Mr. Pierce's case, and begged to be cleared. The judge appealed to Mr. Pierce who gave his permission, and the sheriff departed to obtain that of the other counsel. It was not, of course, a criminal case. When we left the judge, and just as we passed the still lighted courthouse, the jurymen came out, most assuredly not singing "we won't go home till morning."

I was too reasonable to take a man out of his way who had been pleading for hours, and I found my way to the tavern alone. A room with a parlor attached was given me and the landlord was as civil as— as—an expectant waiter.

Concord to Charlestown, by stage, 50 miles

If anyone were to ask me anything about the road from Concord to Claremont [*the equivalent of today's Route 114; they were heading slightly north of west*] I would say it is 50 miles in length, that there is a lake called "8 mile pond" on the way, and that it is generally pretty. For my own part I saw little of it, for the conversation between Judge Gilchrist and myself never flagged. [. . .] At Claremont, a private conveyance was waiting to take him to Charlestown, 10 miles further down the Connecticut, whilst I was obliged to wait 3 or 4 hours for the stage. [*The stage would pass through Charlestown, but the judge's carriage could not carry all RCR's luggage.*]

On my stopping at Charlestown I found a very kind farewell note from the judge waiting me, wishing me a pleasant and safe voyage, and an invitation to call on him if ever I have the opportunity.

Everyone has heard of the valley of the Connecticut, with its beautiful villages and farms, and Northampton—the beautiful unrivalled Northampton. Then why say any more than that I reached New Haven at 11 on Thursday morning, and New York at 2?

[*With those few lines RCR sped through the rest of his journey, rushing to get back to New York, in which he lost track of the days. With the help of his other journal for MPH I deduce that from Charlestown he reached Hartford, by stage, (130 miles), on Sunday 27 September, where he found himself without money. The landlord of the United States Hotel, with great reluctance lent him $8 on the security of his watch, and the next day he took the train to New*]

Haven, (37 miles) and a steamer to New York (80 miles). He excused this sudden collapse of his chronicle with the words:]

The valley of the Connecticut dismissed in 9 lines! Oh, fie! I hear some say—but I cannot help it. I am sick of description. The scene is before my mind in all its beauty, but my pen has run over the adjectives so often, they have become "Dull, stale, flat and unprofitable," and I for one will give a silver penny to the man who will invent some new adjectives and another if he will bring them into general use.

I had resolved to run down to Philadelphia before embarking at 5 o'clock on Tuesday evening 29 Sept. I found myself in a tête-a-tête with Mr. J. J. Smith, Jr., one of the kindest friends and most delightful men I ever met with. [. . .] In the evening I spent two hours with Mr. and Mrs. Furness. [. . .] I returned with Mr. Smith, and spent the night at his house, first accompanying him to see the Automaton chess player, which a few gentlemen have purchased. Having promised not to reveal, I was initiated into the secrets of this most intricately beautiful contrivance. Brewster has managed to give a statement like the actual fact, to be sure, but not even approaching it in actual fact or ingenuity. It never has been completely guessed, or even hinted at. [. . .]

I spent a most delightful evening bidding farewell to my other friends, and expecting to find Dr. Gibson in New York, for he had crossed me on the way, I stepped into the railway car, and six hours over the worst-managed road I was ever on, landed me once more [*on Tuesday 29 September*] in the gay city of New York.

[*Presumably RCR had found time to dispatch $8 to the inn at Hartford, for he found his watch waiting for him.*]

15

Homeward Bound

Oh! how my heart bounded within me as the goodly steamship the "British Queen" left the wharf in East River at 5 minutes past two on the first day of October. [*The "British Queen," when launched on 24 May 1838, was the largest ship in the world, described as "a most beautiful specimen of London shipbuilding." A three-masted wooden bark, it had a splendid figurehead representing the young Queen Victoria.*] Verily it seemed as if Transfusion was a reality and that I had within me the soul of some happy schoolboy on breaking up morning! I shall not soon forget the first time I entered the word Home in the hotel book under the head of Destination. On this occasion there was the same kind of feeling, carried out to a greater degree. Nothing could disturb my equanimity—I verily believe I could have shaken hands with the greatest bigot on earth.

I am not going to say one word about latitude, longitude, courses, Variations of the Needle &c &c.

We found that the great businesses of the day on board the ship would be

Breakfast	Nine
Lunch	Twelve
Dinner	Four
Tea	Seven

with such eating and drinking ad interim as the exhausted stomachs of the passengers might need.

When we had fairly cleared the land, and I had taken my last look at what I had so eagerly taken my first a year ago, the Highlands of Neversink, I went down to dinner, and when all were assembled on deck after that meal I took a slight glance at the passengers. About ⅔ of them I found to be Germans and French, by the help of my list in the Morning Herald of the day, and the rest English and Americans. A gentleman, Dr. Ellerson by name, came up to me and presented Dr. Gibson's card of introduction, saying that he had also met me

186

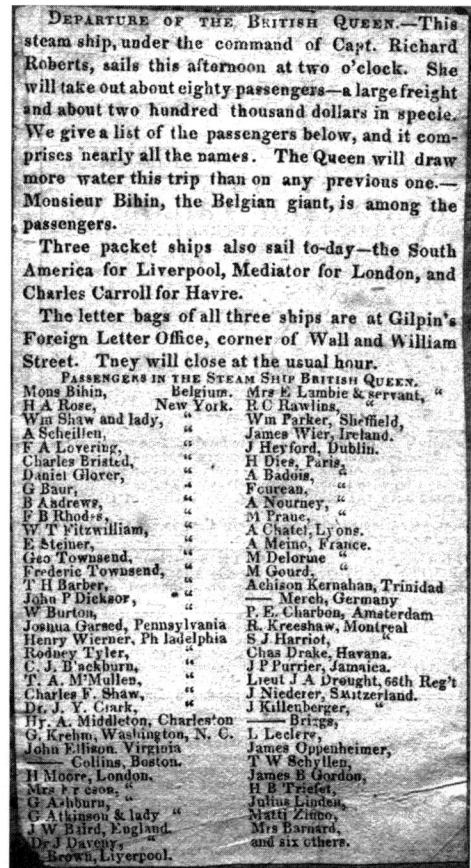

Clipping from the *Morning Herald*, 1 October 1840.

before at the White Sulphur Springs. I found that he was going to England for some 5 or 6 months, and was a pleasant man in conversation. We took adjoining quarters at the dining table and passed the meal always pleasantly.

This is now the 5th or 6th day out, so I have had some opportunity of observing. At the head of the table at our end sits the surgeon of the ship, a queer little fellow about 30—a regular Londoner. To his right on the first and second days, but alas owing to indisposition never seen since, was the celebrated Belgian giant, M. Bihui, seven feet six inches in height, and stout in proportion, and his wife six feet at least. The giant must be a good property, for he is not more than 35. He did not make, that I could perceive at a stolen glance, a great impression upon a sirloin of beef, but he reversed the order upon a fine fat woodcock, and instead of "making no bones of it" he made it all bones.

So much for the giant, who is pleasant and agreeable, though he speaks but little English, and his wife equally so, without speaking English at all. One thing in the economy of the giant's comfort on his voyage cannot be pleasant—as there is no berth in the ship long enough or wide enough, he is obliged to sleep on a series of mattresses on the second deck.

Next to the giant and his wife is a Lieut. or Major in the 66th Regiment, a pleasant-tempered young man who enjoys a glass of hot brandy and water, and who assured me that the Irish Catholics had been too well used, and that if anyone ought to know the true state of the case, he ought, as he had land in Ireland as well as England. I bowed low to an authority so excellent as an Absentee Protestant Landlord of the True Tory Stamp.

Next to the officer is a most singular character, a narrator of marvellous anecdotes, whose memory is so short that he will sometimes relate the same incredibility two days running. [. . .]

Saturday 10 Oct Up to yesterday morning at breakfast, the sea had been so smooth that we had not used the grooves for the dining table. For the last 24 hours, though we have had little or no wind, we have been going through a heavy rolling sea. Last evening, just as the sun had set, we came up with a brig, the singular and unaccountable position of whose sails had been remarked ever since she came in sight. It was almost dusk when we arrived abreast of her, and within fifty yards of her beams. Not a seaman was visible on her decks—the helm was deserted, the deck unmanned, the boats gone. She had been abandoned, and as the long heavy surge raised her up, the water rushed through her seams on all sides, showing us that she was waterlogged. We sailed quite around her, but could distinguish no name, but the initials "I. S." were carved upon her stern. It struck a melancholy chord in my heart as we went once more on our course and left the lonely vessel heaving up and down in the long rolling swell, her masts and yards plainly visible against the purple sky where the sun had lately gone down. Alas! where were the crew? Had they escaped, or had their sun gone down while it was yet morning?

[*Three other sightings of this apparently British brig, timber-laden, adrift in mid-Atlantic were reported in* Lloyds List. *She was still afloat three weeks after the 'British Queen' sighted her, but must have foundered eventually.*]

Sunday 11 Oct From midday yesterday the wind and sea were gradually rising, and when I went up after tea to walk on the deck, I found it blowing very stiffly, with a dirty, ragged-looking sky to the south and southeast—our course lying due east. At 8 o'clock, the dead-lights on the stern were knocked in, and, the ports on both sides of the ship well examined, I lay down on one of the sofas in the cabin, and when I awoke the ship was rolling and pitching so heavily I did not care to find my way up to my berth in the fore-cabin. I therefore wrapped my coat around me, turned round, and was soon asleep again.

At 12 a lurch of the ship roused me. I found the cabin perfectly dark. To go to sleep again was impossible. At this time I was lying right under the cabin windows at the stern, so I kept still for some time, listening to the still-rising gale overhead, and the "heavy dead digs" which the sea ever and anon bestowed on the goodly hull beneath. I might have lain about an hour, holding on to a rail over my head, when suddenly a sea struck the ship right across the bows, which made every timber in her hull tremble again. The next moment the returning surge met the whole breadth of her counter [*part of the stern above the waterline*], stove in the centre dead-light, and in came a deluge of water. Down I went on the floor, spluttering the salt liquid out of my mouth, floundering about like a stranded whale at low water.

It was still dark, but I fortunately caught the leg of the dining table, and grasping my cap with equal good fortune at the same moment, I was soon on my feet again. Two or three others had been lying in similar positions, and we hastened on deck to inform the Captain. On the middle deck we found almost all the passengers watching, through the upper companion, the flapping of the main spanker, off which every fresh gust of the furious gale was tearing a fresh ribbon— while the broken end of the gaff, suspended by its unyielding chain, was swinging about like the new-fashioned stylus round the neck of a modern American bluestocking.

It was now 2 o'clock, and the gale had not abated one jot, but the engines were still working, though slowly, and our course, "onward, yet onward," was unchanged. A single glance at the boiling surge from the middle deck told me that it was a greater sea than I had ever witnessed before, and prepared for a drenching. I ascended to the upper deck, away flew my cap before my head was well above the head of the companion ladder. Fortunately it had caught in the lee gangway nettings, and I worked my way over to it. Head and cap could hardly have been more soaked than mine were when they met again. And now, with my hands well worked into the running rigging of the mizzen mast, I stood and witnessed the wildest scene of grandeur the ocean had yet unfolded to me. Before me was the immense length of the hull of the ship, looking small compared to the immense seas, which came "fathering and sounding on" towards us.

Surrounding the main mast was a group of men getting in the flying remnants of the main spanker, now and then utterly veiled by the showers of drenching spray. Three times did she roll, until the top of her huge paddle boxes lay level with the foaming, bursting tide; but up she rose again, and the loud crack of the paddle boards breaking up some smaller sea came borne by the gale to my ear.

It was four o'clock before any abatement took place, and at daylight I worked my way to the fore cabin. Baugh! What a sight! My inkstand upset on the basin, followed in its course by my journal and other books lying loosely about—all the drawers in the chest of drawers out, the bed soaked through and through—my only pair of dry boots converted into water ewers, my band box approaching rapidly a pulpy state, and the whole room presenting an aspect which might have given a less squeamish character than Beau Brummel a cold to enter it. Well—the gale blew off, the state room was dried, and instead of a cold I picked up a a hint—viz., "if the weather is remarkably fine at sea, use it to get your berth into the most perfect order."

The same reason which had kept my state room in such disorder as to reduce everything into a state technically called "pie" by the printers' devils when the gale came on, has been visible in everyone's appearance and conduct ever since we came on board. On the second day, save myself and one or two others, everyone appeared in their usual land dress, and many have seemed to vie with one another who should dress in the most expensive and fashionable style. The idea is, and has been prevalent in everyone's mind that they are travelling in a steam ship, and that the voyage will be completed in a certain, definite time. Already, Oct. 16, has betting commenced as to the hour of our arrival, and a grand lottery of 48 half-hour chances is to be drawn with great pomp, tomorrow morning at 11 o'clock.

Thursday 16 Oct. 1840 A fortnight out today, and land approaching. A bird that ventured too far landed upon our quarter-deck this morning. We are bowling along with the same glorious weather which has marked the greater part of the voyage. The dinner table today was decked out with vases of lovely flowers, lovely, although the handwork of some child of earth. A number of toasts were proposed, and everything showed that there was some change somewhere, for some reason or reasons, generally well known by the passengers.

Friday 17 Oct. This afternoon at 5 o'clock I clearly saw the Land's End in Cornwall. Oh, never was mariner, ancient or modern so enraptured.

> Oh dream of joy is this indeed
> The lighthouse top I see?
> Is this the kirk, is this the hill,
> Is this mine own countree?

Saturday 18 Oct At half past nine o'clock today we stopped the engines at the beautiful village of Cowes, and two hours afterwards set foot on English soil at Southampton, after an absence from my native land of thirteen months and four days.

[*The irrepressible statistician concluded the voyage and his American travels with a copy of the ship's log.*]

Log of the British Queen, New York to Southampton.

Date	Latitude	Longitude	Distance run.	Revolution	Winds.
Oct 1	Discharged Pilot o 5 Pillo Sandy Hook				
2	40.15	71.12	130		
3	40.29	67.22	180		
4	40.55	62.55	204		
5	41.50	58.14	216		
6	43.00	53.58	202		
7	44.35	49.00	230		
8	46.18	44.20	218		
9	47.50	40.36	187		
10	49.17	36.05	203		
11	49.47	32.30	141		Heavy Gale 1 a.m. to 4 a.m.
12	49.50	27.30	200		
13	49.59	22.20	210		
14	49.38	17. 8	203		E
15	49.32	11.50	206		E
16					
17					

[*Richard Rawlins had toured the U.S. and Canada for eleven and a half months, devoting five months in all to Cincinnati, three months to New Orleans, two months to New York, Boston, Philadelphia, Washington, Montreal and Quebec, and a total of two months travelling between these cities and other places of interest. With the concern for detail that typified all his observations he rounded off his diary with an analysis of his journeys.*]

The following table was prepared upon the plan of one which I found in the American Almanac, compiled by a foreign gentleman who travelled some 10,000 miles through the United States. The statements which I had already myself arranged somewhat resembled that of the table, but were not quite so full full and explicit, and even now I am without any data as to what should be allowed for stoppages. Upon railways the stoppages are much longer than upon English railways, but I am quite unable to make any statement as to the time occupied by stoppages.

Statistics of Travelling in the United States.						
Mode of Conveyance	Number of miles	Time hours. min.	Average Speed ph our Miles. Hund.	Cost for one person Dollo: Cent	Average Cost p mile Cent. Centimes	Number of Tracks or Conveyances
Railways.	1,062.	71.35	14.96	46.96	4.33	19.
Steamboats 5964 in: On Rivers.	4,965	538.30	9.28	129.05	2.55	16
.. Lakes &c.	999	100.30	9.94	29.00	2.94	9
Stages	1,764.	407.12	4.32	114.91	6.55	
Canals	398	109.00	3.71	16.00	4.00	3
Private Conveyances Horseback, chaise, &c.	170	. . . .	. . . .	. . . .	. . .	. . .
Totals.	9,358	1226.47	av: of the whole, 8.44	$335.92	av: of the whole. 4.07	

Railway Travelling in America is rendered very unpleasant by the incessant clouds of sparks sent up from the wood, which is the sole material consumed in the fireplaces. The carriages used upon some of the railways are of great length.

Stage Travelling is by far the most unpleasant mode of passing over the ground. In winter stages are exceedingly cold, as the wind is continually insinuating itself under the edges of the oilskin sides, and in summer you must either have the said oilskins down, and be suffocated with the heat, or rolled up and have the benefit of the full rays of a scorching sun, and in dry weather clouds of dust. But I doubt whether a worse case than any of these is not when it is raining on a hot summer's day, and these oilskin blinds have all to be down. The heat and steam from the hot ground can then be almost unsupportable, and you feel as if you would almost sooner be drenched outside than parboiled within!

Canal Travelling is very pleasant when the weather is not too warm, and you can sit out and read, particularly through fine scenery, such as you have upon the Pennsylvania canals. But the great drawback on these occasions is the night accommodation. The berths are composed of mere wooden boards fastened three tiers high on the sides of the cabin. On a warm summer's night the heat and the close feeling of the densely crowded apartment gives the unfortunate who sleeps on the top board the constant feeling of suffocation; and if he should so far forget his miseries as to go to sleep, he will not only run the risk of "dropping off" with a vengeance, but will speedily awake with dreams of Burke and Hare [*the Victorian "body-snatchers" who sold corpses to medical schools*].

Travelling by Mississippi or Ohio steamboats, were it not for the danger of being blown into nothing, or dropping down below the surface of the water, either suddenly, in consequence of a snag piercing the bows of the vessel, would be by far the pleasantest mode of locomotion. A spacious and airy cabin seventy feet long or thereabouts, 12 or 14 feet high, and as many broad, affords a delightful promenade when the sun is not too hot to walk the upper deck. [. . .] The galleries built all round the steamer entirely open to the air, but sheltered from the sun, also afford a pleasant shelter for morning readings and watching the banks of the great rivers as you float down the majestic current, or stem its mighty force on your return.

The steamers in use on the eastern rivers and seas and on the Great Lakes are entirely different from these just mentioned. They are without any exception in the east (and with few exceptions on the Great Lakes) upon the compression principle, and the arrangements for cabins and berths more nearly accords with the Glasgow and other steamboats with us. I have elsewhere noticed the speed with which passengers are landed and received off the New York steamboats. No sooner is the steamer under weigh again than a man goes about ringing an enormous bell, and after every ring he shouts "Gentlemen who have not paid their fare, will please to walk to the captain's office and settle!" The end of this sentence is always in the highest tenor, and has invariably the effect, common as it is, of exciting a laugh from the passengers. Negroes delight in saying it in the most comical manner possible. You then are in duty bound to go to a small office on deck and pay your fare in exchange for a ticket, with the name of your destination legibly printed upon it, without which you are not permitted to land. Your baggage is immediately carried away to the baggage room appointed for all luggage destined for your stopping place. At the door of this baggage room a porter is in constant attendance to give out and receive trunks. I should have mentioned that a similar system exists in almost all the railways in the Union. The trunks are placed in wagons made for the purpose, not on the top as with us. [. . .]

I have before alluded to the practice of eating by the roadside upon railways. No sooner does the train stop at a station than the doors fly open and away go the passengers helter-skelter into the refreshment room to take oysters, coffee, cakes or whatever they can get. The bell rings, and out they rush, their hands laden with whatever they have been eating. This practice of stopping often, and on occasions for some time, diminishes badly the already very low speed attained on most of the railways I travelled upon in the United States.

Rawlins signs off his journal for Mary.

Postscript

One of the first questions that come to mind after reaching the end of the *Journal* is *How* was it possible for a young foreigner to gain such ready access to so many distinguished people? I have speculated that the memory of his grandfather's support for the struggle for independence might have opened doors, but there is no direct evidence for this. The key might lie with John Champion Vaughan, with whom the Rawlins family in England had maintained close ties, and Richard planned a visit to Cincinnati ahead of his mission to New Orleans. He was keen to learn as much as possible about the political and religious scene in Ohio, and his cousin was an excellent tutor, introducing him to every influential person in his circle. Rawlins in turn impressed them with his knowledge, ability, and personality, and they willingly wrote letters of introduction for him to take to Washington, where, step by step, he reached the Oval Office. But in fact the easy access to people in high places was not uncommon. The Presidency was a relatively informal institution: General Jackson would travel by public steamboat and train, and Frances Trollope's husband, a 45-year-old attorney, was able to waylay him on a steamboat in 1829 and engage him in easy conversation. Thomas Hamilton was about the same age when he met Jackson casually in 1833, writing in his *Men and Manners in America* that year that "the President told me he was always at home of an evening, and would be glad to see me whenever I chose to drop in." When he took up the offer, he found Jackson's openness remarkable: "nothing is more striking to a European than the utter absence, in this country, of official reserve." Captain Marryat, however recorded that his successor, Martin Van Buren, had decided that a line must be drawn somewhere: the White House had become open house to anyone wishing to accost the President, and henceforth entry to Presidential parties was to be restricted, to stop "the mobocracy" from attending.

All of the early visitors who had been able to get their impressions of America published, were, of course, much older than Rawlins, and their reputations had preceded them, so that allowing for his youth and relative obscurity, his achievements in meeting and conversing with top people must rank at least as high as theirs. Moreover he had opportunities to mix with and sound out the opinions of lesser mortals which more distinguished travelers may not have had.

After disposing of the commodities that Rawlins bought in New Orleans the partnership of Rawlins Brothers found little new business, and in 1841 they wound the company up. Then, trading as J. H. and R. C. Rawlins, they acquired the paper mills of John Green & Co., a business which they ran for the next forty years. Richard took on an additional job as cashier for Rawlins and Son in 1843, when his brother Charles wanted to devote his time to politics, principally in the cause of Free Trade, and that year he and Mary Hunt were married.

John Vaughan had also turned to politics: the Liberty Party put up a candidate in the presidential election of 1840, but failed to attract support, and in 1844 Vaughan took over the editorship of Cassius Clay's *True American* to further the "free-state" cause. That year his mother and sister (Aunt Vaughan and cousin Virginia) sailed for Liverpool, where they stayed with Richard's parents for two years or more. On their return to the States, after spending a summer in Mobile, Alabama, they were en route to Camden when their steamboat caught fire, and they both perished.

Vaughan made such an impression as editor of the *True American* that in 1848 the Liberty Party nominated him as Senator for Ohio. He was however beaten by two votes by another Cincinnati lawyer, the intensely ambitious Salmon P. Chase, who had been adopted by a coalition of Democrats and the new Free-soil Party, but whose views on slavery were identical to Vaughan's. The political temperature continued to rise over the next few years; the Missouri Compromise was continually threatened by the expansionist claims of the slave states, and Vaughan was in the forefront of the battle to curb them. At the same time he took up the cause of democracy in the Balkan states, having befriended the Hungarian exile Louis Kossuth, and his daughter Virginia took on a dangerous mission to Europe on his behalf.

The slavery issue was now becoming inflammatory: the Kansas-Nebraska Act of 1854 rode rough-shod over Missouri Compromise, by allowing Utah and New Mexico to decide for themselves whether to be slave or free, and allowing migrants into Kansas and Nebraska to take their slaves with them. What had begun as a dispute between states was likely to become a dispute within territories seeking statehood.

The time had come for a full-blown political party to stem the tide, and Vaughan was one of five influential men, including Joseph Medill, owner of the *Cleveland Leader* and the *Chicago Tribune,* who called for a convention, which took place in Pittsburgh in December 1855, and created a provisional National Republican Committee. Salmon P. Chase, the Democrat Senator for Ohio, threw his cap in the ring, mainly on the slavery issue, and although he wanted the party to be called "Free Democracy," he became the first Republican Governor of Ohio. After the first Republican National Delegate Convention assembly in Philadelphia in June 1856, the Free-Soil and Liberty parties disappeared and the anti-slavery Democrats joined the Republicans. Chase unsuccessfully sought the presidential nomination.

Vaughan continued to exert his influence through the press, turning the *Cleveland Leader* into a great city daily, and doing as much for the *Tribune,* and along with Medill played a major part in preparing the ground for Abraham Lincoln, whose policy was not to deny the rights of existing slave states, but to resist extension, and ultimately to abolish the system. This drew Vaughan to Kansas, which had now become a real battleground between the Free-Soilers and the slaveholders. Until then the territory had been exclusively Indian, but now that the door had been opened for settlers of both persuasions to move in, some resorted to violence. Vaughan established the *Leavenworth Times* near Kansas City, to help stiffen the resolve of the endangered "free-state" men. After a bitter struggle the free-state men won, and, in 1861, Kansas became the 34th State of the Union. Vaughan was narrowly defeated in the nominations for its first senator, but the "War Between the States" was now inevitable.

He continued to run the *Leavenworth Times* during the Civil War, but what he did afterwards has not been discovered. All that is known is that when Samuel Bernstein (who had been a friend of his and his son Champion in Leavenworth) returned to his native Cincinnati in 1886, he saw a piece in a local paper saying that "Col. John C. Vaughan, father of the Republican Party and leader in its pristine purity" was the inmate of an "eleemosynary" (charitable) home just round the corner from his own house. The only other resident who knew of Vaughan's distinguished past was another "free-soiler," a retired school teacher, now paralyzed. From then on Bernstein visited Vaughan every week until his death in 1892, survived by his daughter Virginia, who was still trying to make a living out of writing, in Boston.

Richard was an active member of the Liberal party, and in 1883, after retiring and disposing of the paper mill he acquired two Staffordshire weekly newspapers, which he edited in the Liberal cause for the next five years. He died in 1898.

* * * * * * * *

This book was about to go to press when I received from the Library of Congress extracts from *The Papers of George Washington*, Vol. 8, published as recently as 1999 by the University Press of Virginia, which give credence to Rawlins' recollections and shed new light on Richard Champion's public activities as a U.S. citizen.

Within two years of settling in Rocky Branch, near Camden, S.C., Champion made up for any disappointment at not becoming the first British Consul-General by being appointed clerk to the Camden Court of Common Pleas and General Sessions. He also served in the South Carolina General assembly from 1789 to 1790, and was a delegate to the State Constitutional Convention. From March 1791 to his death later that year he was Commissioner in Equity and Registrar of the Court of Equity. His reputation must surely have survived in the memories of some people.

Shortly after his inauguration as President, George Washington undertook a tour of all the States, and in May 1791 he was to visit Camden, when Champion asked a Major William Jackson to convey a letter to him, together with a copy of his *Considerations on the Present Situation of Great Britain and the United States.* The letter was fulsome in praise of Washington's achievements, but also set out his own contribution to the cause, "united to this Country by Blood, Affinity, and by an early Attachment to Liberty."

He also handed Jackson a parcel containing two biscuit porcelain portrait plaques, one of Washington and the other of Franklin. He explained that he had never heard whether the ornamented plaques that he sent by way of Paris in 1778 had arrived safely, and that he had brought these unfinished examples with him from England. Apologizing for the doubtful likeness of Washington, he hoped that the President would accept it as a curiosity, and that Jackson would accept the other for himself. Champion was casting his bread on the water in the hope that he might "have the Honor of being presented" to his hero.

Replying from Philadelphia on 19 July, Washington acknowledged the receipt of the letter and the book, but made no mention of the plaque, and an editorial comment in *The Papers of George Washington* confirms that no acknowledgment of its receipt has ever been found. It is possible that Washington, having in his possession the original, decorated plaque, graciously declined the gift. Did Jackson keep them both?

The editor also commented on the dubious likeness, speculating that it may have been modeled on a fictitious mezzotint published in London in 1775. He also revealed the provenance of the original plaque, which had been hung in a Mount Vernon sitting room, and became Martha's property after the President's death. It remained with her descendants until it was returned to Mount Vernon in 1995, on loan from an anonymous donor.

These late revelations must surely add weight to my belief that Richard Champion's reputation as a supporter of the Revolution paved the way for his grandson's reception in the United States.

Index

Adams, John Quincy, U.S. President (1827–29), 131, 177
André, John, 44–45
Arnold, Benedict, 44–45
Auburn, NY, 50; Penitentiary, 51–52
Avery, Mrs. W. H., 107–8, 116

Banks, stability of, 28–30; Second Bank of America (1816–36), 36, 87, 129. *See also* Sub-Treasury Bill
Beecher, Harriet, 121
Bernstein, Samuel, 69, 198–99
Biddle, Nicholas, 120, 129
Brock, Sir Isaac, 62; Monument, 62, 153
Brownson, Rev. Orestes Augustus, 171, 174, 177–78
Buchanan, Mr., Speaker, House of Representatives, Ohio, 74
Burial at sea, 22
Burke, Edmund, British M. P., 11

Calhoun, John C., U.S. Senator, 69, 133, 135–36
Canals, 48–49, 54–55, 73, 123, 194
Catskill Mountains, 47, 167–69
Champion, Jane, 9, 13–14, 69
Champion, Richard, merchant and shipowner, ally of Edmund Burke, supporter of American colonists, Deputy Paymaster General, founder of Bristol Pottery, emigrates to U.S., 10–13, 199
Champion, Sarah, 13, 69. *See also* Vaughan, Sarah
Channing, Dr. William Ellery, 170–71
Channing, Rev. William H., 1780, 172–73, 177

Chase, Salmon P., U.S. Senator, 197
Cincinnati, Ohio, 69–89; common schools, 70, 72–73, 77, 82, 121–22
Clapp, Rev. Theodore, 116
Clay, Henry, U.S. Senator, 131, 133, 134–35
Columbus, Ohio, 74; penitentiary, 75–76
Cookworthy, William, 11
Cranch, Justice, U.S. Supreme Court judge, 130–31, 133, 137, 138
Cranch, Mr., artist, 88
Crawford, Thomas, 181–83

De Saussure, John, 13, 32, 117
Durham, Earl of, 155, 158

Fox, Charles James, 11
Franklin, Benjamin, 11–12, 37, 40, 85
Free Soil Party, 197
Furness, Rev. William H., 39–41, 185

Gibson, Dr., 20, 25–26, 27, 28, 36, 128–30
Gore Hall, Harvard University, 172
Greene, Hon. William, 75–77, 87, 133
Guilford, Nathan, 82, 122, 130

Hamilton, General, 31
Hammond, Governor, 69
Harrison, Governor William H., 75, 81, 84, 121, 164
Hunt, Mary Prout, Rawlins' fiancé, 9, 10, 88–89, 105, 151, 197

Jackson, Andrew, U.S. President (1828–37), 106, 196

Kościuszko, Tadeus, 44, 46

201

La Fayette, Marquis de, 38
Liberty Party, 197
Lincoln, Abraham, 198
Lloyd, John, 10, 12, 13
Longworth, Nicholas, 79–80, 86
Lowell, Massachusetts, 174–76

Mackenzie, William Lyon, 155
Marryat, Captain Frederick, 14, 196
Martineau, Harriet, 14; on Cincinnati,
    78; on New Orleans, 89; 119; on
    Niagara Falls, 61; on prisons, 51–52;
    on U.S statesmen, 136–37
Martineau, Rev. James, 14, 171
Miami, Ohio, 150
Missouri Compromise, 70, 197–98
Montreal, Quebec, 161
Morris, Robert, 11
Mount Vernon, Virginia, 137, 200
Mount Washington, 181
Mure, William, New Orleans cotton
    broker, 28, 29, 31, 33, 41, 96, 115

Natural Bridge, Virginia, 145
New Orleans, Louisiana, 96–119;
    House of Assembly, 100–2; ceme-
    tery, 104
Niaraga, 57–61
Niblo's Gardens, New York, 29–30
Norris, William, locomotive pioneer, 20
North, Lord, British Prime Minister,
    (1772–82), 11

Owen, Robert, British industrial rela-
    tions pioneer, 175–76

Papineau, Louis, 154
Peale Museum, New York, 30
Perkins, Rev. James Handyside, 85, 149,
    150
Philadelphia, 36–41
Pierce, Franklin, U.S. senator, 135,
    183–84
Portage railway, 123–25
Portland, Duke of, British Prime Minis-
    ter (1783), 13

Quebec, 157–61, Citadel, 158–60

Railways (U.K.), Liverpool to Manches-
    ter, 10; London to Liverpool, 10
Railroads (U.S.), general, 193; Bal-
    timore and Ohio, 141, 152; Bal-
    timore and Susquehanna; 126–28,
    Boston and Lowell, 174; Hudson and
    Mohawk, 47–48, 49–50, 166;
    Nashville, 102, 114–15; New Jersey to
    Philadelphia, 34–35, 41; Niagara to
    Buffalo, 63
Rawlins, Charles Edward, entrepreneur,
    father of Richard Champion Rawlins,
    9, 13
Rawlins, Charles Edward Jr., 9–10, 13–
    14, 36–37, 40, 60, 85, 96, 147
Rawlins, James, 9–13; as partner in J.
    H. and R. C. Rawlins, 197
Rawlins, Richard Champion; educa-
    tion, and apprenticeship, 10–16; as
    partner in J. H. and R. C. Rawlins,
    197; as editor of Liberal newspapers,
    199; "Recollections of Seventy Years,"
    9
River travel, Hudson, 43, 166, 169; Mis-
    sissippi, 91–95; Ohio, 90–91, 121–
    22, 149; St. Lawrence, 153
Rochester, New York,53

Saratoga Springs, New York, 165
Sing Sing Penitentiary, 43
Slavery: abolition of in West Indies, 10,
    84; Abolition Party 117; opposing ar-
    guments in United States, 69–70,
    110, 116–18, 197
Slaves: auction of, 98–100; conditions
    of in "Success" plantation, 108–10
Smith, J. J., 37–39, 41, 185
Stage coaches, 52–54, 64–65, 78, 126,
    141, 146, 152, 180, 193
Steamboats, 120, 154, 161, 179, 194;
    "Boston," 122; "Canadian Eagle,"
    156; "Champlain," 43–44; "Ellen
    Kirkman," 113; "Erie," 152; "High-
    lander," 156; "Leviathan," 46;
    "Odessa," 149; "Persian," 107;
    "Queen of the West," 90–95, 120–21;
    "Swallow," 169; "Troy," 167; "White-
    hall," 163

Steamships, "British Queen," 21, 42; "Great Western," 10, 21, 42; "Liverpool," 21, 23
Stetson, Charles, 71, 149, 150
Stowe, Calvin Ellis, 121
Sub-Treasury Bill, 130
Sugar plantation, 111–12

Thanksgiving Day in Ohio, 73
Trollope, Frances, 80; bazaar, 80, 84

United States, frontier with Canada, 131, 182

Van Buren, Martin, U.S. President, 53, 130, 196
Vaughan, John (of Philadelphia), 36–40
Vaughan, John Champion, cousin to Rawlins, 13, 69–70, 75–77, 84–85, 196–99

Vaughan, Sarah ("aunt Vaughan"), 13, 32, 69, 121, 197
Vaughan, Virginia ("cousin Virginia"), 13, 69, 121, 197

Walker, Judge, 71, 81–82
Washington D.C., 128; Houses of Congress, 129; White House, 130
Washington, George, 11–12, 38, 45, 122–23, 137–38, 199; commission as Commander-in-Chief, 131
Wayer's Cave, Virginia, 143
Webster, Daniel, U.S. Senator, 40, 136, 172
Webster, Noah, lexicographer, 15
Wedgwood, Josiah, 11
West Point Academy, 45–46
White Mountains, N. H., 179–83
White Sulphur Springs, Virginia, 147
Wistar parties, 36